LITERARY
CASH

OTHER TITLES IN THE SMART POP SERIES

Taking the Red Pill
Seven Seasons of Buffy
Five Seasons of Angel
What Would Sipowicz Do?
Stepping through the Stargate
The Anthology at the End of the Universe
Finding Serenity
The War of the Worlds
Alias Assumed
Navigating the Golden Compass
Farscape Forever!
Flirting with Pride and Prejudice
Revisiting Narnia
Totally Charmed
King Kong Is Back!
Mapping the World of Harry Potter
The Psychology of The Simpsons
The Unauthorized X-Men
The Man from Krypton
Welcome to Wisteria Lane
Star Wars on Trial
The Battle for Azeroth
Boarding the Enterprise
Getting Lost
James Bond in the 21st Century
So Say We All
Investigating CSI

LITERARY CASH

Unauthorized Writings Inspired by the Legendary Johnny Cash

EDITED BY

BOB BATCHELOR

BENBELLA BOOKS, INC.
Dallas, Texas

BenBella Books, Inc.
6440 N. Central Expressway, Suite 617
Dallas, TX 75206
www.benbellabooks.com
Send feedback to feedback@benbellabooks.com

Printed in the United States of America
10 9 8 7 6 5 4 3 2 1

Library of Congress Cataloging-in-Publication Data

Literary Cash : unauthorized writings inspired by the legendary Johnny Cash / edited by Bob Batchelor.
p. cm.
ISBN 1-933771-03-8
1. Cash, Johnny. 2. Cash, Johnny—Fiction. I. Batchelor, Bob.

ML420.C265L57 2006
782.421642092—dc22

2006032612

Proofreading by Erica Lovett & Jennifer Thomason
Cover design by Laura Watkins
Text design and composition by John Reinhardt Book Design
Printed by Bang Printing

Distributed by Independent Publishers Group
To order call (800) 888-4741 • www.ipgbook.com

For media inquiries and special sales contact Yara Abuata at yara@benbellabooks.com

CONTENTS

Fiction

Nonfiction

ACKNOWLEDGMENTS

AN EDITOR OF AN ANTHOLOGY like *Literary Cash* accumulates many debts. I am wholly indebted to BenBella Books publisher Glenn Yeffeth and our editor Jennifer Thomason. From my first phone conversation with Glenn, he supported the project and realized its merits. Jennifer has been a guiding light in the process of developing the manuscript and turning it into a fantastic book. In a really short time, Glenn and his staff have built a phenomenal publishing company—one that writers yearn to work with.

I am equally indebted to the twenty writers who helped turn the idea for the book into reality. Each contributor has my eternal thanks. Lauren Baratz-Logsted and Greg Logsted, Gretchen Moran Laskas, Deborah Grabien, Gayle Brandeis, and Russell Rowland deserve special kudos for their roles in making the initial proposal sparkle.

My family has not only supported me as a writer, but also inspired me to greater heights. My parents, Jon and Linda Bowen, are constant sources of encouragement. My little brother Bill has been a true friend. My mother-in-law, Nancy Roda, is a thoughtful supporter, as was my father-in-law, Gerald R. Roda, who unfortunately died before this book was published. I think he would have been proud to read it, as I would have been to hand him a copy. Thanks also to David, Ann, and John Roda.

I'm lucky to have a lifelong friend like Chris Burtch who shares a love of music, sports, and history. Thomas Heinrich has been a great pal and sounding board. Anne Beirne and Chuck Waldron have provided wonderful friendship over the years, as have Rodd Aubrey, Peter Magnani, Lawrence S. Kaplan, and Richard Immerman. I'd also like to thank my colleagues in the School of Mass Communications at the University of South Florida.

My greatest debt in the world goes to my two best girls: my wife, Kathy, and daughter, Kassandra Dylan. To call my wife an angel is to sell her impact on my life short, and Kassie (my little baby) is constant joy. My love for them is boundless.

INTRODUCTION

ON JULY 4, 2006, WHILE THE nation celebrated its birthday with barbeques, county fairs, and fireworks, thousands of fans found time to slip away from the revelry long enough to buy Johnny Cash's *American V* record, fittingly released that day. Although put out nearly three years after his death, the buzz surrounding the album placed it among his finest work. Since Cash recorded most of the material on *American V* after his beloved June Carter Cash's death and before his own death shortly thereafter, the work carried both a legacy and a mystique.

After the success of Cash's earlier American Recordings albums produced by Rick Rubin, the critical acclaim surprised few people. More shocking, however, in an era dominated by bubblegum pop, cookie-cutter country, and hip hop, *American V* debuted at number one on the Billboard albums chart.

More than fifty years after his first single and on the heels of the biopic *Walk the Line*, starring Joaquin Phoenix and Reese Witherspoon, Cash arguably remains more popular than ever. The evidence is as clear and strong as Cash's deep baritone voice.

Bigger than the songs he wrote and sang, the movies and television shows he starred in, or the books he authored or were written about him, Johnny Cash is an American icon. He became a star at a time when no template existed for how that role should be played, so he plowed ahead with unbridled fury.

Early in his career and for far too many years, pills and alcohol beat Cash down. The emotional roller coaster of performing in front of countless adoring fans, followed by interminable bus rides and zigzagging across the country, cost him his health, his first marriage, and nearly his life. But his addictions could not put out the fire that fueled his creativity and his longing to tell America's story of the saint, sinner, working man, or king.

Cash kept on telling stories even when the hit singles seemed to dry up, finding ways to remain relevant to new audiences. Decades before Madonna won praise for constantly reinventing herself as a performer, Cash moved back and forth from the stage to starring in his own television variety show to movie roles that stretched the public's idea of celebrity. Only Elvis Presley, his comrade and friendly rival, had ever successfully moved across genres so easily, building new audiences on every front.

By 1980, the forty-eight-year-old Cash became the youngest living inductee admitted into the Country Music Hall of Fame. As similar accolades poured in, some musicians might have given up the fight, especially if their new songs received as little airplay as Cash's in that decade. Everyone recognized his historical significance, but felt that his best days were also in the past. Cash stumbled through the '80s, musically adrift and beginning to suffer physical setbacks, including double bypass surgery and relapses into painkiller addiction. Cash never gave up, despite not quite finding his place in the "me" decade. He could have quit at any time while remaining a legend for the rest of his life and beyond, but Cash still had stories to tell.

Cash's resurrection began in the early '90s as he took chances with his music that would have seemed foolish when he was younger, like singing on U2's 1993 *Zooropa* album and working with rap and hard-rock producer Rick Rubin at American Recordings. Rubin saw Cash's voice as his primary gift, which called for little more than some interesting lyrics and a lonely guitar. Together, they recorded Cash's first album for the label, *American Recordings*, in a stripped-down style that focused on the singer's powerful voice. The album received critical acclaim and reintroduced the legend to a new generation of music lovers. Two years later, Cash and Rubin released a sequel, *Unchained*, backed by Tom Petty and the Heartbreakers. Ironically, although country music stations would not play his songs, Cash won a Grammy for Best Country Album.

Cash suffered several additional physical ailments as the new century began, including a misdiagnosed disease that nearly crippled him. At the same time, however, his work achieved new levels of dignity and emotion. Cash's physical pain came forth in his voice on the discs *American III: Solitary Man* (2000) and *American IV: The Man Comes Around* (2002).

The defining moment of Cash's later career was his recording of the Nine Inch Nails song "Hurt." Cash turned Trent Reznor's song about heroin addiction into an appeal to God for redemption and a retrospective on his deep love for June Carter Cash. Cash's voice is pleading, replete with wisdom, but also filled with knowledge that the end is near.

The "Hurt" video gives viewers a powerful image of Cash not giving in to fate, even as the walls crumble down on the lithe, powerful man he had been. His hands shake as he pours wine from a goblet. Cash's mottled skin and white hair stand in stark contrast to his "Man in Black" persona. He looks frail for the first time, but does not hide from the shocking image.

The video also shows glimpses of June Carter Cash, who died of complications following heart surgery on May 15, 2003, at the age of seventy-three. Cash would follow four months later, officially from diabetes complications, but more likely from a broken heart and the yearning desire to see June Carter Cash at Heaven's Gates. Posthumously, Cash won best video of the year at the Grammy Awards and the Country Music Awards.

Over the years, Cash aged, mellowed, then raged some more, but ultimately became, at various times, the nation's conscience, critic, patriot, and elder statesman. Successive generations "found" Cash, keeping his legacy alive from the birth of rock music to the iPod age.

Johnny Cash and Bob Dylan shared a special friendship that lasted across the decades. In 1999, at an all-star tribute to Cash, Dylan's respect resonated in his voice as he launched into "Train of Love." Lightly strumming his guitar and bouncing from one foot to the other, Dylan told Cash, "I used to sing this song before I ever wrote a song and I wanna thank you for standing up for me way back when."

Over the years, Cash often discussed their unique friendship and points where their careers intersected. In his 1996 autobiography, Cash talked about singing on Dylan's *Nashville Skyline* album and having the young folk singer on his popular variety TV show. Music bonded the two legends, but they also found common ground based on a healthy respect for history, religion, and ideas.

Ironically, the birth of *Literary Cash: Unauthorized Writings Inspired by the Legendary Johnny Cash*, came about as I read Dylan's 2004 memoir, *Chronicles*. For the first time, fans got a glimpse into Dylan's private life and influences. For the reclusive, elusive star, writing such a book seemed about as improbable as singing on an underwear commercial, but yet there it was. The book sparked yet another resurgence in Dylan's popularity and only increased his iconic aura.

Immediately, Dylan's lengthy discussions about songwriting touched me. As a person who takes on the solitary task of writing books and then putting thoughts out into the world, I could relate to Dylan's feelings of anguish about writing his own material, particularly early in his career. "It's not like you see songs approaching and invite them in. It's not that easy," he explained. "You want to write songs that are bigger than life. You have to know and understand something and then go past the vernacular" (Dylan 51).

Chronicles is littered with references to writers that motivated Dylan: Faulkner, Kerouac, Chekhov, Poe, and many more. When I read about how much literature and poetry influenced Dylan, I began to think about my writer friends who draw inspiration from music when and while they write. Talk to any group of writers about music and the examples seem endless, from simply listening to music while creating to using songs to evoke feelings or set a scene. Writers drawing inspiration from music and musicians seems like standard operating procedure.

The light bulb went off. What if we threw a twist into that common equation? I thought it would be great to assemble a group of authors and have them write essays and stories "inspired by" a musician or group. Providing a new spin on the musician's themes and ideas would open the door to a fresh way of looking at the musician's lasting influence. Although I was reading Dylan's memoir, Johnny Cash served as the ideal choice for this kind of book, based not only on his broad range of material, but the wide-ranging influence his music continues to have on so many listeners. Thus, *Literary Cash* was born.

Dylan's remarks and performance were not the only amazing events that night in New York City. One of the most touching moments transpired when June Carter Cash took the stage and sang "Ring of Fire," the song she wrote about Johnny so long ago. Sharing with the audience her personal recollection of Cash in those days, saying that he was "scary," her performance paid tribute to her husband in front of thousands of fans and supporters, but in so intimate a way that it could have been just the two of them at home in Tennessee. The power of her voice and spirit rocked the auditorium.

I can barely sing and only know a few guitar chords. I'm a writer, as are the twenty others who contributed to the book. *Literary Cash* is our way of paying tribute to Johnny Cash, just like the performers that night in 1999 and countless others in a variety of tribute CDs before and since his death. The difference is that our words are set to the page, and theirs were set to music.

There are seven nonfiction essays in *Literary Cash* and thirteen short stories. The former are new and interesting examinations of Cash's life and body of work, ranging from his status as a popular culture icon to his influence on crime narrative and similarities with literary superstar C. S. Lewis. Two of the essays are creative nonfiction, narratives of how Cash's music provided inspiration, changed lives, and gave people from all walks of life the ability to share a common ground.

Since the songs of Johnny Cash inspired the short stories in the collection, we thought it would be fascinating to also present the author's "backstory." Each backstory provides readers a glimpse inside the creative efforts of the writers and the specific songs or feelings that brought the story to life. We liken the backstory to the kind of explanation one hears on VH1's *Storytellers* or reads about in music magazines. We see the backstory deepening the reader's connection to the writer's inspiration and revealing Cash's lasting influence.

Each short story in the book is a new interpretation inspired by Cash and his music. We hope to invoke the spirit of Cash through our words and leave readers saying, "Hey, that story could have been a Johnny Cash song."

At its heart, *Literary Cash* is a labor of love and our way of paying homage to one of the world's towering figures. His music and spirit live on.

—Bob Batchelor

Works Cited

Dylan, Bob. *Chronicles: Volume One*. New York: Simon & Schuster, 2004.

FICTION

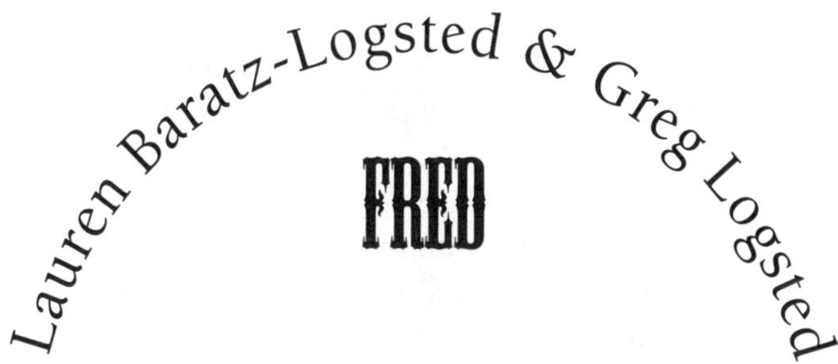

FRED

Lauren Baratz-Logsted & Greg Logsted

BACKSTORY: "Fred" is, of course, inspired by "A Boy Named Sue," and we consider it to be our Critter & Cash story because it owes as much to the Little Critter books we were reading to our young daughter at the time we wrote it as it does to the Man in Black.

BUS STOP. NEW SCHOOL. NEW YEAR. I figure I'll arrive there early, check out the lay of the land. I stand there smoking. I look totally cool.

I try leaning against a tree. I'd have preferred a building or a wall, but lush green lawns surround me. Looking cool in the country takes work.

Other kids arrive. Some look cooler than me, some not so much. They all know each other. I know no one.

It's the same every year. My mom keeps moving us to wherever she can find work. Four years ago it was Texas. Eight years ago it was Arkansas. This year it's Connecticut. I guess I'm now a Connecticut Yankee. Lucky me.

The other kids huddle together in two separate circles: the cool and the not-so-much. I know what they're doing. They're trying to decide whether they should talk to me, include me. I smoke my cigarette, look off to the side, pretend I don't care.

I'm thinking style over substance.

I'm doing my best James Dean, working the retro-sexual look. I'm getting a headache. Also, my shoulders are starting to get sore from leaning against this damn tree.

Finally, one guy, who seems to lack both style and substance, asks me if I have an extra smoke. I reach into my pocket, still leaning against the tree. It's a difficult move. I pull it off nicely, maintaining my cool façade. I give him one and he asks my name. This is my big moment, the one I've been waiting for. The spotlight suddenly burns brightly. I imagine a large hushed audience eagerly awaiting my response.

Yes, this is my chance to reinvent myself yet again.

Each year, each new school, I try out a new name, ride that sucker as long as I can. It usually isn't very long, but I'm determined this year will be different. It's my last year of high school. I want to make it count. After this, I'll be out in the real world and it won't matter any more. I'll be able to be who I want to be. But I still just want this one year, to be like everybody else.

I look him in the eye as if this is some kind of contest, as if the first one who blinks loses. Cigarette smoke drifts into my face. I give him my best Clint Eastwood squint. My eyes start to water.

"Jack," I say. "My name's Jack."

I've given this one more thought than usual, since every four years I tend to go all presidential.

Eight years ago, when I was ten, I went with Bill because I didn't want to be Bob, because, you know, Bob's your uncle. But then Bill turned out to be a horndog. Then, four years later, I went with George, because Al was a weird yanker. We all know how that turned out: shocked and awful. Now I sure as shit don't want to be George again, and I've never wanted to be Ralph, but John? There are Johns all over the place. It's such a common name. It's what you piss in. It's also the name given to those pathetic souls that pick up prostitutes. So I've decided to go all retro and sexual, only not as one word this time, back to someone who was a horndog *and* never lost any respect over it. I'm going to be Jack. If I was five years old this would be a problem, there would be Jacks all over the place because of that stupid movie where that ship went down, like some guy letting some girl he's only known for a couple of days live in his place is such a smart thing to do. Although, maybe that's the way to go, meet a beautiful girl, fall in love, get laid, and die in the middle of a frigid ocean. Hell, I'd rather do that then spend the rest of my life slowly dying in an office cubical or selling life insurance.

"Cool," the guy who bummed one of my smokes says. "I'm John. Why don't you come over here?"

And just like that, I'm in and what did I tell you about there being Johns all over the place.

I have so planned this out. I've covered every damn base. It isn't so much a deception as it is an act of protection or even desperation. Either way, just consider it a condom for the soul. I'm hoping my actions will silence their words.

The week before school started, I showed up for orientation, made sure to introduce myself to every teacher for every class I was going to have. It was like I was running for office, shaking hands to beat the fucking band.

"Hi, I'm Jack. I'm going to be in your calculus class."

"Hi, I'm Jack. I've got you for poli sci."

"Hi, I'm Jack. French is my favorite subject. Now if I could just talk to you for a moment about *un peu de* side *issue*?"

And they all understood. Of course they understood. Who wouldn't? After all, they're not sadists. They get Jack.

I look at my schedule, find my way to home room. I have my foot in the door, I'm almost in, and that's when I see the fucking fly in my own ointment. Shit. I tell myself it'll be okay. I tell myself all I have to do is step back out again, wait for the teacher to come along, get her alone, and talk to her in private for one little minute about my little *issue*.

There is always one thing you miss, I think, no matter how carefully you plan. You don't take DNA into consideration. You ignore the fact there might be a resistance movement on the ground. You forget fucking Florida.

And you talk to every goddamn teacher you're going to have in advance, but you never talk to the home room teacher, BECAUSE THE GODDAMN HOME ROOM TEACHER WASN'T ASSIGNED YET!

But it'll be cool, I tell myself, it'll be fine. I'll just stop the teacher before she goes inside and she'll totally understand. And here she comes now, and she's kind of pretty in her turquoise paisley dress, red hair flaming down her shoulders. I smile my most seductive smile, the one I've practiced in the mirror, hoping I look hot as opposed to terrified.

"Hi, I'm. . . ." I start but I get no further.

"Just get in there," she says. "If I'm late, you're late."

I sit there in home room, slouched in my chair, waiting for the fucking world to open up and swallow me whole.

But then I hear Red calling out the names, and I start to think, *Hmm. Maybe today will be different; maybe today someone else will be sucked into that humiliating vortex.*

There's a Chin from China.

There's a Pepe from France.

One name follows another. Each name is like stepping out further across a frozen lake of thin ice. Each step brings me closer to that fateful fall.

Fuck! There's an Armpit from India. Who does that to their kid?

Doesn't anyone else think this is funny? But Chin they all think is cool. And sure, they razz Pepe a little, but he smiles so wide and takes it all so well, you can tell people are gonna wind up liking him. But come on now, *Armpit*?

I snigger a little bit but then I realize I'm the only one laughing.

"What an incredibly cool name," says John from the bus stop. "Armpit. It's like your whole name is just one big fuck-you."

Yeah, John, fuck you, too. I suppress an overwhelming compulsion to just turn around and poke him in the eye. Perhaps I should. Maybe his howls of pain would end this roll call of impending doom.

Unfortunately I don't and here it comes, because Armpit's last name is Gandhi, or something like that, so I know it's coming, the ice is popping and snapping around me. . . .

"Sue Garland?" Red says, looking up with that questioning look she's already used like fifteen times. The first several times she used it, I liked the way it made her look. It made me want to fill it, like Bill would've done. Or Jack. Hell, George might've even gone for it, only to pray for forgiveness afterwards. Or maybe he'd just say he did it because God wanted him to. But now I hate that open mouth.

I slouch lower in my seat, thinking that if I can just slouch low enough, maybe I'll become invisible or turn to dust or something and just blow away.

But there's not low enough I can go in this world to hide, thanks to my fucking dad.

Finally, while everyone else is still looking all around the room, trying to figure out which of the girls is Sue Garland, I raise one single finger. I own it.

And that's when everyone starts laughing. Fuckers wouldn't laugh at fucking Armpit, but now they're laughing at me. The ice buckles beneath my feet, then breaks and plunges me into the frozen murky depth below.

"Jack," John laughs, scornfully. "Fucking Jack," he laughs again before turning away.

I really *should* have poked that asshole in the eye.

And that's it, you know. That's the way it's going to go until fucking June. Guys won't hang out with me because I'm a boy named Sue. Girls won't go out with me because I'm a boy named Sue. It's the way it's always been. Why did I ever think any of that'd change now?

I'll probably die jacking off. Alone.

And so it goes on.

I spend my time at home playing the guitar my dad left behind. I suck at it, but there's nothing else to do, so I play anyway. I also drink a lot of Jack Daniels. Fucking Jack.

At school I spend my time alone, counting. There are 262 days until graduation. I, as the teachers always tell us, do the math. If my calculations are correct, there are 22,636,800 seconds remaining until graduation. I spend my classes counting that number down. One day I get caught up on a new concern: Is there a leap year day coming in February? It throws me off until I can find the answer and when I do, I'm lost and have to recalculate all over again. I don't do so well in my classes. Nobody talks to me, except for teachers and my physics lab partner, and he only talks to me when he absolutely has to. Of course it goes without saying that I'm constantly mocked, mainly in the halls, but sometimes in class. Gym's the worst. I've considered coming to school with a baseball bat. Have myself a little "call me Sue and see what I'll do" hit parade. But that's just my fantasy. I know I'll never do anything remotely like that. It seems that I've got the baseball bat but I lack the balls. Besides, if I can just count down the seconds—how many more seconds are left?—I'll be able to finally graduate. I'll move on with my life. I really will be able to finally reinvent myself.

I spend my time, when I'm not playing guitar, fantasizing about my special baseball league, or counting the seconds, coming up with a list of new possible names.

Autumn in New England. The sky is a hard blue crystal, the clouds are puffy, the leaves are changing on the trees, and the temperature is ninety degrees because, you know, there is no global warming.

I stand outside in cutoff shorts and no shirt, because I can. I can go with no shirt because it's ninety degrees and I can wear cutoffs because, no longer having to worry about looking cool, I can just wear whatever's comfortable, rather than wearing those too-long baggy shorts everyone else wears that just have always looked dorky to me anyway and only wind up making my thighs sweat. There are definitely membership privileges in being the only person no one wants to talk to.

I stand on the cement porch, looking at the day, and that's when I spot the moving van next door.

The moving guy is carrying a red cushiony chair, with a teapot balanced on it, toward the house. He looks so big, his nose almost like a giant horn, it's like he's a big rhinoceros or something there in his overalls. I stand next to the bushes and watch, wondering who's moving in. Piano, Victorian floor lamp, end table that looks like it's made of brown plastic instead of wood, a rolled-up carpet—everything comes down the ramp of the van, across the sidewalk, and into the house. The sun is on the other side of the sky now, the ramp is flipped back up into the van, the van is pulling away.

It's then I finally notice the girl.

She has on striped overalls with a yellow tank top underneath, her breasts straining against the fabric. Her hair is blond, long, straight, with nothing done to it like she doesn't even have to worry about fashion. Her eyes are blue, but real warm like and not the cold you sometimes get, and if she's wearing any makeup I sure can't see it from where I'm standing. She's barefoot, too, just like me.

She looks to be my age and, you know, way better than the old guy who lived there before.

Her smile is open, wide, and she lifts her hand in a friendly wave.

"Hey!" she says.

I think about waving back, even get my hand halfway up. But then my mind jumps ahead to Monday. I see that, no matter whom I introduce myself as now, Monday will come, the bus stop will come, and she'll find out who I really am. Maybe she'll even join the others and mock me too. It seems to be the only sport my school excels at.

I can't take this anymore.

So, instead of waving back, I do what anyone else would do in similar circumstances. Well, I guess anyone else who's become the joke of this town and every other town he's ever lived in; anyone who has to put up with the daily putdowns and snickers behind his back. I do what now comes natural: I turn my back on her and walk away. I try to pretend she's not even there.

I can hear her calling out, "Hey, wait a sec! Where ya goin'?"

This is just getting too damn embarrassing. I really should have just talked to her. I wanted to. I'm such a fucking loser. Loser, loser, loser! I keep walking and she keeps calling out to me. I start walking faster. All I want to do is get around the side of my house and out of sight. She keeps calling out to me. I pretend not to hear her. Finally, mercifully, I manage to walk around the side of my house. My heart is pounding. I'm dizzy. I just want this all to end. My eyes tear up. I take off running. I'm not even sure why or where I'm going. I just want to be gone.

I sprint across my yard, all the way to the picket fence that borders our property with the neighbors on the other side. I hit the fence hard, pull myself up, clear it, crash into the garbage cans on the other side. I'm halfway across the neighbors' yard when I turn around. There's no way, I think, she'll clear that fence, but she does, no problem, doesn't even have the problems I did with the garbage cans. Now I see a dog clear the fence, too. I don't know this dog, but now he's running with us, too, as I take off again.

For fun, let's just call this dog Blue.

Why the fuck is she chasing me? If I'm lucky I'll come across a hole I can crawl inside of...and die. I'm definitely keeping my eyes open.

I get to the briar patch on the other side of my neighbors' yard and crawl through. I hate the roots digging at my knees, the branches scratching at my back, that stupid blackbird cawing away on top. And I really hate all the bugs that I'm sure must be all around me, even if I can't see or feel any of them.

I'm sure the briar patch will stop her. No way will she struggle through all this.

But I'm on the other side and now I hear a rustling and there's Blue and there's the damn girl, too, wearing a determined expression on her face.

Fucking girl.

Across from the briar patch, there's an apple orchard and, even though I'm beginning to suspect I may be the weirdest guy who ever lived,

I climb it. When I look down, far below me, I see the girl struggling to keep up. The dog's not even attempting this one, just goes straight over to the flat roof of the cider house and scrambles up onto it, like he knows that's where I'm going to land next.

Fucking Blue.

I lower myself from the slender trembling branch onto that flat roof and I'm on the far side when I hear the girl land with a thud.

This is it. It's time to play for all the marbles.

I jump from the roof, hit the ground, and there she is right behind me. I grab onto a long rope, dangling down from one of the trees, and ride it across the rocky stream, Blue dangling off the end, almost pulling me down.

Girls suck at climbing ropes. I know this from twelve years of gym class, twelve years of guys saying, "Sue's the only girl who can climb to the ceiling." I've always figured the reason girls suck at climbing ropes is cause of their breasts. Their breasts get in the way, weigh them down, make their bodies unevenly distributed. Even when they're younger, before they have real breasts, it's like they have shadow breasts, sabotaging their ability to climb.

The girl with the breasts straining against her yellow tank is not slowed down in the slightest.

Blue and I tumble down the grassy hill, landing, my back getting bruised by the rocks, in the rocky stream that snakes around the hill from the other side.

Just as I'm coming up for air, the girl comes tumbling down the hill, landing right on top of me.

There's nowhere for me to go now.

"I like your shorts," she says, breathing hard. "What's your name?"

Why, oh, why, I think, couldn't this be 22,636,800 seconds from now? She's the perfect girl and if this were only 22,636,800 seconds later, I'd be beyond graduation, I'd be free, and this could all work out.

But this isn't 22,636,800 seconds from now. It is now, as in right now, and there is nothing else to do but to tell the truth. Hell, she'd find out on Monday anyway.

"My name is Sue!" I blurt, a touch maniacally.

She looks at me, startled.

"Well, go on now," I say, "laugh. That's what everybody else does."

And there she is now, she's doing it, just laughing in my face. I'm so used to that, though. Why should life disappoint me now?

Then she does the strangest thing. She leans over and, her hair brushing against the damp sides of my face, kisses me smack on the nose.

"Hey," she says. "My name is Fred."

•

LAUREN BARATZ-LOGSTED lives in Danbury, Connecticut, with her husband, Greg Logsted, and their gorgeous daughter, Jackie. Lauren is the author of the published novels *The Thin Pink Line*, *Crossing the Line*, *A Little Change of Face*, and *How Nancy Drew Saved My Life*, all dark comedies; *Vertigo*, a literary novel set in the Victorian era with erotic and suspense undertones; and the forthcoming young adult novel *Angel's Choice*. Lauren also has an essay in BenBella's Jane Austen theme anthology *Flirting with Pride & Prejudice* and is the editor of and a contributor to BenBella's *This is Chick-Lit*.

GREG LOGSTED lives in Danbury, Connecticut, with his wife, Lauren Baratz-Logsted. He tries to convince their daughter, Jackie, that he fights robots for a living but in fact owns The Other Guy Cleaning Service. Greg is a lifelong music fan, currently working on his first novel.

Gayle Brandeis

TUMBLING

BACKSTORY: Johnny Cash's "I Still Miss Someone" inspired this story. While the song explores missing someone after a relationship ends, the story explores missing someone (in this case, the main character's husband) after his untimely death.

THE ROCK TUMBLER CLATTERED INSIDE THE linen closet. Celia put her pillow over her head to drown it out; it sounded like a blender trying to make daiquiris out of marbles. When she bought the rock tumbler for her son, she thought it would have to run for a couple of hours, maybe a full day. She had no idea she was in for weeks of tumbling, weeks of constant abrasive clank.

Her sleeping son dug his toes into her sweatpants. Brian had no trouble with the sound; he slept through her crying jags, he slept through this incessant grind. She pulled her leg away. Some threads, snagged in his sharp toenails, snapped, but he didn't stir.

Celia slipped out of bed and plodded over to the linen closet. When she opened the door, the decibel increase sent goosebumps up her arms. She threw a mattress pad over the tumbler and carried it over to the coat closet. It felt alive in her hands, a snarling, breathing animal. The bright orange extension cord, still tethered to the outlet near the coffee machine, thumped behind it like a tail.

In the span of a week, Celia had moved the rock tumbler from the kitchen counter to the kitchen cupboard to the bathroom counter to the cabinet under the bathroom sink to the linen closet in the hopes of lessening the noise. She was beginning to run out of hiding places; their one-bedroom apartment was far too small for this kind of racket.

She jammed the tumbler into the closet, fortified it with a ring of galoshes and snow boots. Rubber won't burn, she told herself. If the engine caught on fire—and how could it not? How could such a crappy little engine withstand such work?—it would just melt the rubber. She stumbled back off to bed, half convinced. The noise wasn't any better. If anything, it had grown more fierce. She buried her head under her pillow, dragged the pillow under the covers. She felt like she was full of ants, full of bees, like she was going to burst out of her skin. When Brian shoved his feet between her legs again, she let him keep them there.

In the morning, Celia dragged herself to her dentist appointment. Dr. Haverford's gloved fingers brushed her lips on their way into her mouth, and tears sprang to her eyes. She wished Dr. Haverford would take off his gloves. How long since she had felt adult skin on adult skin? She pressed the tip of her tongue to the latex. The surface was powdery, surprisingly bitter. Saliva pooled inside her cheeks. Dr. Haverford suctioned it out. He was always so gentle with his instruments.

"When did you start grinding your teeth?" Dr. Haverford stretched the corner of her mouth with the stem of a mirror.

"I didn't know I had," she said.

"They're wearing down." He ran his fingers along the ridges of her molars. She half expected them to bend and vibrate in the wake of his touch, like sea anemones, or the teeth of a comb.

"You've been under a lot of stress," he said. "It's understandable."

His glasses made his eyes look three times larger than they were. They made him look like a Keane painting. A Keane painting of a paunchy middle-aged dentist. She wanted to kiss his eyeballs, dig her hands in his curly hair. So strange and unsettling, these flashes of desire.

"Have you been experiencing any headaches?" he asked her. "Any jaw aches?"

"Headaches," she said. She could hear the rock tumbler rasp under her skull.

"I'll make some impressions," he said. "I'll fit you with a bite guard so you won't grind these beauties down." He touched her shoulder before he left the room. She felt the heat of his hand linger in the weave of her shirt, then dissolve.

Celia wondered what her teeth would look like all ground down. She imagined her mouth full of pointy quartz nubs.

Brian had wanted a rock tumbler because he wanted to know what the inside of his rocks looked like. He had amassed an impressive collection of rocks. He found them everywhere—parking lots, the schoolyard, the soccer field, and the courtyard of their apartment building. His pockets were always full of gravel; Celia's purse was, too.

Brian liked to bring the rocks home, hold them under the kitchen tap cupped in his palms. He liked to watch their hidden colors emerge. Some were banded with red; others had hidden brown blotches, greenish speckles, pearly swirls. Then they dried and looked dull again. He wanted to polish them up, take that dullness away for good.

Celia found a tumbler on clearance after the holidays. She was a bit disappointed with the quality of it—the base, which looked like solid metal on the box, was just molded plastic, painted silver; the red plastic barrel seemed too flimsy to hold stones. Brian was thrilled until he found the bag of dusty rocks inside.

"Do I have to use these, Mama?" he asked.

They flipped through the instruction booklet together. "Looks that way," she read. "'These stones have been specially selected for tumbling. Do not mix with different materials.' Sorry, honey."

"But I want to use *my* rocks," he said. He had specially selected a number of rocks himself, had arranged them in an old Frango Mints carton. The rest of his rocks were in shoeboxes under the bed, marked igneous, sedimentary, and metamorphic. Whenever Celia saw the words, she misread them as ingenious, sedentary, and metaphoric.

"Tell you what," said Celia. "We'll do these rocks first, just to make sure it all works out, and when they're done we'll do your rocks. Deal?"

"I guess so," he slumped against her.

The instructions called for petroleum jelly, which Celia didn't have. She had an old bottle of Astroglide in her cosmetic case, but the thought of it depressed her; she was sure it would be welded shut by now. Plus, she didn't want to have to answer Brian's questions about the name. Is it for astronauts? Is it for meteorites? Questions like the ones Brian's dad asked when Celia first came home with it, excited and shy. Her OB/GYN had told her the dryness she had been experiencing was normal, part of perimenopause; she handed Celia the Astroglide and said, "Have fun." Celia was slightly freaked out by the diagnosis, but she followed her doctor's orders well. She and David were silly together that night, giddy with the slipperiness, saying things like "3-2-1, blast off!" and "Houston, we have no problem. No problem here at all." Brian was four then, sound asleep on the couch.

Four seemed so much younger to Celia than six. Four was still a baby. Six was a real boy. A real reading, thinking boy. She and Brian had both grown up a lot in the last two years. The last year, in particular.

Celia found a tube of cherry-scented Chapstick in her purse, the rim of the cap lightly encrusted with sand. She dragged the waxy cylinder around the axle on each end of the barrel, swept it inside the rim of the lid. It left a clotty fragrant smear.

"Now the thing won't get chapped," she told Brian, hoping she hadn't just gummed everything up. She wondered if there was another cherry-scented rock tumbler anywhere in the world.

Dr. Haverford carried two small trays of pink goo into the room.

"Open," he whispered, and her entire body softened on cue. He slid one tray into her mouth, pressed it against her top teeth, her palate. The goo tasted of plastic and mint. It felt pleasantly heavy, like amnesia. She remembered having impressions taken as a teenager at the orthodontist's. She had gagged during the process, had almost thrown up. Since then, she had grown accustomed to having large things in her mouth. She thought of David, the heft and funk of him. She felt a stirring between her legs, a wetness. So her body remembered how to do this after all.

Dr. Haverford gently tugged the tray from her mouth. His fingers on her lips. His breath in her hair. Her teeth felt suddenly naked, exposed. She could see the edges of them etched into the pink, a severe half circle. She pictured plaster being drizzled inside, filling the crevasse, hardening.

Dr. Haverford eased the lower tray into her mouth, wrapping her teeth in a humid clinch. He suctioned more moisture from under her tongue.

"The bite guard will be ready in a couple of weeks," he said. "But there are some things you can do in the meanwhile to stop the grinding. You can put a warm washcloth on your face before bed. You can take a nice bath, cut down on the caffeine. Drink a glass of wine. If you relax yourself before you sleep, your teeth should relax while you sleep."

"I don't sleep," she said. The tray made her sound like she had a major speech impediment. His magnified eyes filled with such sadness, she had to look away. She could hear the rock tumbler turning miles away, never stopping, like a heart.

Celia and Brian rinsed the dust off the bag of stones and put them in the barrel. They emptied the bag of coarse black grit over the stones. They covered it all with water. They set the barrel on the base and turned on the tumbler. It started to turn and clank. Water began leaking out of the lid immediately.

"Oh no!" yelled Brian. "It's broken, Mama! It's not going to work!"

"It's okay," said Celia. She remembered reading that leaking was normal. Leaking was part of the process. She felt her own self leaking. Always leaking. A normal part of the process, people told her. "It will seal itself in about half an hour. The grit and water have to form a bond."

Brian curled into her lap. With each turn of the tumbler, a hint of candy and medicine tinged the air.

The first grit cycle was supposed to take two to four days, but when they opened the barrel and took a look on the third day, the rocks were still rough and pitted. They let the tumbler grind for a few extra days before they poured the contents into a bucket, scooped out the rocks, poured the gritty gray water down the toilet. Some of the rocks were smooth, bits of pink and green shining through. Others still looked brown, dull, even after all that tumbling.

The second grit cycle was supposed to take twelve to fourteen days. Celia didn't know how she was going to handle it. "Remember," the instruction book said, "in mere days you are doing what nature takes thousands of years to accomplish." Her jaw tightened and clenched. She could feel her mouth fill with dust, the edges of her teeth eroding.

"Would you like to see your impressions?" Dr. Haverford asked at her next appointment, a couple of weeks later.

"I don't know," she said. "Did I make a good one?"

"You always make a good impression, Mrs. Nurenberger." Dr. Haverford smiled before he walked over to the closet, and, to her surprise, every warm feeling she felt toward him vanished. She didn't want her love to be requited.

"I have a surprise for you," he said when he returned. She was worried—what did he have for her? Candy? Flowers? A ring? What would she say?

He placed two plaster sets of teeth on the little tray by the chair. She recognized her own teeth, the ones that overlapped a little on the bottom that had drifted back as soon as she had stopped wearing her retainers.

"Whose are these?" she asked, pointing to the strange mouth beside hers.

"Those are Mr. Nurenberger's," he said softly.

And there they were, David's teeth, the span of David's gums. How could she not have known? The little chip on his front tooth. The slight protrusion of his eyeteeth. The filling on the side of his molar. The teeth her teeth had clinked against. The gums her tongue had run across. The teeth that had cradled his tongue, sheltered by his lips. She picked up the plaster and held it to her chest. She kissed every canine, every incisor. She pressed the impressions of his mouth against the impressions of her mouth. The feel of plaster on plaster was an insult. She hurled both mouths against the wall and watched them explode.

Celia had been avoiding going to Evergreen. She hadn't gone since the funeral. Brian, who was sick that day, had never been there. She thought it was time. It was time to visit David's real set of teeth, his teeth and bones surviving underground while the rest of him rotted away, his lips, his tongue, all the parts of him she had touched. Celia felt nauseous. In the parking lot, a couple walked by, leaning into each other, eyes red and teary. He had his arm around her waist; she had both arms slung around his neck. Celia felt a tidal wave of jealousy. The couple was obviously grieving, but at least they were grieving *together.*

It took Celia a while to find David's site. She plowed forward, Brian trudging behind. A cold, wild wind swept leaves into the air around them, but Celia didn't shiver until they finally found his name chipped into gray granite. The thought of a chisel against stone made her teeth hurt.

Brian reached toward the rocks on the gravestone. Celia wrapped her hand around his wrist and pulled it back.

"Those are Daddy's rocks," she said. Her voice felt insubstantial in the wind. "You need to leave them there."

"Why?"

"To show that people have been here to see him. To show that we remember him." She wondered who had been there. His parents, probably. His sister. Cousins. Friends. Not his wife. Not his son.

Brian nodded. He started to pull rocks from his pockets, dozens of rocks, and set them on the gravestone. Rock after rock after rock. So many rocks. David's skin used to be so soft....

"Where did you get all those?" Celia asked him.

He didn't say anything. He just kept unloading more rocks, laying them on top of the granite. She didn't know how he could fit so many into his small pockets.

"Did you get those from other people's graves, Brian?"

"I didn't know," he said. "I didn't know you were supposed to keep them there."

Celia imagined she should tell him to put them back where he found them, to spread them back over other people's markers, but as she watched him lay down one stone after another on top of his father's gravestone, she thought, *David, these are all for you.*

When they got home, Brian asked, "Where's Daddy's rock?"

"We left the rocks at the cemetery, honey," Celia said. She felt drained. The rock tumbler growled and rattled in the closet, jangled and clacked.

"No, the rock that was in him."

"The gallstone?" She had almost forgotten about the gallstone, had pushed it to the back of her mind the way she had pushed the baby-food jar holding it to the back of the kitchen cupboard.

It was supposed to be an easy operation. Laparoscopic—one day in the hospital, minimal recovery time, and minimal scarring. But there was a problem with the anesthesia and David never woke up. The dark jade stone was the only part of him she was able to bring home. That first night, she put the stone in her mouth, hoping for a last taste of his body. The stone tasted chemical, as if it had been soaked in formaldehyde. She spit it out and shunted it as far away as she could. Her tongue felt numb for days.

"Can we put it in the tumbler?" asked Brian.

They were going to start the polish cycle soon. They had to scrub out the barrel, rinse off the stones, and prepare them for their final week-long fling.

"I don't see why not," she said.

Before David's operation, they had looked up the word "gall" in the dictionary. It meant many things. "Something bitter to endure," for one. "Bitterness of spirit," for another. "A cause or state of exasperation." Also, "to wear away by friction, to become worn by rubbing."

"I am getting rid of my bitterness," said David. When Celia kissed him, his mouth tasted like soup—salty, savory, not bitter in the least.

The bite guard was not easy to get used to. At Dr. Haverford's office, it felt smooth, simple between her teeth, but at home it felt like she was biting down on an airplane wing. She couldn't sleep—not only because of the noise, but because she was sure she was going to choke on the plastic.

When it was time to start the polishing process, Celia could barely keep her eyes open. She asked Brian to tell her about the different kinds of rocks as she poured the contents of the tumbler into a bucket. She hoped his voice would keep her awake.

"Ingenious," she said. "Tell me about ingenious rocks."

"Igneous," he corrected. "Igneous rocks are rocks that were made from lava. Lava that cooled off."

"And sedentary?" She ran her hands through the wet stones.

"Sedimentary. Those are rocks that are made from pieces of other rocks."

"What about metaphoric?"

"Metamorphic, Mama," he sighed. "Those are ones that change. Like they end up in a different place and it makes them change. Like they're buried underground and they get hot and they melt and change."

"Sounds metaphoric to me," said Celia. She tried not to think of David underground, melting, changing. She felt like she was melting, herself, she was so tired. She scooped the stones from the bucket, the stones that had grown smoother, more colorful, during all the tumult—marbled shades of magenta and cobalt and amber and emerald. She poured the dirty water down the toilet. She rinsed the bits of grit off the stones. She washed the inside of the barrel with soap and a brush. She climbed up onto the step stool, and pulled the baby-food jar down from the kitchen cupboard, knocking down a box of corn meal, a bag of split peas in the process. She left the spill, a spray of sand and pebbles on the counter, alone.

The gallstone, released from its jar, was a much deeper green than any of the stones from the tumbler. How could a body produce such a beautiful thing—a beautiful thing that could cause such pain? She rinsed the stone off, pressed it quickly to her lips, and handed it to Brian. He solemnly placed it in the barrel on top of the other stones. He poured a cup of clean water over them, then the bag of polish. He closed the lid and turned the tumbler on.

The familiar clanking filled the room. Celia's lips tingled. This time she didn't find the noise so jarring. It sounded rowdy, robust, alive. This time David was there inside it, after a long, long silence, making himself heard once again.

●

GAYLE BRANDEIS is an award-winning author, whose first book, *Fruitflesh: Seeds of Inspiration for Women Who Write*, has been adopted by writers worldwide. Gayle's novel, *The Book of Dead Birds*, won Barbara Kingsolver's Bellwether Prize for Fiction in Support of a Literature of Social Change in 2002, and was published by HarperCollins. Her poetry, fiction, and essays have appeared in dozens of magazines, anthologies, and Web sites, including Salon.com, Nerve.com, *Hip Mama*, and *The Oy of Sex: Jewish Women Write Erotica*. Gayle's second novel, *Self Storage*, will be published by Ballantine in January 2007. Gayle, who was named a Writer Who Makes a Difference by *The Writer Magazine*, is Writer-in-Residence for the Mission Inn Foundation's Family Voices Project, and teaches writing throughout Southern California. She lives in Riverside, California, with her husband and their two children.

Gretchen Moran Laskas

THINGS MIGHT HAPPEN

BACKSTORY: The story of a liberating divorce has become something of a staple in short story collections. Being contrary by nature (a family failing?) I wondered what a "stay together" story might be like. Country music in particular offers several excellent examples of such works, but there was one in particular men seemed drawn to: Johnny Cash's "I Walk the Line." Since the male character in this particular story exists completely off the page; since he is a man without a voice amidst all the rapid-fire female ones (another family failing?), letting Johnny speak for him evens the playing field a bit.

RITA WAS NINE YEARS OLD WHEN her parents finally divorced. As far back as she could remember they had been fighting over every little thing—the light bill, the new shower curtain, the dogs Daddy bought and tried to train (but they only messed in the house the more he used the whistle). What Rita remembered after he left was how quiet everything was, how peaceful. When she would come home from school, the only sounds in the house were gentle, feminine ones: the whirl of her mother's sewing machine in the upstairs bedroom, or the clicking of the crock-pot turning on and off.

When Rita was fourteen, her father came back and her parents remarried. The fights were the same (although there weren't any more dogs) and Rita began to avoid the house altogether, taking a job at the mall and staying out late with friends. All of them had parents who had either stayed together or fallen apart, not the stop and start of Rita's life. She would sit on the bleachers outside the school, moaning about the latest round of vicious name-calling in the kitchen. What she didn't mention was how most mornings, her mother smiled as she fixed breakfast, and her father had taken to whistling.

Perhaps he missed the dogs?

Rita found the whole thing humiliating.

When Rita married John two years ago, she told him that she would never put her kids through all that. And she won't, or at least, she wouldn't, because she and John never had kids. Good thing, too, because their marriage is all over. Rita plans to get divorced and stay that way.

"I don't see his truck," Rita says as she pulls the car into the driveway of the doublewide where she had lived since they were married. She shuts off the engine and sits a moment, looking at the house, with the door closed up tight and all the curtains pulled. When she left, a week ago, everything had been wide open; she had nothing to hide, after all.

"During the day is always the best time to come," Traci tells her. Traci is her best friend from high school and has offered to let Rita stay with her for a few weeks. Traci has been divorced twice, and has an apartment in Morgantown with big patio doors that look out over a ravine and a washer and dryer that stack one on top of the other. Everything in the apartment is beige: the walls, the carpet, the sofa and chair. Only the end tables are shiny black plastic.

"Men don't just miss work on account of a little marriage going sour," Traci says. Her eyes are angry and narrow. Traci was off today, and Rita called in to the veterinary clinic where she works as a receptionist and said that she was sick with a migraine. So it is obvious to both of them that they care more. They are here and John is not.

Rita pulls out her keys, and has a moment of pure panic. What if John changed the locks? What if she can't get inside, where all of her things are, everything she owns but the few mismatched items she threw into the suitcase before she left? She'd packed clothes for work, for instance, but not her comfortable shoes. Toothpaste, but no mouthwash. For three days now Rita has been stealing Traci's mouthwash, just a little at a time so Traci won't notice, and wearing her Reeboks with skirts and trying to hide her feet behind the front desk at work.

But Rita's key works just fine, and the air inside is cool. After the soothing beige of Traci's apartment, the doublewide almost blinds her with its color. The bright gold couch and the green chair are right where she left them. The curtains are red and gold striped, and the wallpaper is green with red flowers. Rita is embarrassed to have Traci see the place, although it is spotlessly clean, which Traci's apartment is not. Rita is not surprised to note that the room is actually cleaner than when she left it—John is probably pleased that he can run the house the way he likes. The brass lamps gleam when she turns them on. When Traci pushes the tape player (John doesn't like CDs and spends hours scouring stores for tapes and even vinyl records), Rita hears Johnny Cash.

"Turn that off," she snaps at Traci, who looks up, surprised. Usually Traci is the angry one. But Traci can't know that John used to sing the song "I Walk the Line" when they were dating, how much Rita had loved it then. He seemed so confident, so sure of himself. So unlike her father. What she hadn't known was that he would want her to walk the line, too. Being married to John was like joining the army, she'd told Traci last week.

Rita can see Traci looking around, and knows that Traci doesn't think much of the doublewide. To Traci, doublewide will always mean trailer, which is true, but isn't true at the same time, because the rooms are bigger, more like a house. They walk down the hall to the master bedroom. The bed is made, the covers pulled tightly, and Rita finds it hard to believe that the bed is soft or that she ever slept in it.

"So what did John do to you?" Traci asks, sitting in a chair and watching Rita open drawers and drop clothes into a laundry basket she took from the closet. Rita thinks that Traci should offer to help, or at least give advice, having gone through this twice before. What does one pack for a divorce that fits inside a laundry basket?

"Do to me?" Rita asks.

Traci is looking at the bed. "What was the straw that broke the camel's back?"

"Oh," Rita says, wondering what to say. "Nothing shocking. I mean, it's not like he ran off with another woman or something."

Traci leans forward in the chair. "Did he ever, you know, do anything to you?" she asks. Her voice is lower, as though there is someone else in the house listening besides Rita.

"Do to me?" Rita says, and realizes that she just said this a few seconds ago. But it is like Traci knows a language other than English, which she expects Rita to understand, now that she is getting divorced, too.

"Did he ever, you know, hurt you in any way? Hit you?"

"Of course not!" Rita says, her voice loud. Traci falls back against the chair, as though Rita's denial has pushed her there. "John isn't like that," Rita tells her in a softer voice. "I mean, with John, he just gets quieter when he's upset." Rita realizes that Traci, her best friend, doesn't know John at all.

"Sometimes those are the worst ones," Traci says. She nods her head as though she and Rita are agreeing on something, and maybe they are, Rita thinks. After she folds her jeans and underwear and puts them in the basket, she's dismayed by how full it is. She hasn't yet packed the clock that had been her grandmother's, or the quilt her great-aunt Mary had made. Her closet is still filled with clothes.

Traci is looking over her fingernails, and Rita worries that she might be bored. "I don't think it was any one thing," she says, trying to get Traci interested again. "But lots of little things. You know, like one night we were sitting in the kitchen and I noticed that John seemed to be listening for something." Her voice wavers a little, and Rita fights it for control. "And it made me upset that he wasn't listening for me, because obviously, I was sitting right there."

When Rita has said this, Traci is still looking at her fingernails, although she nods and sighs. Rita goes into the bathroom, knowing that she has let Traci down in some way, but unsure of how to fix it. She opens the medicine cabinet and stares at the tiny bottles of mouthwash that John uses. He has this idea that things will keep longer in smaller packages. Everything in the cabinet is arranged by height. "Look at this," Rita wants to show Traci. "This is what my life is like." But she admits that the order makes everything easy to find, and the tiny bottles will be easier to pack.

Rita takes a few bottles and some more toothpaste. She takes the Advil, too, because John never takes anything when he gets a headache. All this in hand, she stares at the pink plastic container holding her diaphragm and the half-used tube of KY Jelly. She can't imagine having sex with anyone right now, but it seems strange to leave it here for John. Maybe if she takes it, he'll think that she is having sex with someone else, and Rita is surprised how excited this idea makes her. Maybe then he will call and yell and scream and make a fuss.

She sits down on the toilet, glad to have a minute alone to think. What would it take, she wonders, to make John kick up a fuss? It just isn't his way. John doesn't worry about something so much as he does something about it. He's always trying to keep things from breaking down. Like the Y2K crisis, when the news started reporting about that, he went every week to Wal-Mart and stocked up on gun shells, dried fruit, and kerosene. When Rita asked him about this, he didn't say much, just that he wanted to be ready, *just in case*.

"In case of what?" she asked him.

"Things might happen," he answered. "We need to be prepared." After that he started buying canned goods, stacking them under the kitchen sink when he ran out of room in the cupboards. Rita teased him about eating canned baked beans until the next millennium. John didn't think that was very funny.

Just when Rita thought he might be calming down, there came the terrorist attacks. After 9/11, John began again. Rita watched the piles of sheeting plastic grow, and the mounds of duct tape. Bottled water filled one closet. He talked about buying a generator. "I promised I would take care of you. I just want to do my best."

"How is putting me in a plastic bubble going to take care of me?" she'd demanded.

"I'm just following the list," he replied, holding it up. The words DEPARTMENT OF HOMELAND SECURITY ran across the top.

My home was certainly secure, Rita thinks. Still, she'd managed to get in easily enough with her own key.

She goes back into the bedroom, where Traci is standing up, looking down at the bed with its pillows set so neatly. "When I was married to Dave," Traci says, still staring at the bed, "he held me down and raped me over and over until I told him that I loved him." Her voice is low and flat, as though someone has taken it out of her mouth and stepped on it.

Rita feels a wave of sympathy and puts her arms around Traci. When Traci pulls away, she is calm again. She tosses her head over in the direction of the laundry basket. "Are you ready? I want to go home."

"I'm ready," Rita answers. And even though she isn't, she feels she ought to be.

Back in Morgantown, Rita and Traci stop for a cup of coffee. Coffee is one of those things that Traci takes very seriously, and both she and the clerk look disappointed when Rita asks for a plain cup, black. Traci orders a double latte with hazelnut cream.

"You don't have to prove anything to me," Traci tells her. They are sitting in the booth at the coffee house, which seems to be filled with students from WVU. Rita is startled by how young they look, how intense.

"I'm not proving anything," she says, sipping her coffee. It is not as strong as she normally drinks it.

"You've been doing it all week," Traci tells her. "Like the button you sewed on last night, on that blouse. It was like you had to sew on that button or else your whole life was going to come apart."

"That's my favorite blouse," Rita protests.

Traci shakes her head. "I know what it's like, you know, going through all this. And I know when someone is ordering a plain cup of coffee just to punish herself." She puts her hand over Rita's and gives it a quick squeeze. "It's all right, that's what I'm telling you."

Rita looks down at her mug of coffee and can see her own face wavering back at her. It's true that she used to drink her coffee full of cream and with two sugars, back when she was in high school and working with Traci at Montgomery Ward, standing outside the store giving away toasters and baking dishes to anyone who opened a charge account. She isn't sure of the exact moment she switched to black coffee. John always took his black and sometimes, when she didn't want a whole cup of her own, she would take just a taste of his. But Rita can't remember when she decided that his was better.

"Look at that," Traci whispers, and points to their left.

Coming into the coffee shop is a tall man wearing a worn flannel shirt and the sandals you wear with socks—something that Rita can't imagine doing. With him is a young girl, and Rita first thinks that it's his daughter until she sees them sit down and open up some books. She guesses it's a professor and a student.

"You can bet he's sleeping with her," Traci says, her voice low, but not quite a whisper this time.

The man is wearing a wedding ring, and the girl is not, Rita notices. Still, she is unsure. The girl's eyes are bright and watch the man carefully, but all of the students in the bar seem to have that look, as though they are waiting for something big to happen to them. As though a package is coming for them in the mail.

"How do you know?" she asks Traci. Rita watches them in small glances, trying not to be obvious about it. She is waiting to see if they touch, but they don't.

"You forget that I was married to one of them," Traci says, and that tone is back in her voice, that tone she used at the doublewide, in Rita's bedroom. She glares at them without even pretending that she isn't.

"Was that Dave?" Rita asks. Was it a professor that tried to rape you? Was he dressed like that? These are the things she really wants to ask, but doesn't because she's embarrassed that she can't remember. Traci has a life that such stories seem to run together instead of sticking in your mind.

"Morrie," Traci says, dropping her eyes now. "You'd think that I would have known better, seeing as he was married when he started seeing me."

"Oh," says Rita. She has not known this.

"I didn't do anything wrong," Traci is quick to point out. "Morrie had already left his wife." She looks back at the couple. "He wasn't wearing a wedding band, for heaven's sake, and his divorce was almost final."

"I see," Rita says, although she doesn't. For the first time, she thinks about John taking off his wedding band. He could see other women, like Morrie dated Traci. Now that she's gone, he's a free man.

Another student comes in, a boy this time, and sits down next to the girl. The professor smiles and says something and they all laugh.

Two weeks later, Rita is still living in Traci's apartment. Traci hasn't said anything, but Rita knows she will have to find her own place soon. Nothing as nice as the doublewide, or even like this, but something. Maybe John will give her part of the furniture. She'd like the kitchen table and chairs, which are painted blue with gingham seat cushions on them.

Traci is dating a new boyfriend, an assistant buyer at Ward's, where Traci still works as a floor manager. Twice they have come back to the apartment and had sex in Traci's bedroom, which is right beside Rita's. Rita can hear everything, and judging from the sounds, the sex must be pretty good. They are in there right now, and Rita is trying to talk to her mother on the phone while standing on the little balcony. She hopes that her mother can't hear them.

"He hasn't even called or written or anything," Rita says. Rain is falling and she has to keep a finger pressed against her left ear as she talks in order to hear what her mother is saying.

"Well, what can you expect? I blame myself, your marriage going bad," her mother says.

Rita was a bit surprised, at first, that her mother wasn't more upset about the divorce. Instead, her mother seems to feel guilty, as though she is the one getting the divorce instead of Rita.

"It's not your fault," Rita tells her, and there is a snuffle on the other line, as though her mother is crying.

"Your Dad and me, well, we weren't the best example," her mother says. There is the sound of a nose being blown and a slight cough. "But I do hate the thought of you being there in West Virginia without any of us to help you." Rita's parents now live in Florida, in a trailer that is a real trailer and not a doublewide.

"I'm fine, really," Rita assures her.

"When I think of how humiliated you must have been, your parents getting divorced and all. Why didn't you tell us, sweetie?"

"I'm fine, Mom," Rita says again. "You and Dad did a great job. I'm not upset with you."

She isn't upset, not about the divorce. When her parents remarried again when she was fourteen, well, that was embarrassing. Her mother wore white and her father bought them all enormous bouquets of flowers. After the wedding, there was a reception in the church basement with a cake two feet tall, with a pale blue fountain inside.

"This is the wedding I always wanted," her mother said over and over. "This is much more real than the first time, driving over the mountain into Oakland."

Her mother is still talking, but Rita has removed her finger from her ear and can no longer hear her. The rain is falling harder now, and the storm drain at the bottom of the ravine is filling up with water, brown water, the color of the latte with hazelnut cream.

She goes back inside, telling her mother good-bye. When she closes the patio door, she listens in the direction of the bedroom, but all is quiet now. Rita walks around the living room, straightening the pictures on the end tables. All of the pictures are of Traci. Traci sitting on the beach with a string bikini on, her long legs blending into the sand. Another of Traci wearing a baseball cap, smiling shyly at the camera, as though it had surprised her. Traci sitting on the steps of the state Capitol building down in Charleston.

Rita wonders who took all these pictures. Who stood on the other side of the camera, telling Traci to smile? She notices that some of the pictures have been cut, so only Traci remains, happy, waving to the person looking at the picture.

The sounds start again in the bedroom, and Rita is restless. She looks around the living room, but the beige color makes everything run together and there is nowhere to focus her eyes except on the pictures, and Rita is tired of looking at Traci looking at her. She goes back out to the balcony.

The rain is gushing now, washing like curtains down from the roof. Down in the ravine, the creek has become a raging river. Rita watches it rise, sees the water cascading down the steep slopes of the ravine, making the river bigger and bigger.

With this rain, flooding is a possibility, although it is hard to believe that the water could reach this far up. Still, it could happen, that roaring coffee-colored water, pouring in here, making the beige couch a darker brown and swirling away the pictures.

As Rita watches the water, she thinks about the water coming up and up and up, not only into this apartment, but spreading throughout the whole valley like a great, ancient river. Everything would vanish. People would drown.

But John has a boat. They've never used it, but Rita knows that it would be in tip-top condition, because that's just the way John is. And the Homeland Security supplies don't sound so silly now—after all, they could put the dried fruit and the bottled water into the boat. They could take the cans and some matches and a gun with shells. A fishing pole, a tent—John will know where everything is. She would even pack some of the tiny bottles of mouthwash. It is antiseptic; it could help keep things clean, and John would like that. No matter what happened, they would be prepared.

Rita picks up her purse and scribbles a note for Traci. She does not bother to pack her suitcase. What good would her suitcase be in a boat? Outside, she gets into her car, and drives as quickly as she can for the doublewide. She hopes she is not too late. Rita hopes there is still time to launch the boat and set it floating down the river before the water covers the world.

•

GRETCHEN MORAN LASKAS is an eighth-generation West Virginian, the setting for her first novel, *The Midwife's Tale*. Her young adult novel, *The Miner's Daughter*, about the coal camps of West Virginia in the Great Depression, will be published by Simon and Schuster in 2007. Her short fiction has been published in numerous literary magazines, including *Salt Hill*, *Pleiades*, and *Mobius*, and is included in the anthology, *American Girls about Town*. Laskas now lives in Virginia with her husband and son. *The Midwife's Tale* has won Appalachian Book of the Year, the Weatherford Award for Fiction, for outstanding contribution to Appalachia, and has been nominated for Southeastern Booksellers Book of the Year and the Virginia Library Award. It also received a Library Journal starred review and was selected as a "Must Read" by *Working Mother Magazine* and was a Featured Alternate Selection of the Literary Guild and Doubleday Book Club.

Russell Rowland

ONE MORE WRONG THING

BACKSTORY: Growing up in Montana, country music was a big part of the soundtrack of my childhood. And there was no bigger star during those formative years than Mr. Johnny Cash. We watched him stroll out at the beginning of his variety show every week and announce in that wonderful baritone, "Hello, I'm Johnny Cash." Much to my dismay, I turned out to be a tenor. But Johnny continues to inspire, as he did with this story.

WHEN THE COP APPROACHED JIM HANDY on the street, he had a woman with him. A woman Jim recognized. He'd passed her on the sidewalk just a few moments before, and had smiled at her. He had in fact given her his best smile, knowing that she'd probably ignore him, that she'd just keep on walking, because that's what downtown people do when people smile at them. Now, however, things did not look good. The woman was scowling at him, her brow lowered over her eyes like a visor.

"Just what the hell do you think you're doing?" the officer asked.

"What do you mean?" Jim replied.

The cop pointed, down—at Jim's crotch. Jim didn't want to look down there with this woman standing there, right in front of him. But the officer was angry. Both of them were. Jim could see that for a fact. So he looked, and imagine his surprise when he found that his zipper was wide open, and spread apart like a goddamn barn door. He was on full display.

Jim quickly tucked and zipped. And then, flustered, his face burning up, and realizing that he must have been careless after he stopped at the coffee shop and used the restroom, Jim shuffled his feet, wishing he could hide somewhere. The cop was staring at him, waiting for some kind of explanation, but Jim's jaw hung loose. Something needed to be said. Finally, Jim managed to speak. His voice rasped, nearly a whisper.

"I had no idea," he said. "Really."

The look that both the cop and the woman wore told him that they didn't buy his innocence for a minute.

Jim tried to explain. It had been a difficult morning. An argument with his wife. He was distracted. And he was wearing loose pants. It was an honest mistake, forgetting to zip up. Wearing boxers. It could happen to anyone. It was also a warm summer day, so there was no cold air to alert him.

"He tilted his head," the woman said with disdain. "He was definitely trying to get me to look."

"I'm going to have to take you in," the cop said. He turned to the woman. "Do you mind coming in, too? To make a statement?"

"Gladly," she said. "Anything to see this... this... maggot put away. Just give me a minute to call my office," she added, and the cop nodded. She pulled out her cell phone.

"This is awful," Jim said, and his mind was working, trying to figure out how he was going to explain to his boss, to his wife, to everyone. But a look from the cop told him he'd better watch his step, so Jim didn't say another word.

It had already been a strange morning—besides the argument with his wife, which led to a very unpleasant conclusion, there had been so many odd thoughts going through Jim's head.

Every morning, Jim rode the bus downtown to work. Usually, like everyone else, he walked to the bus, got on the bus, and rode the bus with his eyes to the ground, or in a magazine—anywhere but on the eyes of others. But that morning, each time the bus came to another stop, and the hydraulic puff of air sounded when the door sucked to a close, Jim felt closed in. He kept going over the argument with Alice, and all he had to do at work, and for once in his life, he wasn't comfortable burrowing further into his head. He needed a distraction.

Jim noticed a young father on the bus with his three small children. The children were adorable—about the same age as his kids. And having a great time, although the bus was packed. They giggled and made faces, and pulled their voices up and down into funny caricatures.

The people on the bus were not amused, not being accustomed to interruptions in their silent meditation. Especially from children. The presence was unusual, and the children's giddy mood made a lot of people uncomfortable. They frowned, or fidgeted.

But not Jim. He smiled to himself when the little girl, about seven, threw her arms around her younger brother, nuzzling her face into his neck. It tickled the little boy, and he giggled, tilting his head toward her to try and force her face away.

Even the father was playful. He held a baby about nine months old, and blew raspberries onto its chubby tummy and its cheeks. And he touched the little girl's neck with his finger and wiggled it, tickling her, too. The girl squealed, and people on the bus cringed, or hunkered deeper into their newspapers.

But Jim smiled at the little girl. Then he looked up, and noticed one other person on the bus who was smiling. An older woman. Her powder blue eyes were aimed directly at Jim, and she nodded, acknowledging that she appreciated this diversion as much as he did. Jim nodded back, but he suddenly felt uncomfortable, as if he'd been discovered doing something forbidden.

For the rest of the trip, Jim tried to catch the father's eye. Jim wanted to let him know with a look that he admired the way he handled his children. And the fact that Jim couldn't get his attention made him admire the man even more. Because the father didn't even bother to look around the bus. He didn't give a damn whether anyone was uncomfortable with his children's behavior or not. He never took his eyes off them, and the smile on his face was one of pure joy—pure, unwavering, unapologetic joy.

The children and their father got off the bus, and one stop later, the older woman made her way toward the exit. As she passed Jim in the aisle, she looked up. "Thank you for the smile." She gripped his arm.

Jim nodded, but he was embarrassed. And he was puzzled as to why her compliment would embarrass him. And when he realized why, he was troubled. It was because she had drawn attention to him. Even though it was only momentary, she had diverted the crowd's eyes to Jim, and he was aware that just because he appreciated those children, and wasn't as bothered by them as the others, he was really no different than the rest of them. When it came down to being singled out, Jim was just as frightened, just as determined to be another anonymous presence on another commuter vehicle to another mundane day of work.

The discovery shook him, and as he crawled out among the striding mass of white collars and suits with clean lines, Jim couldn't stop wondering when and how he had become one of them. How and when had he become so scared? And how could he allow this to happen?

These were the thoughts that passed through Jim's head as he strolled down the street that morning, looking for life in the unsmiling, serious faces. And he was trying to remember the last time he'd done something spontaneous.

And it was then, when that thought hit him, that he noticed the woman in question, his eventual accuser. She was quite beautiful, with the kind of sleek black hair Jim liked, and dark red lipstick against her pale skin. Quite out of his league, he knew. Even if he had been single. But with this thought of spontaneity fresh in his head, and the fight with Alice still lingering, Jim followed an instinct and smiled at her. And to his surprise, she started to smile back. But her expression changed quickly. Jim attributed this to a realization that she had let down her guard and smiled at a stranger on the street. He assumed she had been overcome with her own fear, and regretted smiling.

And so it happened. Jim was arrested. His first time. And it wasn't as bad as he'd always imagined. Not at first anyway.

When the cop took him by the arm and "helped" him into the back of his car, Jim was surprised that it didn't bother him much. Not even with all the people gawking—actually, they didn't really gawk. It is important in the downtown environment to appear as if nothing fazes you, to keep your fear masked with a stiff indifference. Being distracted by the world around you shows weakness, a vulnerability that could lead to failure. So people didn't stop, or gather. They glanced furtively. But Jim didn't feel the need to tuck his chin into his neck, or pull his jacket over his head.

And it was then that Jim first began to feel a hint of freedom. On the ride to the station, Jim started chuckling thinking about it. The cop glared at him in his mirror.

"You think this is amusing?"

"I'm sorry," Jim said. "It's too complicated to explain."

The cop glared again, and muttered.

And the more Jim thought about it, the more he felt that he could make the most of this adventure. After all, most of the people Jim knew had never been to jail. This could be an opportunity to give everyone some insight into what it's like. Excellent party conversation. He'd always been curious himself. When they got to the station, the cop took Jim's statement, which was pretty straightforward. Jim surprised him. He admitted his crime.

"I thought you said it wasn't intentional," the cop said.

"I know," Jim answered.

"You know?"

"Yes."

"You know what?"

"I know that's what I said."

"But it was?" he asked.

"Yes, I think so," Jim replied.

"You think so?"

"Yes."

Jim had noticed by now, from his nametag, that the cop's name was O'Hare. He was thick, and his complexion had that Irish ruddiness. And as he got flustered, he reddened even more. Jim wanted to explain that he wasn't trying to make him angry, but he knew the cop wouldn't understand. So although he was cooperative, the more Jim talked, the more upset the cop became.

Jim's accuser was not amused, either. In fact, she found his manner offensive. She had already given her statement, talking through clenched teeth, and glaring at Jim from the sides of her eyes. And then, as if she couldn't bear to leave until she saw him behind bars, she waited while O'Hare questioned Jim. He could hear the breath racing through her nose.

"You want to make your phone call now?" O'Hare asked.

"I waive that right," Jim said.

"You don't want to make a phone call?"

"No."

"What about your job?"

"They'll be fine without me."

The cop tightened his lips. Then he glanced at Jim's hands. He pointed. "How about your wife?"

Jim shrugged.

The woman jumped in. "I wouldn't want to call her either, if I had this kind of news," she sputtered.

"Do you have a lawyer?" O'Hare asked.

"No."

"You are despicable," the woman growled, her voice barely audible.

"A lot of people don't have lawyers." Jim tried smiling at her, to lighten things up. But this drew the most hateful scowl yet.

Finally, the woman shook her head, in that shivering way that people do when they've endured more than they ever thought possible. And she left. Jim felt bad. After all, she was the victim of something she didn't understand. She had no way of knowing that she had run headlong into a situation that involved more than a simple matter of indiscretion. It was fate. She just happened to be in the way.

O'Hare looked Jim over. "So you want to post bond?" The cop told Jim how much it was.

"No," Jim said.

O'Hare kept his gaze fixed on Jim, his murky blue eyes boring into him. "No?"

Jim shook his head.

"Listen," O'Hare said, leaning forward in his chair. He had one of those swivel chairs, and the springs groaned loudly when he tilted his ample weight. "You don't have any priors. All you have to do is post bond, and you can go. You come back for your court date, pay your fine. . . ." He threw his hand in the air, indicating the end of it.

"No. I'd rather not do that," Jim said.

O'Hare raised his brow. "So you'd rather spend the night in jail?"

Jim nodded. "Yes," he said. "That's what I'd rather do."

O'Hare swiveled, and locked his hands together on the desk. He studied his fingers, as if trying to determine whether he had them in the right order. "Do you have any history of . . . mental disorders . . . anything like that?" he asked.

Jim informed him that he did not, and O'Hare nodded. Then his head changed its direction and started shaking back and forth. "All right," he said. "No phone call?" he asked, making sure.

"No," Jim answered.

The second thing Jim noticed about his jail cell was how much it looked like he expected it would. Jim had never seen a jail cell. Except on TV, or in movies. But it seemed familiar in the same way that a neighbor's living room does, even though you've never been inside. Familiar because of the assumptions you've made from observation.

It was gray, of course. Everything in the cell was gray. Even the sheets, although clean, were gray. Gray from being thin and from being washed with gray things over and over again.

Jim stood on the gray cement and took it all in, which only took a second or two. Then he addressed the first thing he'd noticed about the cell, which was the other inmate. A tiny man. He sat cross-legged on the lower bunk, and the mattress hardly showed his weight. He had slicked black hair, sideburns, and his bone-thin, tattooed arms jutted out of a sleeveless T-shirt.

He squinted up at Jim, showing his teeth, as if the sun was in his eyes. His teeth were tobacco-stained. Everything about him appeared to be stained with tobacco. His fingers, even his nails. And his skin. He was so tan that Jim couldn't make out the tattoos.

Jim was still feeling a bit giddy from his newfound freedom, so when he spoke to the tiny man, he flinched at the lightness of Jim's mood. Jim imagined what he must think, seeing this clean-cut man in dress clothes.

"Hello," Jim said.

And after he jumped, he responded with his own, "Hullo."

Then it was Jim's turn to flinch. Because from the depths of this almost childlike man, whose chest was no bigger around than a basketball, came a voice as deep and smooth as Jim had ever heard—the kind of voice that pulls you into an immediate state of awe, and respect. He sounded like Johnny Cash.

"Handy," Jim said, offering a handshake. "Jim Handy."

The other man's head tilted slightly to one side, and he measured Jim with an, "Are you one of them queers?" sort of look. But he shook Jim's hand.

"Name's Elvin," he said. "Elvin Taylor."

Jim hitched up his pants. "So what are you in for, Elvin?" He delighted in being able to ask this classic question.

Elvin's deep-set, coffee-brown eyes remained fixed on Jim, the skin below them hanging like the seat of a truck driver's jeans. He grinned and looked Jim up and down, shaking his head. "You never been in jail before, have you?"

"Well...." Jim said.

Elvin just looked at him, then rubbed his eyes. He shook his head again. "What did *you* do?" he asked, and his voice rumbled through the cold walls. "Park your Mercedes on the sidewalk?"

Jim dug his hands in his pockets and paced across the cell, smiling at his joke. "Indecent exposure," Jim said.

Elvin laughed. "Another pre-vert...two pre-verts in the same cell. Imagine the possibilities. And my last night, too."

Jim laughed, but rumors about prison made his laugh nervous.

Elvin shook his head. "Don't worry, pal. I'm jokin'. I'm not a big believer in 'any hole is better than no hole.'"

Then Elvin laughed loud and long, and his rich voice almost shook the heavy cinder. The echo was so loud, it seemed that the walls actually shook.

"So it's your last night?" Jim asked.

Elvin nodded, still chuckling.

"How long have you been here?"

"Just a couple days," he said. "This time."

"For?" Jim asked.

Elvin took a deep breath and looked away from Jim, toward the corner of the cell, as if they were outside, and he could survey the horizon. He let the breath out slowly, through his nose, and turned his look back to Jim. "I'm a lover," he said, and a mischievous smile followed. A wink.

Jim laughed. "I didn't know that was illegal."

"It is if she's married to a cop," he said, leaning toward Jim confidentially. "The laws are a little different in that type of situation."

"Ohhhh." Jim nodded. "I see. So what did they get you for?"

Elvin sighed. "Well, I also have a bit of a problem, you know." He held a fist up to his mouth and tipped his head back, miming a swig.

"Ah," Jim said.

Elvin dug into his shirt pocket and pulled out a pack of Pall Malls. He held the crumpled pack out to Jim, and he shook his head. Elvin lit one up.

"You ever tried to quit?" Jim asked him.

"Smoking?"

"No." Jim repeated his pantomime.

"Oh, that." One side of his mouth stretched into his cheek, and he shook his head. "Hell yeah, I've tried. I been to all kinds of treatment programs, halfway houses...."

He told Jim more, and Jim could hear in that solid, marble voice a combination of things—a helplessness, but also a bit of rehearsed rhetoric, a speech Elvin had probably used countless times in treatment, and in front of parole boards, to girlfriends, to convince people that he really was trying, just to get them off his back. Jim could see that Elvin had no intention of quitting drinking.

"So have you spent a lot of time in prison?" Jim asked.

"Oh, hell yeah. I'm a wanted man in more states than I've even been to." Elvin laughed again, and Jim was intrigued by how proud he seemed of this fact.

A silent moment passed, and Elvin had nearly finished his cigarette when he started coughing. It began as a regular cough, a smoker's hack, but it quickly escalated until he was hunched over on his bunk, clutching his throat. His body quaked, and jumped, and Jim stood helplessly watching, not feeling as though he knew this man well enough to approach. Elvin coughed for a good minute, and finally a spray of blood spewed from his mouth. Jim jumped back, but then his concern overcame any desire to avoid getting involved. He stepped forward, sinking next to Elvin on the bunk.

"What should I do? Should I call the guard?" Jim asked.

Elvin waved his hand, and Jim assumed from this gesture that this was a routine occurrence for him. Elvin seemed to expect that the fit would pass at any moment. But the coughing continued, and suddenly a stream of thick red flowed from his mouth, splashing onto the concrete with an echoing slap. Elvin Taylor's tiny body then tumbled forward into the pool, where he landed on his back with a boyish thud. Just like that, he was dead.

Sitting on his gray bunk, just across from where Elvin Taylor sat a few minutes before, Jim Handy stared at the still-damp gray floor, where a gray mop had just swept away the thick blood. The guard had been annoyed at having to clean up after Elvin. He hadn't been very thorough, and a few dark red streaks still crossed the floor, not quite dry. And staring at that spot, Jim could still see the shocked expression and the hunched figure of Elvin Taylor.

It did not escape his attention that in the matter of a few hours, he had met with two life-shifting experiences. Besides never having been in jail before, Jim had never seen anyone die, either. The idea that the day in jail would be something of a lark was gone. The situation didn't seem humorous any more, and Jim found himself thinking about the consequences of his arrest.

His boss would be upset, not so much because Jim missed a day of work but because he didn't call. Alice would be angry for the same reason. Jim could hear her now: "You didn't call anyone? Anyone at all?"

She wouldn't believe him, Jim suspected. She would think he was keeping something from her. She had been thinking that a lot of late. For good reason, he knew.

Sometimes Jim thought communication was highly overrated. Especially in marriage. They say it's the key to a good marriage, but he found it such an incredible chore. Because of the repetition. The discussion that is the same discussion you had a week before, and the week before that. Jim always supposed that some people found reassurance and stability in this kind of repetition. But to him it was annoying. And sometimes unbearable. To the point that he often refused to participate.

His wife Alice was one of the people who liked repetition. She liked order. She liked routine. But she didn't seem to acquire the sense of security she expected from these things. So her solution was to seek more order. More routine. More discussions.

They had discussed once a month for as long as they'd been together—ten years now—whether or not Alice was becoming more like her mother. Jim had told Alice several times that he would not discuss it any more. He had told her that in some ways she was like her mother, but that in many—in most ways—she was not. He had told her that he didn't even care if she ended up being like her mother. Jim was one of the few men he knew who actually adored his mother-in-law.

But Alice was adamant. So they discussed it, even after he'd insisted he wouldn't. And of course the path was always the same. His words had absolutely no bearing on the discussion at all. It was as if she had the conversation mapped out in her head before it even started. It was exasperating.

Jim had a friend, Jerry, who said that all women are this way. But in fact, Jerry was much more this way than his own wife, Sarah. Jerry and Jim had discussed time and again Jerry's doubts about whether Sarah was still in love with him. He complained that she hardly ever told him any more, and that she didn't like kissing him as much as she used to. Jim had told Jerry many times that being in love takes on a very different form after a few years. Jerry would nod and say he supposed this to be true. Then they would discuss it again a few weeks later.

Meanwhile, Sarah happened to be one of the most grounded people Jim knew. She understood that actions are more important than words. This understanding made her words more valuable than most peoples'. Because she didn't talk to try and convince anyone of anything. When she spoke, people noticed.

Actually, Jim was in love with Sarah. But she didn't know that. Nobody did.

He often thought of an afternoon when he went walking on the beach with Sarah. The four of them, Jerry and Sarah and Alice and Jim, rented a beach house for a long weekend. Sarah and Jim were the first ones up early one morning, and they walked. They talked about many things—mostly movies, or films, as Sarah liked to call them. Both of them loved movies, unlike their spouses.

They walked and talked for a couple of hours, and Jim felt as if it was the first fresh conversation he'd had in years. The first conversation that didn't reek of well-practiced paragraphs. He felt as if he had been caught in a maze of these kinds of conversations. Conversations that revolved around accomplishments and qualifications. He'd been to several parties where he had decided by the end of the evening that everyone would have saved themselves a lot of time by handing out their résumés at the door.

Now Jim sat on his gray bunk thinking about that day on the beach. Interesting, because that day was also gray. A foggy day, early spring, so the beach still had that gray wintry blush, and the water also looked gray. The difference, of course, was that the gray from the day on the beach had been a beautiful gray.

He thought about all of these things, and the more he reflected, the more he realized that he should have called Alice. Just out of consideration. She would be worried. Despite telling him that morning that she was going to leave, that she wanted a divorce, she would be worried. Maybe that would make her even more worried.

Jim yelled at the guard. He yelled for a long time without any response. And finally a tall, thick, bored young man ambled into the cellblock, and stopped at his cell.

"What?" he asked.

"I want my phone call."

"What phone call?"

"You know. My phone call. I never got my phone call."

"You never got a phone call?" The guard smirked.

"No."

"Right," the guard said sarcastically.

"I'm serious."

"You know how many times I've heard that one?" He started to walk away.

"Wait!" Jim yelled.

He kept walking. The clunk of his hard soles echoed along the walls. "Go to sleep," he said over his shoulder. "And be careful not to mess up your suit." He laughed.

"Wait!" Jim repeated. "I want my phone call!"

"Shut up," one inmate muttered.

"Yeah. Shut up," another repeated. "Yuppie asshole."

The door slammed shut, and the metallic finality of the noise sent a shiver through him. He was surprised he hadn't noticed it when he first entered the cellblock.

It wasn't until the darkness settled in, after lights out, that the loneliness started to creep up on Jim. He noticed little things then. Like the smells. Smells of men. Sweat and cologne. And a hint of their evening meal, which had been some kind of meat—probably beef, cooked until it too was gray. Each noise was magnified by the echo of the concrete surrounding him. The breathing, sighs, snoring, and moans.

But he also felt a strange sense of security. He felt safe—from Alice's sudden desire to discuss something, or a bad dream from one of the kids. Or phone calls from clients.

Jim realized he wasn't lonely for Alice, or the kids. He was just lonely, and he suddenly felt bad for Elvin, coming to the end that he did. In jail. Elvin didn't even have a chance to say good-bye to his girlfriend, the cop's wife. Maybe he'd never told her that he loved her.

Jim thought about Elvin's bravado. "I'm a lover." Remembering this made Jim smile, and he finally drifted off with this smile on his lips.

The rattle of iron woke Jim. Scared the hell out of him. It was still dark, and for a second or two he wasn't sure where he was.

"Get up, Handy," a gruff voice said.

Jim sat dazed for a moment, trying to make a face out of the obtuse circle of flesh above him. It was clearly the middle of the night. "Why?" he asked. Again, the rumors snuck into the back of his mind. The ones about prison guards this time.

"Someone's here to get you. Paid your bond."

"Oh." After sitting dazed for a second, trying to gather his thoughts, Jim pulled his jacket on, stood, unsteady, and followed, looking around the cell as he left, as if he might have forgotten his briefcase, or his umbrella.

Out in the lobby, he expected to find Alice, but instead it was Jerry and Sarah who stood looking confused and worried. Jerry twisted his hands around in his pockets, and Sarah's brow was scrunched, as if she might suddenly start crying.

"Are you all right?" Jerry asked. "You look terrible."

"I just woke up," Jim said.

"Oh, Jim," Sarah said, hugging me. "We were scared."

"We've been up all night," Jerry said. "Why didn't you call? We had everyone we know calling, trying to figure out where you were. We didn't even think to call the police until a couple of hours ago. It just didn't seem possible that... that...."

"That something like this could happen," Sarah finished for him.

"Can I go?" Jim asked the guard, who handed him a bag with his things. The guard held out a pen, and pointed to a form, which Jim signed.

In the car, riding in the back seat, Jim began to wake up. He thought about how impossible it would be to explain to Alice, or to Jerry, or even to Sarah, how much the past twenty hours had affected him. They could not possibly see it.

"So what happened?" Jerry asked.

"Don't make him talk about it if he doesn't want to," Sarah said.

"I'm not making him do anything," Jerry said.

Sarah turned around in her seat and looked at Jim, smiling. "Do you want to talk about it, Jim?"

Jim glanced out the window, thinking, and he realized something.

"Where are we going?" he asked.

Sarah grabbed his hand, reaching for it and squeezing. "To our house," she said. "Alice told us to take you to our house for the night. She's scared, Jim."

Jim turned to look at Sarah. She was beautiful, even after no sleep. "Is that all Alice told you?" he asked.

Sarah turned back toward the front, releasing Jim's hand. A silence followed, which answered the question. But neither of them would say it. Nor could he. The fact just sat, unstated but present. Alice was leaving.

Jim studied Sarah, then Jerry, and he realized that he might only have one chance to show them how much his night in jail had changed things, how much differently he saw everything. He had to act then, while the feeling was still strong.

So Jim leaned forward, poking his head between the bucket seats. He rested his forearms on his knees. He cleared his throat.

"I'm sorry to have to do this in front of you, Jerry," Jim said, and then he turned to Sarah, ". . . but I have to tell you, Sarah, that I'm in love with you. I've been in love with you for a very long time."

They were all silent for the next five blocks. Jerry drove, and Sarah's head remained locked in its straight-ahead position. Jim did not retreat. He did not look at either of them. He watched the road, waiting for this revelation to sink in. He knew it must come as a bit of a shock. He understood that they probably needed some time to process it, and perhaps to figure out how it would affect their lives.

Finally, Jerry tilted his head toward Jim, half-looking at him. He raised his brow. "Are you on something, Jim? Did you take something today?" And Sarah jumped in as soon as Jerry had spoken, after waiting for him to break the silence. "Did they do anything to you in there?" Sarah looked at Jim, and the concern in her face made him ill.

"No, no, no," Jim said, and his hands tried to wipe away their assumptions. "I'm perfectly sober. I'm perfectly sound." He tried to remain calm, but his heart had sunk. Because he knew that if Sarah didn't see that he was telling the truth, no one would.

"We're sorry about Alice, Jim," Jerry said. "But you've got to pull yourself together, man. You can't let yourself fall apart over this."

"Jerry's right, Jim," Sarah said. "Nothing is worth losing your head."

And with that, Jim fell back into my seat. He was defeated, alone. Now he was sure. Nobody understood.

Of course, the worst thing about Alice leaving, the part that was hardest to understand, was that this was exactly the thing that she hated most about her mother. It is the one thing she had never forgiven her for.

"Did you get any sleep?"

Jim lifted his head from the passenger window, trying to perk himself up. He wore the same clothes from the day before.

"Yeah. Yeah. I slept great," he lied, reaching up to smooth out his hair.

Jerry weaved his way through the residential development where he and Sarah had lived for four years, and Jim tried not to think about Alice hanging up when he called earlier. The last twenty-four hours hadn't even registered in his mind yet, and the hours that he'd spent wandering around Jerry and Sarah's house in the middle of the night had mostly been a daze. He remembered hearing them arguing, but he'd been so busy trying to figure out what he was going to do to even care what they were arguing about. Now Jim felt his palms getting damp. He was short of breath. The thought of going back to the office made his head whirl, as if it wasn't attached to his neck.

"You want to catch the bus at Pine?" Jerry asked.

"That's fine. Whatever is easiest for you."

Jerry cleared his throat. "Listen, Jim . . . we've been friends for a long time, right?"

Jim nodded.

"What you said last night, to Sarah. . . ."

"I'm sorry about that, Jerry." Jim barely had enough air to get the sentence out.

"We both know, Jim. We've known for a long time. We had a pretty nasty argument last night, after we picked you up."

"You did?"

Jerry nodded.

"God, I'm sorry."

Jerry waved a hand. "No, no, it's okay. I mean, I'm not saying it's your fault we had an argument. It was something we've avoided talking about for a long time."

Jim frowned, looking out at the manicured lawns and polished cars parked along the street. Trying to catch his breath.

"But I have to ask that you never bring that up again."

"Oh, no. Of course not."

"Just because you're going through a rough time doesn't mean you can start saying everything that comes into your head, Jim."

Jim nodded, but he felt as if he was about to lose consciousness. A thought came to him that seemed perfectly sound. He concluded that he was close to losing everything. He thought to himself that if he did one more wrong thing, his whole life was going to fall apart. He reasoned this out with the fevered thought process of a man who doesn't see that something has already happened.

"Alice wants to be with you, Jim." Jerry looked over at him. "You realize that?"

Jim's chin fell to his chest.

"You are wanted."

Jim collapsed against the passenger door, and before he thought about it, before he thought about anything else at all, he started talking about how unhappy he was. And from the minute the words started, a realization was born—not one that he could recognize or feel yet, but one that niggled its way into his subconscious. And there was a chance that someday he would know that the feeling he'd experienced the day before was nothing remotely like freedom.

•

RUSSELL ROWLAND's first novel, *In Open Spaces*, (HarperCollins, 2002) received a starred review in *Publishers Weekly*, which called it "an outstanding debut." It made the *San Francisco Chronicle*'s bestseller list, and was named among the Best of the West by the *Salt Lake City Tribune*. Russell recently completed *The Watershed Years*, a sequel to *In Open Spaces*. One of Russell's stories was chosen as one of the notable stories of 2005 by the Million Writers Award, and he was a MacDowell Fellow in 2005. Russell is currently co-producing a feature film with his brother, and consulting with several writers on their own projects. He lives in San Francisco.

Tiffany Lee Brown

RENO

(For Bill . . .)

BACKSTORY: Born in the desert and raised in the dripping greenery of Oregon rain, I spent most of my life in the exaggerated landscape and mindscape of the contemporary American West. My dad, and his dad before him, sold parts for heavy equipment: the immense construction, mining, and farming machines that have—for better or worse—literally shaped the West. We road-tripped relentlessly, visiting guys in shops and warehouses, on jobs and farms. We trailed the smells of diesel, grease, and Orange Goop hand cleaner from Death Valley to Seattle.

I loved these travels and continued them throughout my adult life, camping in the Nevada desert, crossing the California border on Amtrak's Coast Starlight train at dawn, driving all night on I-5, Highway 20, the old Highway 395 winding around Mono Lake's freakishly beautiful moonscape. My haughty teenaged disdain for country music fell away. I rediscovered Johnny Cash. He mined the stoic loneliness of the Western mythscape and harvested its regret in a way that spoke to me deeply.

The opening clause of "Reno" is a direct, six-word quote from the song "Folsom Prison Blues." The story is otherwise independent. Incidentally, that famous, brilliant Johnny Cash song itself may have been inspired by Gordon Jenkins's "Crescent City Blues;" Jenkins apparently received a settlement on an infringement lawsuit against Cash.

I SHOT A MAN IN RENO. The loudspeakers. They blared at me, clogging up the streets with noise, trying to get me to come in. Come in and see their weapons, their jewelry, their gold. There's no such thing as bad credit. Give your son a legacy that will last! But I didn't want to buy a weapon. I didn't want any jewels. I didn't want any of it.

That day I drove all the way down from Lakeview, boiling in the pickup. It didn't have A/C so I splashed water on myself while I drove. I'd gotten good at doing that, driving with one hand while I poured a gallon jug over my head or slapped some water under my pits. I kept a good five gallons on the passenger side all the time.

I drove out to my sister's place in Cedarville on the way back. Three girls were playing in the front yard. I sat in my rig and watched their game. Two of the girls whispered on the porch steps while the third one, the little one, stood above a whirling sprinkler, shivering, her eyes closed. The two girls pushed her down in the mud. The little one crawled, crawled around in the mud, chanting something. She kissed the backs of their hands and stood up. Then all three of them ran around under the sprinkler, shrieking.

The two girls looked about ten or eleven maybe, wearing halter tops, wearing blue jeans that sat low on their hips. The little one had mud all over her Mickey Mouse T-shirt. She tried to stop them from dancing with each other.

"Am I in now?" she asked. "Can I be in?"

Tabby was pretty easy to pick out. She was that third girl, the younger one; her hair was short. Brittney was harder. Both of the older girls looked the same to me: same pink lips, same squashed bug of a nose, same hair parted in the middle and flowing out long behind them. Then one of the older girls slapped Tabby across the cheek and laughed. That one must be Brittney, a lot skinnier than last time I saw her.

I picked up the two stuffed burros off the passenger seat and walked up to the girls on the lawn.

"Hi," I said, "How are you girls doing?"

I held out the burros. The girls didn't take them. Water began to bead up on the little animals' gray fur.

"These are for you," I explained. Then I turned to Brittney's friend. "Sorry I don't have another one."

They still didn't take the burros out of my hands. The water was starting to soak through. Thankfully it wasn't one of those sprinklers that goes tch... tch... tch and then sprays back all over everyone. I can't stand that sound. This kind bubbled up in a spiral and kept spinning. Very quiet.

"Um... who are you?" Brittney asked, adjusting the small nubs under her halter top.

"I'm Terry," I said. "You remember me from Grandma's in Lakeview?"

She looked down and kicked the muddy grass with her foot.

"I brought you a burro," I said, "like I send at Christmas. You guys must have a big collection of these things by now, huh?"

"Um... okay, I don't like know what you're talking about, so... just... wait here." Brittney ran up the porch stairs. Her friend followed fast.

The little one looked up at me. Her voice came out higher than I was expecting, higher and sweeter and younger. "I like donkeys," she said shyly. She held her arms in a cradle shape. I put both of the burros in the cradle and she smiled, rocking them.

My sister shoved her head out the window. "Tabby," she said, "come in the house and play with Brittney. Now."

The girl didn't move.

"Get in here!" her mother warned.

Tabby ran past and waved the burros at me. She whispered, "Don't worry, I'll put them somewhere safe!"

My sister locked the door behind her and walked down the steps. "You look like you could use a bite to eat," she said, "my treat." She waited for me on the road in front of the house. I didn't want to leave the twister of water on the cool, wet lawn. I stood there for a minute, but she wouldn't stop waiting until I joined her on the hot asphalt. "We'll take your truck," she decided, "and I'll walk home after."

First thing she did was hit her head on the gun rack. "For the love of God!" she yelped. "I thought Mom told you to get rid of them things!"

"Mom never asked where the venison came from, she just cooked it," I said. I breathed in and breathed out, without saying anything, to stay calm. Then I said, "Dad left them to me fair and square. It was right there in the will."

"I'm not talking about the... I mean.... They let you have guns?"

"I have every kind of permit ever invented," I said. I reminded myself to breathe in and then breathe out again, nice and calm. I'd only seen my sister once since I got put in the SRC six years before. She and Mom came to Graduation Day. There was a party with cookies and punch, and a banner that said "Congratulations Greg, Terry, and Pam." All three of us were getting out that day. Pam and I moved into the same halfway house. Greg's brother took him out to Winnemucca.

"Of course you do, of course," my sister said. "You and Daddy always had that in common, going down to Willy's, getting your toys."

I spent a load of time at Willy's World of Weapons as a kid. Willy would come out from behind the long counter and shake my dad's hand. "If it isn't Ernie Thompson," he'd say, like it was a complete surprise, "and the little one, too." He'd shake my hand like I was a grown-up, a real customer, and bring me an orange soda from the cooler in the back room. Then Dad and Willy and I would play cards or sharpen knives or clean weapons. We'd discuss the finer points of how to go about things if you were left-handed like Dad and me. I'd hunt through bins full of dusty marbles, plastic Army men, Confederate flag stickers, Bic lighters decorated with Day-Glo skulls and devil-ladies in red bikinis. Willy would bring out anything I wanted from the display cases: silvery handcuffs from a real-live policeman; crusty holsters that Billy the Kid or Annie Oakley or Elvis used to own; blades from Japan that you could throw through the air and they'd rip the other guy to ribbons; a bag-looking thing that had been on a real American's face while he was getting tortured in Vietnam. Willy let Dad have that one for free. The three of us closed up the shop and burned the thing in the back alley. But a lot of the time, we'd just sit there, quiet, glad of the air conditioning.

"We asked you to come," I said to my sister. "You just didn't want to."

"Of course I didn't," she snapped. "That old man smoked like a chimney. I hated that place." She jumped out of the cab. "This truck smells like wet dog!"

My sister was a great one for getting mad. When we were kids, she was always mad at Dad for blowing his hand off in the war, not during action but messing with explosives in the supply tent. He was still a crack shot with his wrong hand, up 'til the day he died. He taught me how to clean and load and fire a weapon with one hand, either hand, leaning in with other body parts for support. "In combat, you can't count on your right hand," he'd say, waving his stump. My mom made him a T-shirt with iron-on velvet letters that spelled out "Born-again Southpaw." He wore it all the time.

Now my sister got mad about the gallon jugs, so I put them in the truck bed. She wiggled away from the gun rack and fussed with her lipstick. Then she got mad that there wasn't a seat belt over on her side.

"I'm sorry," I said. "Nobody rides in this rig but Ratbait, and she's dead."

Cedarville smelled funny. Not like cedar, more like paint. Flakes of old paint so small I was breathing them in. And new paint. New paint to cover the real smell of things. New paint to cover the false fronts on Main Street. My sister took me to Susan's Frosty, where they made the best burger in the state, but I couldn't eat it. We sat inside at first, but the place was packed with hippies coming back from the desert. You could tell they hadn't showered in a long time and they were trying to cover it up. I can handle a little B.O. but what I can't handle is patchouli.

We took our burgers outside and sat at a green plastic table next to the street. Three tiny dogs all piled onto my feet and tried to climb up me until an old lady untied their leashes and took them away. After that I couldn't eat. I can't stand dogs anymore. It doesn't matter what breed. They all remind me of Ratbait.

I watched my sister finish her burger. "You should get another dog," she told me, chewing. "That Ratbait was a big girl and she was a stinker. To high heaven! Whew." She made a motion of fanning bad smells away from her face, her long nails shining in the sunlight. "What you need is a nice short-hair breed, you do know, don't you, that they're less dandrous? Like a little pug. Wouldn't you just love to have a nice little pug?"

"What the hell would I do with a nice little pug?" I asked.

"For starters, you might have someone to talk to," my sister answered.

People in your family can push your buttons; this is something I learned in outpatient, even though I didn't see my family very often. Carolee, my social worker, said it's important to hear your own breathing and take a minute before you say something. Before you do something, something you might get sorry about later.

"I work with many fine animals," I said eventually, "and I am happy to know the fine people of this world. Ratbait was a companion, it's true. She was a true companion."

"You're lucky Mom and Uncle Riley took her in after Dad—I mean, that dog was huge and she went crazy whenever you weren't around. Three years we're talking! But what could we do, any of us?" I watched the bits of mashed-up hamburger and pickle and lettuce stewing around in my sister's mouth. She waved her fingers over her mouth area, shielding it, but you could still see all the food inside.

She swallowed and kept going. "Who was going to hold it all together? Me, that's who. A single mom at the time if you'll remember! With a toddler and a newborn! If Uncle Riley, may he rest in peace, didn't have the bigness in his heart to take in Mom and that dog of yours, if he didn't happen to have that big place up in Lakeview, well, I don't know how everyone expected me to—"

A boy wearing pants made of seashells and silver bells walked out of the restaurant and knocked me into the table, wafting smells of sweat and spices over me. He kept walking.

"How rude," my sister said.

"It's all beautiful," the boy told his friend, stretching out his back before jumping into her van.

I looked at my sister with her blotchy lipstick and mouth full of food. "I'm sorry I couldn't help during all that," I said. "I'm sorry."

"Oh, I always figured someone in this family would get put in the SRC," my sister said. She laughed a little. "I just always thought it'd be Daddy."

I breathed in nice and calm. In my mind I could picture a big red button, a shiny, candy-like button, right in the middle of my chest. I could picture my sister reaching over and pushing the button so hard it went through my ribcage and fell out my back.

"Dad was a good man," I said, very slowly, so she could understand.

My sister stood up and grabbed our plastic trays with the food and paper on them. "I have to get a move on. You need gas before you head out?"

We drove to the gas station and she got her friend there to fill up my rig. I turned and hunched my body around my jeans wallet—I made it out of Levi's pockets in twelfth grade—and pulled out ten bucks. That was the end of my money, but I sure as hell didn't let her see that. Still, she wouldn't take it. She waved her hand like a queen.

"No, no," she said, "You come all the way up here. This is my treat." Her fingernails were long and curved, but cut flat at the ends, with a white strip. Her wedding ring caught the sun's rays in short flashes, like she was sending coded messages to invisible spacecraft.

I said, “I stayed at Mom’s last night. You should get up to Lakeview sometimes. She’s not looking so good.”

My sister fussed with her purse and didn’t say anything.

“She asked me why Dad didn’t visit. I told her he’d been gone six years, six years this week. We even went down to the cemetery.” The headstone had both their names on it, even though Mom wasn’t dead yet. It had her birthday carved on it, then a dash, and then a blank spot.

My sister said, “You’re taking the 395 back down to Reno? If you leave now, you’ll get back before dark, easy.”

“I don’t live in Reno anymore,” I told her. “I got my own place out by the reservation.”

“Walker?” she asked. She sounded fake-surprised, like she hadn’t gotten my Christmas cards from the past three years, like Mom wouldn’t have told her anyway. “What on earth are you doing out there?”

“Not Walker,” I said, “Pyramid. Closer to work.”

“What kind of work can you do out there?”

“I’m in ponies, wild ponies and burros,” I said. “Don’t you read my Christmas cards?”

She looked at me for a long time, like I was some kind of spider she’d never seen before. Then she walked across the road.

“If you drive down through Gerlach instead,” she shouted, “watch out for the gravel! They’re doing construction.” She waved, a fast wave with all her fingers wiggling. I waved back.

I got the gallon jugs and put them back in the cab. Taking the 395 down to Reno wasn’t a bad idea. I could probably make it down there on one tank of gas, and in town I could get some money easier than out by my place.

The ranch had to lay some people off a while back. That’s why I’d been working for free, which was why I ran out of money. I didn’t tell Carolee; there’s no point worrying people. When I first got out of the SRC, it took her fourteen months to find me a job. That’s more than a year. Besides, I loved the ranch and the ranch loved me. The ponies and the burros loved me. The folks I worked for, they liked me, too. They kept saying they might be able to hire me back someday.

The only thing for it was to sell something, and I had a Glock 27 that lived in the glove box. I never thought I’d sell one of Dad’s weapons, but sometimes in life you have to give things up for the greater good. A few years before he died, Dad got the little Glock from a friend’s son, a sheriff out near Klamath somewhere. It didn’t have much sentimental value.

So I drove straight through. I drove straight through Susanville and all the way down to Reno without stopping. I used up all the water in the gallon jugs, pouring it on my skin. Then I got thirsty. Smells stuck themselves onto my body, wedged into my small places, down my back, the crooks of my elbows. Sage, cooking in the hills. Roadkill, roasting on the tar. People, sweating in their cars. I'd never be able to eat with all these smells sticking to me. Or sleep, probably. I hadn't been able to sleep for a few days. That happened sometimes. That happened a lot.

The sun was setting when I pulled into town. The air had cooled but I still felt hot, hot and thirsty. I got off the freeway and parked right in front of Willy's World of Weapons. The whole street shouted at me. Come inside. Give your lady an occasion she'll never forget. Give her a 100-point diamond, set in white-hot white gold!

I took the little Glock out of the glove box and felt its heaviness in my left hand, then in my right, then in my left again. I released the magazine and then I drew back the slide, letting the cartridge plop onto the passenger seat, right where Ratbait should've been. I racked the slide, moving it back and forth one, two, three times, to make sure the little Glock was empty. At that point, my dad would always point a pistol in a safe direction and pull the trigger, to really, really make sure the weapon was disabled. Six years ago, he pointed it at his head. Maybe that was the only safe direction he could find.

The little Glock felt light and gentle this way. I put it in its black plastic box and headed to Willy's World of Weapons. Willy's huge, wooden sign with its peeling, red-painted letters and cartoon cowboy was gone. Instead, a light-up sign wrapped all the way around the building. Willy's had loudspeakers now, too. The voices at Willy's said different things from the voices across the street at The Diamond Rose. Buy this, buy that. But I didn't want a timeless 24-karat gold reminder of love. I didn't want a diamondette tennis bracelet. I didn't even want a genuine bayonet from the Great War. I just wanted my dad back.

Inside, the bins were all gone. The long counter was new, deeper and more square-shaped, with shiny chrome around its edges. The guy behind the counter was young and he wore his hair long. In his ear there was an earring of a little silver feather. He was sitting on a stool, stabbing the buttons on his cell phone. I waited at the counter for a minute or two while he finished his game. He looked mean, mean like one of the orderlies at the SRC, mean like a mustang with colic.

Finally, he gave a big sigh and beeped the cell phone off. I put the black plastic box on the countertop and said, "Hello. What can you give me for a Glock 27?"

He didn't open the box. "We don't need nothing like that," he said. "You can get one of those at Wal-Mart."

"It's law enforcement issue," I informed him. I didn't know what else to say.

He pushed the box toward me and stared at it until I picked it up. "Head east," he said. "Pawnshop by the IHOP. We're strictly collectors here."

They sure didn't used to be strictly collectors. They used to have everything, including orange soda. "Where's Willy?" I asked.

"Whaddya mean, where's Willy?" he said, laughing. "Willy's a name on a sign, that's all Willy is." He stopped laughing and looked me up and down. "I got a willy I could show you."

The sound of the loudspeakers leaked in from outside. Buy this, buy that. Buy a sword from 1623. Buy a classic Smith & Wesson. Support our troops: buy a flag.

"Willy is real," I told him, nice and calm and slow, like I was talking to my sister. "He's real and he's my dad's friend and I want to talk to him. Tell him Theresa Thompson is here."

"You mean the old man?" asked the guy behind the counter. "I can't go tell him nothing. He died since before I started working here. And his name wasn't Willy. Frank or something." He flipped open his cell phone and slumped back onto the stool.

I walked out the door and into the loudspeakers. Buy this, buy that, real gold never goes out of style. I got in my rig, loaded the little Glock, charged it, and put it in my left pocket.

I carried the empty black box back into Willy's World of Weapons in my right hand. Buy an ice cream, buy a fig. Buy an emerald collar for your dog and a triangle-shaped flag for your daddy's coffin. I watched the guy behind the counter play his game for a minute. I breathed in and breathed out, nice and slow. I felt calm. Really, really calm.

"You tell Frank that Ernie Thompson's daughter sends her regards," I told him. Then I shot him, all twelve rounds.

•

TIFFANY LEE BROWN is a writer, performer, and interdisciplinary artist based in Portland, Oregon. She is the editor of *2GQ*, the literature and media arm of the non-profit 2 Gyrlz Performative Arts, and is presently a guest editor for *PLAZM* magazine. Her work is published in periodicals such as *Bookforum*, *Utne*, *Bust*, *Tin House*, and *Art Access*, and in anthologies including *The Bust Guide to the New Girl Order*, *Gargoyle*, *Slow Trains*, *Northwest Edge*, and *The Clear Cut Future*. She has performed at the Portland Rose Festival, Wordstock, Burning Man, Performance Works NW, the Richard Foreman Festival, the Enteractive Language Festival, the Dark Arts Festival, and others. She is currently collaborating with book artist Clare Carpenter on *A Compendium of Miniatures*, to be published by *2GQ* in late 2006. Tiffany would like to thank Soapstone for offering her the wonderful residency at which she was able to finish this piece, and Bill Palmer for his invaluable insights. Tiffany welcomes online visitors at www.magdalen.com and at 2GQ.org.

Steven A. Hoffman

JC WAS THE FIRST GOTH KID

BACKSTORY: My fictional writing is heavily influenced by music. Typically I select a particular artist's music to complement a story. The music helps set tone, emotion, pace, and beat of a written work. With "JC Was the First Goth Kid," I listened to many different Johnny Cash songs for inspiration, both before writing and through headphones (with the volume kept very low) while working on the story. The composition of the musical inspiration influences the story's overall written composition.

THE MORE I TRY TO AVOID choosing my destiny, the more I end up determining my own fate.

I got to my first high-school class early so that I could claim the perfect seat. With no one else yet in the room, I planted myself at a lab table one row behind center. The biology classroom had tables set up for pairs. I chose a left seat to ensure maximum writing space. Arriving first to the class, I also avoided the awkward situation of approaching someone already seated and being told that the other seat was being saved. Instead, a person would choose to sit next to me. The only catch to this method was when a teacher assigned seats. But even then, someone else still determined my fate.

Many high schools in New Jersey are regional, meaning that they draw from middle and junior high schools from around a ten- to fifteen-mile radius. Chances are I would only know about 20 percent of the people in my entire freshmen class. I didn't know any of the students as they entered the door at the front of the classroom. However, all of the other students appeared to know each other as the tables began to fill in around me with banter and excitement. By the time the class was about to start, all of the chairs were taken except for the empty one next to me.

The teacher, Mr. Feinberg, walked in and closed the door behind him. He introduced himself and took roll. With a typical New Jersey attitude he called out each person's first and last name, but from thereafter he referred to us by our last names preceded by either Mr. or Ms. I knew one person, Jennifer—*Ms. Hatch*—from my middle school, and she was a brown-nosing bitch. He then ran through the semester's topics and labs. As he started to describe the dissections we would be performing, the door to the classroom re-opened and in walked a tall lurching Goth kid. In 1980, there was no such thing as a Goth kid, but he exemplified the image and was probably personally responsible for the fashion trend, personality characteristics, and moniker now known throughout the country.

Annoyed, Mr. Feinberg put on a game show host's enthusiasm and addressed the latecomer with familiarity. "Ladies and gentlemen, please welcome Mr. Joseph Carlson. Welcome to class, Mr. Carlson." The teacher's expression quickly changed to serious. "We're off to a good start, I see." Feinberg pointed at the empty seat next to me. "Take your seat so that we can continue."

All eyes were on "Mr. Carlson" and then on me as he approached my table. Walking toward me, he looked about six feet tall, except that he was slouching. Would that make him six-foot-four, maybe? His thick black hair looked like it hadn't been washed or brushed in a few days, maybe weeks. If it weren't so bushy it would probably hang past his shoulders. It was more of a wavy afro that hung down so that no one could clearly see his face. He had on black jeans with tears in the knees and a long black tattered overcoat. A worn black courier bag was weaved through one arm and draped around his neck. In the V of his jacket was a T-shirt with a black-and-white image of an older man with a rough face and thick, slicked-back black hair.

People ignored Feinberg's introduction and quietly gawked at my new lab partner. His back to the teacher, Johnny shuffled closer to me and opened his jacket enough for the class to see that the printed image on his black T-shirt also had an extended middle finger flipping off everyone that looked at him. As he swung around to take his seat he closed his jacket to hide his shirt's message.

Toward the end of the class, Feinberg handed each of us a syllabus and packet of papers and told us to spend the rest of the class time reviewing the materials. He walked over to our table and stood next to me. The teacher looked at me for a second just to acknowledge my presence, and then spoke through me to Joseph, who was facing the tabletop. The kid's hair covered his eyes and any facial expression.

"Mr. Carlson, I know that you had some issues last year. Hopefully, this year will prove to be a better one for you. But you are going to need to adjust your attitude if you are going to make it through my class—and high school."

Staring at Joseph's head, Feinberg was oblivious as the student's grip tightened around a section of his jacket under our desk. I could tell he was making an effort to maintain self-control. I still had no idea what my new lab partner looked like, but I wish I hadn't been first into the classroom and had made an effort to sit next to someone—even Jennifer. The teacher glanced back at my wide-open eyes as they quickly feigned focus on my handouts. I sensed that most of the class was trying to focus its attention on my table while appearing to study.

"Mr. Carlson, please try and be on time. I have no doubt you can and will do well this year." The teacher turned and started weaving through the aisles and rows of desks. I caught Jennifer with her hand up to ask him a question—probably about how the class could earn extra credit throughout the year.

Joseph mumbled, "Asshole," from beneath his 'fro-like locks. I chuckled, more out of being uncomfortable, but I also wanted to show some allegiance to my lab partner since it looked like we would work together for the rest of the semester. He swung his parcel bag around and it dropped onto the table. On the outside flap was a hand stitched "J.C." I snorted air out through my nose and fell back in my seat in surprise. The irony of wearing a T-shirt with some old dude giving the bird and also having the same initials as Jesus struck me as odd.

He slowly turned his head toward me and I realized I had just drawn attention to myself. I looked over at him and sheepishly said, "I'm Gary."

We made eye contact and Joseph responded with a slow hushed, "Hey, I'm JC."

Pock marked, JC's face looked like it had exploded. His eyes retreated back toward his bag on the table. At the time, I didn't notice how sad and hollow his eyes were. I just felt a pang of empathy since I was so self-conscious of my own acne-scarred face, but it was nothing compared to his.

The bell rang, indicating that our first class was over. Feinberg reminded us of our reading assignments as students headed for the door.

Another hushed, "See ya later, Gary," leaked out as JC got up and headed for the door; head hung low, he darted around people as he made his quick escape.

I was glad that I had some aptitude for science, because JC was not the most dependable person to attend class. In fact, he even missed the next two classes that first week. Rumor had it that another teacher later in that first day of school noticed the shirt he had been wearing and the school suspended him for the rest of the week.

The second week of class went much better. He still wore his black overcoat, but under it was usually a plain black T-shirt. JC turned out to actually be a pretty shy guy. And he had a good sense of humor. The first time that we had a lab he pushed me to do the actual experiment while he recorded the notes.

"Why don't you do this part, and I'll write down the results," I offered half way into the project.

"That's okay; I just want to write down the info." His pencil was pushed through his hair like girls do when they have a chopstick keeping their long hair "together" in a bun. I wasn't sure why he had put it there or if I was supposed to notice and say something about it. But it made me chuckle. Self consciously, I looked around to see if anyone saw that he and I were getting along. I noticed that his hands were up in the sleeves of his coat as I continued to work. His long fingers would come out and grab his pencil to jot numbers and notes on our results paper and then disappear.

When he was in class on a regular basis he would do well with his work. We each had some of the highest grades in the class. When he started to miss days of school I ended up doing the work alone but we still maintained a high-A grade average.

For me, high school turned out to be just an extension of junior high. I wasn't a jock. I wasn't preppy. I wasn't a burnout. I wasn't anything. I wanted to fit in, but usually I was just invisible. People were not mean to me, but they weren't overly friendly either. The film *The Breakfast Club* came out soon after I graduated from high school. While I seemed to know each of the characters in the film and could identify who they were in my high school, none of them would have been my friends. If I had to force myself to pick one of the characters from the movie to identify with, it would probably be Brian, Anthony Michael Hall's portrayal of the geek. If I had to pick which character JC most closely resembled, it would be Ally Sheedy's weirdo character, Allison.

I did have friends from junior high—and we met at the cafeteria every day for lunch. The second week of class I noticed that JC also had lunch at the same time as we did. "Why don't we ask him to sit next to us?" I asked our group, referring to JC.

Everyone looked over at him sitting at a table in the far corner of the cafeteria with his long coat on. He was sitting across from Luke Paxton, a freshman who wore a tight gray suit and skinny tie every day. As I walked to math class one day, I overheard Luke in the hallway tell JC that he wished he was the fifth Beatle. I glanced back and realized that not only was Luke's suit like what the Beatles wore in their early years, but that he even had a haircut like they did; it was stringy and hung down evenly around his head. The bangs cut straight across. Luke and JC were expressive when they were together.

"Um, no." My friend, Mark, took another bite of his sandwich. "We don't need to be associated with them. We're not like them. And why would we want to walk around and get harassed every day?"

The rest of the group concurred, and I guess that I agreed. The friends I had, and more importantly, those who weren't friends, didn't bother me. If we were associated with JC or Luke or any of the other "freaks" we would quickly begin to gain more attention—and not in a good way. When high-school students were put into situations where they interacted with these guys—like being assigned lab partners—it was not held against you. It was a forced association and others in the class or school didn't hold you accountable.

In our class, JC always dropped his bag on the table's top. Each class I noticed the stitched J.C. on its cover. He always flipped it open and pulled out his spiral notebook with the red cover. He had used the eraser side of his pencil to *write* the word "biology" on the notebook's cover. The other spiral notebook he would pull out each class had a black cover. He would only pull that one out half-way from the bag, as if trying to hide it. Using the same eraser technique he had written in large letters "JC's Shit" on its cover.

Inside his black notebook were thoughts, doodles, drawings, cartoons, poems, battles, and anything else that seemed to pour from his mind directly onto the pages. The notebook itself was tattered. It had curled edges and was haphazardly stuffed with other loose pieces of scribble. Whenever he had an idea he would open the book arbitrarily and fill pages until he was finished. Sometimes that bothered me because, while we were supposed to be working together on our labs, he would secretly get lost in his black notebook writings, forcing me to do most of the work myself.

I was intrigued by what he wrote in that book, though, and would examine what he had written or what he was drawing. He never pulled the pages away from me or seemed to be bothered by my prying. In fact, I think he was excited that I took some kind of interest, although I would hardly say that it was eagerness that drew me to his pages. It was curiosity.

On one particular day, "*I wear the black for the poor and the beaten down*" was scribbled on the top of a page he was working on. He was creating an illustration of some high school-aged kid wearing a football jersey adorning the number nine. Coming off the page was a strong muscular arm with a hand tightly gripped around the jock's neck. His eyes were bulging and his tongue was hanging out of his mouth. JC was a good artist. "Did you write this?" I asked.

JC looked over at me with a patronizing look. He held up his pencil to indicate that he did, in fact, write it.

"No, I mean, did you write *this*," I pointed to the line at the top of the page and dropped the tip of my finger down hard on the word *black* for emphasis.

"No, that's from the other JC." He continued with his caricature, working on another arm coming from the opposite side of the page wielding a sharp knife. Its tip about to poke one of the bulging eyeballs.

I would finally be able to ask about the JC stitched onto his bag without appearing to pry. I traced the two initials on his black bag, not completely realizing I was doing it. "I didn't think you were the religious type."

JC froze his hand; pencil on paper and stared into my eyes. His gaze made me look down quickly and withdraw my hand from his bag. "My type," he said softly. "I thought you were different. What *type* do you think I am?"

I was stunned that he misinterpreted what I said with such defense, but with a second to think I understood why he would make the assumption he had. "I didn't mean it like that. I just didn't think that you would write quotes from the Bible, that's all. In fact, I wasn't quite sure if the initials on your bag were your initials or Jesus'. Now I know. Sorry I asked." I started to turn back to our assignment when he laughed.

His hurt look shifted to one of fulfillment. The fisherman who's perfectly created lure snagged the trophy walleye. "Neither," he spoke confidently. "There's another JC that guides me in life—my spiritual advisor, my mentor, my man."

I was confused. This was the first time he had talked with me; really talked with me. I was titillated by his remarks. I thought they were profound. But the vain part of me, the peer-pressured and social-accepting part of me, took control and the judgment that was slapped to the forefront of my head was, *freak*. Blankly, I responded with, "Huh?"

"Johnny Cash!" JC was pretty worked up now. "He's the man."

Tonight Show host Johnny Carson would have made more sense to me. We lived in New Jersey, not Tennessee. I couldn't figure out how a country singer was his mentor. I hid my surprise the best I could, but I could see disappointment in JC's eyes that I had reacted so poorly after he revealed such a deep and personal part of himself to me. The pencil went back into his hair and his hands retreated up into the sleeves of his coat. I sought some type of recovery. "That's cool. I don't know anything about him. I didn't know that people listened to country music around here."

The bell rang and JC quickly shoved his stuff into his bag. As he got up to leave, he turned back to me and his hushed voice returned. "Never mind. . . . I thought you would understand."

That evening, after I completed my homework, I sought my nightly solace by selecting the music that would help me to sleep. Among cases of music cassettes I had narrowed my choice down to an album by one of my three favorite bands: Yes, Rush, or Genesis. My mind momentarily switched gears to my confrontation with JC and the announcement of his liking the "other" other JC. How could he relate to a country artist? I thought that they just sung about dead dogs, alcohol, and scorned love. A hot flash spiraled through my body as I realized my stupidity. How could I criticize JC for his particular interest in music and his spiritual guidance when I would be so pissed off and offended if anyone mocked my music? Besides, I was drawn to groups from England and Canada that sang about By-Tor the Snowdog, Starship Troopers, and lambs that lie down on Broadway. What I got out of my music, I decided, was just as personal and important to me as Johnny Cash lyrics were to JC.

The next time we had class together we had a fetal pig put in front of us to dissect. JC was standoffish and cold. I felt bad about how I behaved and in typical teenage manner fumbled through trying to reconcile. "I've never heard any songs by Johnny Cash. Is there a radio station I might find him on?"

Suspiciously, JC paused. He shook his head and said quietly, "Nope. But Sam Goody has some of his albums."

"I'll have to check it out this weekend. I love going to Sam Goody." I took the dissecting blade and poked at the rubbery pig. I used the tip of the knife to lift its exposed genitals. "Any thoughts?" I asked, handing him the tool.

Male. He noted the single word answer to the first question we were supposed to complete about the pig's gender in his red notebook. JC took the blade willingly from me and like an expert cut an incision vertically through the pig's stomach as we had been instructed. "I think," he said pondering my question, "that we should name our pig Sue." The word *freak* came to the forefront of my mind again as I tried to figure out why he would, first, want to name our lab animal, which we would completely dismantle, and second, why he would choose a girl's name after we determined it was a boy pig. My puzzled look brought a rare smile to his broken-out face and for a second I saw a spark of light in his eyes. "Look for one of Cash's records with the song 'A Boy Named Sue' on it when you go to the mall." He again looked like he had caught the trophy fish, and I kind of liked being part of the effort.

Later that day, walking to class, I passed JC being harassed at his locker by a couple of the school's football players. It was game night, so all the players wore their jerseys with pride, like they were going off to war. Jennifer Hatch, and the other groupies, fawned or drooled or did whatever they did to be cool. When I saw that one of the meatheads giving JC a hard time had the number nine on his back I recalled the notebook illustration from earlier in the semester that JC had been working on that depicted the jock with bulging eyes being choked.

"Hey, Pubehead," Number Nine said loud enough for all around to hear. "Why don't you brush your hair or wash your face once in awhile. Maybe if you didn't jerk off or eat chocolate so much you wouldn't have so many zits." He was as close to JC as he could be without actually touching him. JC continued to pull books out of his locker and ignored the comments, as any of the smart freaks or geeks—myself included—would do instead of returning the verbal jab or fighting or running away.

Number Nine started to pull a taped photograph from JC's locker door. The photo's image was similar to the one on JC's T-shirt he wore the first day of class that had the man giving the finger. Only this one had the same man with a guitar around his neck. Noticing all the other photos of the same guy that filled JC's locker, I assumed that the worn-looking man must be Johnny Cash.

"What a fag," Number Nine said, holding up the photo and showing it to the small crowd. "Most guys would have a chick on their locker door. This guy's got an old dude."

JC grabbed for the photo and swiped it back out of the jock's clutches. The football player went for JC's ever-present black overcoat. Number Nine yanked a lapel toward him and JC's arm came out from one of the sleeves as he was twirled around by the force. The entire group froze as JC's emaciated body was partially visible. Because JC was somehow exempt from gym class, he always had his coat on and his body was always covered. Clinging to him was a faded black T-shirt, too small for his stick-like frame. His exposed arm and neck disclosed blotchy acne scars and thin red two-inch marks like paper cuts or shaving nicks. His forearm had a scar about a quarter-inch thick and four inches long that, I have to admit, instantly reminded me of the incision he had eagerly given Sue only a couple of hours earlier.

Number Nine let go of the coat, not saying a word, and JC retracted his arm back into the sleeve. With a head-nod, the football player signaled to his friends that the fun was over and it was time to move on. No one said a word. Throughout the entire incident JC's face never showed any expression other than distance. All of us who were not part of the popular crowd experienced some kind of torment from time to time, but his face told a story that this was just part of his daily routine. As everyone left the scene, I moved in and approached JC as he was reaffixing his tattered photo to his locker door.

"Why do jocks have to try and dominate everything?" I asked trying to show empathy. "I mean, if they already have all the power in the school, why do they have to rub it in our faces? High school is bunk, and I still have three years to go!"

JC stared into his locker, frozen like he was counting to ten. I heard him whisper to himself a mantra: "If you have political convictions keep them to yourself."

I pointed to a photo of the young Johnny Cash, looking down, solemnly. "Is that from one of his songs?"

"Yeah, it is. He's done some bad things in his life, but what he sings about just," he paused a moment. ". . . it's just something that I connect with, I guess. He looks and dresses different and his thoughts are different, but why does everyone have to be a jock to be accepted?"

JC looked at me, but I wasn't sure I completely understood what he was talking about. The bell rang, indicating that both of us were officially late for wherever we were supposed to be. As JC shut his locker, Mr. Feinberg rounded the corner of the hallway. In typical high-school fashion, teachers always missed the fight. "Ah, my two trouble-makers." Mr. Feinberg stopped and intercepted our departure. "I understand that you, Mr. Carlson, have been causing some more trouble in the hallways."

"Yep, it was me," JC said in a firm-yet-quiet monotone voice almost mocking the teacher. "I'm the guilty party for trying to go to class. I decided to bully a couple of jocks because they just didn't seem to be getting enough attention. I showed them." JC adjusted his coat and looked down at the teacher.

Mr. Feinberg winced a "those darn kids" expression. He reached into his pocket and tore off two tardy passes and handed one to each of us. Finished with his business, he turned around and retreated from where he came. We looked at each other and smiled. Instead of heading to class, JC went back to his locker and opened it. He pulled something from it, walked back over to me and handed me a cassette. I could barely read the handwriting listing all of the songs, but on the spine of the tape I could easily decipher "JC's favorite JC moments" printed in my lab partner's scratches. "This might be a good way to learn a little bit about Mr. Johnny Cash," JC spoke confidently. "It's got some of his best songs. And now you don't have to buy a record unless you want to."

I listened to the tape and had to admit to myself that the songs weren't particularly pleasing to my tastes. I would stick to progressive rock, but I felt good that I at least appreciated and respected his tastes.

The rest of the school year was pretty much more of the same. We did our labs together and both ended up with an A in the class. He hung out with Luke and a few other unique people and I continued to have lunch at the other end of the cafeteria with my friends.

Over the next couple of years we would say "hi" to each other if we passed in the hallway, but that was the extent of our contact. At the end of my junior year, I flipped through my yearbook and JC popped out at me. He was given the distinction of "Class Individual." Each year various seniors are selected as class jock, most talkative, class flirt, etc. Scattered throughout the senior photos are these stand-alone snapshots with the caption underneath declaring their claim to fame during their tenure. JC's photo made me laugh. He was standing beside his locker and there were papers and books piled out of it down to the floor. He was staring straight into the camera and with an outstretched arm he was giving the photographer (and the viewers) the finger. The photo had a black bar over JC's hand to mask the profanity.

This story could end right here, but there is a reason why I was recently thinking about my classmate, JC. Over the past few years, there has been an awakening, for people like me, and a re-awakening, for others, of Johnny Cash and his music. With the recent death of Cash and the gradual maturing and broadening of my musical tastes, I picked up one of his most recent compact discs. It had Johnny Cash singing a cover version of the Nine Inch Nails song "Hurt." That song alone is chilling, but listening to it being sung by a man who must have known he was on the last leg of his life was simply haunting. I wondered why I had never really given Cash a listen throughout the years. That's when it occurred to me that I had been given that tape by JC and hadn't found it at all interesting at the time.

Of course that tape reminded me of JC, whom I had not seen since my junior year in high school. I hadn't lived in New Jersey since I graduated from college and that was more than fifteen years ago. Perhaps, with an e-mail or a phone call I could touch base with him and see how he was doing. I could thank him for turning me on to Johnny Cash and find out what other artists he was into lately.

With the convenience of the Internet, I did a search for JC. Scanning the results, I scrolled through artists, biologists, professors, and even a violin maker all with his same name. Upon review of the linking Web sites, none of these Joseph Carlsons were the JC I knew from school.

I decided to query the Web site of the newspaper that covered the area of New Jersey where I had lived and search for him on that site. I was partially successful. While the newspaper did produce one link to the Joseph R. Carlson I knew, upon reading the linked article my eagerness to connect with the 1983 "Class Individual" proved to be impossible.

September 14, 1993
Joseph Richard Carlson was found dead in his studio apartment last night. Neatly stacked around his bed were volumes of spiral notebooks, magazines, journals, books, and music recordings of the legendary country singer Johnny Cash. The naked body of Carlson, a care provider at a local residential substance rehabilitation home, was covered with hundreds of two-inch small cuts and scars. Officials confirmed that the cuts were self-inflicted over many years and were not the cause of death. A neighbor, who asked not to be identified, described Carlson as quiet, friendly, and never appeared to have guests in his apartment. Co-workers of Carlson at the treatment home also mentioned that Carlson was quiet, but a good listener, caring, and quite respectful of the residents. They also recalled his passion for the life and music of Johnny Cash and how he would light up whenever Cash was mentioned. Everyone who knew Carlson indicated that regardless of the weather, he wore a long black coat; apparently a tribute to Johnny Cash. Laid out along side Carlson's body on the bed was the old overcoat. On top of the coat was a typed note. While authorities ruled out foul play, they would not reveal the cause of death or disclose the contents of the note. An unofficial source indicated that the note contained lines of lyrics sung by Johnny Cash. A framed photograph of Mr. Carlson and Mr. Cash together hung above Carlson's bed. Mr. Cash was contacted and asked about Carlson. "While I don't recall meeting Mr. Carlson, I am saddened to hear of his passing," Cash said. The estimated time of death was September 12, 1993.

•

STEVEN A. HOFFMAN has lived in seventeen states and countries and has been very happy to call Sioux Falls, South Dakota, home since 1997. When he's not writing, he oversees a seven-gallery visual arts center, a science center with three floors of hands-on exhibits, a domed large format theater, and a performing arts center with 300- and 1,900-seat theaters. Professionally, Steve has curated performing arts series, festivals, events, and individual performances for more than fifteen years. Steve holds degrees from the University of Illinois and University of Wisconsin and has worked and taught in Chicago, New York, Ann Arbor, Michigan, and Madison, Wisconsin. He is actively involved with a variety of local and national boards, associations, and panels and has previously been published in several literary and trade publications. Since living in South Dakota his appreciation for country music, fishing, and hunting has steadily grown. Steve can be contacted at SH.writings@hotmail.com.

Amanda Nowlin-O'Banion

THE WALLS, TEXAS — 1987 (EXCERPTED FROM *THE GREENEST GRASS*)

BACKSTORY: I grew up in Huntsville, Texas, where there are eight state prisons in and around town—incarceration and country music are two cultural facts of everyday life. Johnny Cash's "Folsom Prison Blues" rightly illuminates the predominant metaphors in my life as a teenager: the ever-present prison system, iconic music, a dying railroad, and testing of personal freedoms.

MEG'S HAIR WOULDN'T BEHAVE IN THE WIND. It was long and messy and strawberry except for the under duff that rested against her neck. The underneath always grew in darker and straighter than the top. In the visitors parking lot she shook it out of her face and threw her head around like she was in a shampoo commercial. She made a ponytail, tied it in a knot on the back of her head, and tucked it under an Astros cap. The air felt vacant and it made her want to empty her head. She didn't want to take anything personal Inside. She watched a freight train 500 yards off. It slugged along carrying away food-crops the prison grew; beans, greens, and sauerkraut stirred with shovels by inmates in rain pants and no shirts.

She walked toward the entrance of "The Walls," officially called the Huntsville Unit of the Texas Department of Criminal Justice. The state had just changed it from the Texas Department of Corrections. At some point it became obvious there wasn't much correcting going on. She looked back down the highway. Driscoll, her home, seemed a lot farther than forty miles away.

The '85 Bronco behind her was a gift she'd received that morning. It was used, but was shiny and clean in the driveway where her parents unveiled it and sang to her. Her sister, Maryanne, had climbed into the passenger side and swished her butt on the seat, forming it to her. "This is awesome!" She turned up her collar. "You're going to have to take me everywhere."

Meg's dad had arranged for her to leave school around third period. It took her all of what would have been fourth to remove her makeup, change into the oversized sweat suit he told her to wear, and drive to Huntsville. She was acutely aware she'd never before had occasion to make herself look like a boy.

The short shrubbery up the sidewalk didn't budge in the breeze, its waxy leaves stiff as cow chips. Before she reached the door she bent down to pluck a leaf to see if it was real.

Her Uncle Dan had a badge made for her specifically for this visit. It was only in case of an emergency, stamped "OFFICIAL" across the top with her junior class picture on it. Her dad had said if they needed to get her out, she'd have to prove who she was. She clipped it on her pullover so her picture faced her heart. It felt like a passport, like she was going across the border. Leaving town was all she hoped for. It felt good, but not nearly as good as it would feel to be on that train, even though it carried mealy turnips and blinky milk. She was going to meet a legend and she was scared.

The correctional officer at the gate looked at her closely after he flipped up her badge. She relaxed her face and gave him her best girl smile so he could see it really was her in the picture. Her sister called that particular smile her "cruise face," referring to the insincere grin she wore in most family vacation photos. They'd never actually been on a cruise, though. The first officer called over another officer to escort her. "Keep your head down and let the guard walk between you and the inmates. Don't respond if they talk to you." His name badge was turned backwards, too.

The prison system was notoriously short of guards. Meg looked down at his holster, wondering if he had graduated high school. It held a billy club and a radio. She knew they didn't have guns. Growing up forty miles from the state pen and having an uncle who'd been a warden for ten years made it very easy to learn a lot about the prison system. Plus, she'd been to visit twice on field trips. Most local schools had a few places they visited repeatedly. In Driscoll the drill was: second grade, Ice Creamery in Brenham; fourth grade, NASA Space Center, Houston; sixth grade, Prison. Eighth, tenth, and twelfth grades were repeats in the same order. Just a month before on her senior trip she'd seen her father in the hallway. Lately, he spent a good portion of his workweek there consulting with the prison construction team. Or so he said.

Meg had been preparing all week to meet the other reason her father was here. It put a grim shadow over things. His mistress worked for her uncle. It made her hands cold. There was an upside though, and she couldn't forget that. A private meeting with David Crosby wouldn't have been possible if Meg hadn't discovered the affair.

Meg had seen inmates all her life. Summer mornings when she was in junior high, there was always one tending the yard at her uncle's place. Until the eighties, wardens had houseboys who cooked and cleaned for them, but the state stopped using them after the Menedez hostage crisis when the assistant warden's kitchen man smuggled a revolver Inside in a rotten ham. The ordeal left two librarians and a chaplain dead.

The walkway to her uncle's office was dry and white and concrete. The ceiling was easily fifty feet high, the left wall climbing forty feet of sheer cinderblocks. The top ten feet were enclosed with the glass used in high schools in the fifties; some green panes, some white panes, some transparent, all old and yellowed. The high band of natural light made Meg feel she was looking up from the bottom of a well.

The right wall housed inmates in four stories of cells that looked over where she walked. Each was empty. She didn't pass anyone on the way in. A staircase at the end of the corridor led up to a metal door with mini-blinds and a Lexan window thicker than praying hands. It was the only thing on the wall. There, the hallway made a sharp turn to the right and led to what smelled like the showers. Soapy steam clouded that direction. That meant naked men. The cement stairs were steep and beaten, and there was no rail. As she walked up them she pressed her left shoulder and leg against the wall and tried not to look down. The thrill vanished. There was something off about a place that didn't have a rail on a thirty-foot staircase surrounded by bald concrete. She wondered if all the men from those empty cells had to shower at the same time.

The guard, ragged in the ordinary ways of rural Texas, spoke again. “Mr. Meri should be up in a minute. When we get to his office have a seat. I'll lock you in.”

They approached a secretary. This was her. She sat typing something from a yellow pad. The guard led Meg past her desk. Her nameplate said “Eve.” Here she was. She was redheaded, too, but from a bottle. She was young and smiley. Meg pushed the tip of her tongue to the roof of her mouth to keep from screaming. Eve triggered the lock from a button under her desk and said hello. Meg actually bit down on her tongue, but it didn't work. The restraint she mustered only turned her face slightly before she let out a soft “Eat shit,” which she tried to cover with throat-clearing. Had her father told Eve that Meg knew? Meg exhaled in a way she thought could collapse her lungs. Then she remembered she hadn't come here to screw with this woman. She had a real reason and she wouldn't let anything get in the way.

The officer left Meg in her uncle's office. She took off the cap, let down her hair, and pulled out a tube of lip gloss and a compact from her pocket. The applicator was like a tiny sword. She pouted her lips and pressed the furry tip full of clear, thick goo to her mouth. She rarely wore it on days like today, windy ones, because her hair would stick to her mouth and spread gloss all over her face. Meg held up the mirror for a long time, smacking and touching her hair. Maryanne didn't know about Eve. Meg couldn't stop picturing her sister. She knew she wasn't beautiful like Maryanne, but her hair was so overwhelming it sometimes fooled people into thinking so, and she hoped it would fool David Crosby, too. Maybe just seeing someone who lived his own life would show her a way to make it through the last few months living at home.

She put the mirror away. There weren't any pictures of her cousins. Her dad said there wouldn't be because Dan didn't want “nobody looking at his babies.” The room was humid and smoky, all of it the color of vegetable stew with creamy brown paneling halfway up the cinderblock walls. There were three chairs; a steamed-carrot-orange desk chair and two heavy looking cooked-celery-green vinyl armchairs.

Her father's Martin guitar was in the corner just like he said it would be. She unbuckled the case and pulled it out, immediately fretting a G, strumming it with the fat part of her thumb. She'd only started playing in the last few years. Her dad had played when she and Maryanne were little and was taking it up again, playing weekends with a bluegrass band in Huntsville. Unbuckling that particular case had come to feel like opening a tear in space that she could step through. The fullness of sounds from an expensive guitar rang like promise. Regardless of his requests, Meg and her dad never played together outside of the living room. Their uses of the Martin were completely different.

She turned it over in her hands, started with C, then moved to F, and finished with B, which she was sure stood for *bitch* because it was so hard to play. She worked at fretting it, then strummed and sang, "Biiiiiitch," in perfect tune. "Eveisa Biiiiiitch."

The dusty yellow blinds swung left then right when the door opened and her uncle appeared in the doorway. His tag was turned backwards, too. "Ah, mi Rosaquita! You're here." She never understood why he insisted on calling her Rosa. He said it was the color of her hair and that Meg didn't translate well. She didn't hate the nickname, it was his Spanish that bugged her. Her hair wasn't pink. And he was always trying to speak with an accent, as if it made him one of the boys in La Raza on the Inside. He used the same tone with the hands at her grandfather's ranch. Her uncle had tried to talk her dad and grandfather into joining his Spanish lessons, but only Meg took it up, and it wasn't so she could talk to Dan.

"So, le adonde?" She turned her head to the side and tapped her feet together.

"He's coming, relax." He looked at her as he walked across the room to his chair. "Why is your hair down? Didn't your dad tell you to put it up?" He sat and leaned forward. "Are you wearing makeup?" His lead hands spread out on the desk and he breathed hard through his nose. His ears moved when he breathed like that. She hadn't spent much time alone with him and she felt mildly weird about it, like being blood kin meant she was supposed to be friends with a stranger when really the only thing they had in common was the Spanish.

"I put on a little lip stuff when I got in here. I don't want to scare him." She laughed and reminded herself how she'd gotten here. It was about straddling power and politeness.

"Meg. He's an inmate. You need to get that through your head." He waited for her to nod. "He's here for doing SMACK," he said loudly. "Shit'll kill you dead. He's not cool and you shouldn't worry about looking *any* way. You'll wipe that off your face and we'll march out if you can't get a grip on that. Got it?"

She wanted to ask him if he really thought it was a good idea telling her how to behave, but because she was in such a strange place and she didn't want to jeopardize the meeting, the sod was yanked from under her. "It's not like he's violent, he was a dope head." She decided to test his tenderness. She imaged poking the end of her lip gloss sword into his chest to see how hard she could press him.

He clenched his teeth but still managed to enunciate clearly. "Got it?"

Meg wasn't used to losing control like this. Since she'd hinted to her dad that she knew Eve's kid, she had learned to negotiate a variety of situations. The problem was she hated how it made her feel to watch the strongest man in her life squirm. But more, she hated that he'd cheated on the weakest woman she knew. She looked down at the strings on the guitar and plucked the low E, punctuating her vowels. "I got it, I got it."

"Now, put your hair in a ponytail." He breathed hard and leaned back in his chair. His girls wore ponytails. He knew what they were called. "He's going to be playing your dad's guitar. Here's a rubber band." He tossed it across the desk.

She rolled her eyes away from him. "I know." She took a rubber band off her wrist, put up her hair, and left his where it lay. It was easier to look between his eyes than at them. "I think I want him to autograph it, maybe." She hesitated about telling him anything straight. It felt like her guitar. It could've been hers if she'd asked right, but she didn't, wouldn't ask her dad for his guitar. Somewhere, in the already grown-up part of her, she figured he needed it as bad as she did.

Before he responded there was a knock. It was the same officer who had escorted her in, and just as the door opened she noticed a substantial space between his front teeth, and she wondered if he could slide a nickel in there. She lost the thought when she saw he wasn't alone. Behind him, a thin, beardless, short-haired David Crosby, with shackled feet, walked shyly into the room. A man who looked nothing like the clips she'd seen on cable TV. Her father said he looked different, but Meg hardly recognized him at all. She curled back in her seat when he made himself a full step closer. Her face was blank and timid and she couldn't think of what to say, which she certainly hadn't expected. Her uncle filled the void, crossed the room, and pointed to one of the celery-green vinyl chairs. "Please." They did not shake hands.

"Thanks." He kept standing.

"This is my niece, Rosa. Today is her eighteenth birthday and she'd like to hear you play."

Meg's eyes widened but she didn't say anything. She didn't want him to think this was her idea, dragging him in here. It was, of course, but she didn't want him to know it. The decision was showing itself to be a questionable one anyway. He'd been taken away from something. She was intruding on his routine. She wished she could tell him she recognized that. She thought for a second. If they'd been outside, he'd never talk to her, which she guessed was fine. She understood she wasn't famous and didn't deserve this kind of attention. She hadn't thought of their meeting as an inconvenience to anyone before now, but suddenly she wanted no part of it, and it was too late to leave. The same train tracks that moved field crops carried passenger cars to Dallas every other day. She wasn't going anywhere now but it made her sick that she didn't know the departure schedule.

"Hi Rosa." He said it with a Z, like a country man saying, *rows and rows of cotton, Roza.*

She pulled her shoulders back and put the guitar on the ground, leaning the neck against the desk. "Hi." She waved. "My name's really Meg." She was intimately aware of her surroundings. She put out her right hand the way she thought women properly shook hands in old movies, like they were waiting for someone to kiss them. Her other hand wound a fistful of hair around her palm. Something in him was alive in there. It captivated and terrified her.

Mr. Crosby looked at her uncle for permission to approach her, and Dan said nothing of it when he shook her hand firmly then went back to his seat. "May I?" He nodded at the Martin.

"Yeah, yes." She reached down, handling it more gently than she ever did, and gave it to him across the span of about six feet. They both leaned into it so that they were hardly standing perpendicular to the ground anymore, like alpine ski jumpers. She tried to remind herself he was a normal person.

He sat down with the instrument and for a moment he just looked at it, looked at it like he'd picked an apple from an oak tree. He let the air leave his lungs the way people do when they are ready to let themselves cry; that last little bit of air no one ever really exhales unless they're trying to let go of something, or in some cases trying to get a hold of it again.

"Don't you play in here?" she asked. He was in the prison band. She knew that. And he played with a $700 Ovation kept by the chaplaincy. He could have had his own guitar, but didn't.

"I do. Warden lets the band stick around even though there aren't any more music classes." The prison school system had recently nixed music from its curriculum. According to locals, the prisons like their musicians pretty well. In the thirties a female vocal group of inmates traveled the state performing for dances. And recently in Huntsville they were talking of painting a mural of Huddie Ledbetter in the downtown square. Her mind raced through the lyrics of "Midnight Special" and she thought it should shine its light on David Crosby. The song said if the night train's headlamp shone through the bars onto someone, they'd be set free. She didn't know if the train ran here at night.

Mr. Crosby pulled the pick from the end of the neck, then rubbed his forehead with the back of his hand. His fingers were almost maroon, like they'd been bruised for fifty years, and then Meg thought it was possible they had been bruised that long from smashing them into the strings of so many guitars. Her stomach dropped. Or he'd been made to shell peas. Purple hulls made fingers that color. Or pecans. Inmates regularly gathered them from the grounds outside the walls of The Walls. Shelling was punishment.

Eve was looking in through the blinds. Meg felt hot, she stared hard at her uncle until she got his attention then nodded to the door. He stood up, made a pitiful face at Eve, and twisted the blinds shut. Meg didn't feel bad about it at all.

Mr. Crosby flat picked, slow, inaudible notes at first, notes it looked like he could hear only through the camber of his belly on the back of the guitar and the pads of his fingers that silently punched along the strings. The notes grew louder and closer together until he seemed satisfied. He looked up like he'd returned from traveling, his face wet and red and glowing. "Warden Meri said you like this one." He went into it loud and fast and without a hitch. She knew the tune in four counts. "Aye, ye, ye, ye, ye, Canten y no llores, porque cantando. . . . "

Mr. Crosby smiled as big as he sang. It made his eyebrows lift and his hairline tilt back. The thing hiding in him was coming to the surface.

Meg let go of her hair and rolled her eyes at her uncle again like she might find a reason under her lids that he was such a jackass.

Mr. Crosby stopped in the middle of the second verse, laughing. "That's all I know."

Meg clapped for him. Her uncle clapped too, loudly. "That was great," she said, careful of her voice, thinking about the open window behind her that looked out over the recreation yard. Anyone out there could surely hear the music. What did they think about this? Maybe it happened all the time. Meg focused her mind beyond the yard to the train. There were people going up and down, north and south, moving slowly, but freely as they pleased. The men in the yard had things hiding in them like Mr. Crosby had with his music. But she didn't believe all they hid was good.

He gave a little bow from his seat with the guitar in his lap, leaning forward and stretching his arm to the side, pick between his first finger and thumb. "What next?"

There was a knock at the door and her uncle moved quickly across the room to open it. It was the same skinny officer with the large space between his teeth. She thought maybe it could only hold a dime.

"Sir, Mr. Meri? You hear your radio?"

Her uncle looked at him through lowered lids, he was obviously mad the guard had interrupted.

"Yes, I turned it down." His hands crossed over his stomach.

"Well, sir, there's a situation."

He didn't seem overly concerned. "A fight?"

The guard looked at Meg and Mr. Crosby and then to her uncle, "A little more than that."

Dan reached down to his belt where his radio was clipped and turned the dial. The room filled with crackling, official sounding voices. He turned it down.

Meg knew he didn't want to leave them alone.

"Get an officer in here and we'll talk outside."

The officer leaned in close to Dan, but Meg could see what he said by watching his mouth. "There's a shit fit's moved out to the yard. We don't have no one extra right now." There was a pause. "They cut a teacher."

There was luggage on those train tracks, luggage that belonged to old people and to children. There were Snoopy suitcases out there.

Her uncle prepared himself to step outside. He looked at Meg and then at Mr. Crosby. "I'm going to be right out there, but you so much as fart, and you'll be in ad seg the rest of your stay." There were people who cut hair and did nails on those tracks. He looked at Meg, her face all turned up, wide-eyed. "GOT IT?"

They replied simultaneously, "Got it."

He pulled the officer to the lip of the staircase and shut the door halfway.

Meg could hear murmurings but couldn't make out anything. Ad seg was administrative segregation, twenty-three hours a day in a cell. There, men only ate meal loaf, a mixture of all the food from the day baked in a bread pan.

Her uncle returned. He clenched his jaw and narrowed his eyes at Meg and she knew he was going to leave them. "You'll wait in here till things settle." He turned to Mr. Crosby. "You're staying, too." Then looked back at Meg, "I hate to do this to you, honey."

She cringed at the sound of him calling her "honey." Maybe this was just a set-up to scare her. Maybe Eve would come in, excuse Mr. Crosby, and have a talk with Meg about blackmail and extortion.

Her uncle took a zip tie from the officer's belt and secured one of Mr. Crosby's wrists to the arm of the chair. He leaned down and whispered to Mr. Crosby, looking at Meg again. Her eyes felt hard and dark. She imagined them like synthetic emeralds in costume jewelry. Before he was finished she was holding strands of her ponytail in front of her face, inspecting them for split ends, attempting to ignore him and the look on Mr. Crosby's face. "He's harmless, honey, every muscle he's got's eaten from drugs." He moved around his office gathering a key card and a bullhorn. Meg heard the door lock after he shut it. She wondered what he was going to say into that bullhorn that would undo what was happening. She guessed he was a different person here. Or maybe he wasn't.

She stood up and eased across the office to a window that overlooked the rec yard. She put her hand over her mouth. Two men lay on the ground like full sides of beef. Officers tried to separate the inmates around them. They weren't dead, but it made her knees wobble. She remembered she'd heard gangs required a murder for initiation.

Mr. Crosby shook his head. "You ought to sit down." He said it in a quiet voice, and she did.

She wondered how he made it around people like that everyday, but swept the thought from her mind before coming up with an answer.

"It's probably not a big deal. Just taking precautions," he said, waiting a few seconds before continuing. "He deals with this stuff a lot." He stopped and looked at her from one side and then the other. "You're not eighteen, are you?"

"Yes, I am." Her face stretched out to refute him and she touched it with her hands. Did she look older? "Today is my birthday."

"Is he really related to you?"

Her expression scrunched up her nose like she'd smelled stink. "Yes, unfortunately." She knew where he was going.

"Doesn't look like you come from the same bunch. Red hair, white skin. The Boss looks Mexican."

This confusion was familiar and it relaxed her enough that she moved to her uncle's chair. It'd been a long time since she'd met someone who didn't know her family. "Nope, but he looks it. And all the Spanish would make you think so, but he's as Irish as the rest of my mom's family." She picked up a glass paperweight from his desk, inlaid with the state seal. "I got the eyes from my mom. No one knows about the hair. We're supposed to be black Irish. My sister is dark." She looked at his arms, scarred from years of hard everything. "I can't believe he tied you down. I mean I understand why, but. . . ." she caught herself and ducked her chin.

"Don't be afraid."

She could tell he was equally as uncomfortable. "Oh, I'm not." She was half telling the truth. "There's an inmate who sometimes cuts the grass at the ranch and I like him a lot."

He nodded strangely and then focused on the guitar. "Do you play? You could show me what you got?"

"I don't think I could. I play with my dad sometimes. You've played on TV."

"Everybody starts someplace. Maybe I can give you some tips."

She didn't know how she felt starting *here*, but she picked up the guitar and sat down. She hid her eyes behind her hair then glanced at her fingers on the neck. "Here's one of yours." She played slow at first, like he had before and then louder and with more confidence and by the time she reached the chorus of "Suite: Judy Blue Eyes" she was singing to where he could almost hear her. Her voice sounded distant under her breath. She liked that.

He smiled and clapped his free hand on the arm of the chair. "Fun."

What did *fun* mean?

A loud noise came from the yard but Meg couldn't bring herself to look.

He helped her change the subject. "Your uncle doesn't seem crazy about you being here. How'd you talk him into it? Maybe you can tell me how to talk him into letting me go home."

"My dad asked him to do it. He's been doing a lot of cheap work for the state, running construction for them or something. I guess this is some kind of trade." Everything about being here felt uncomfortable. She hated this now.

"Your dad must really trust your uncle."

"Dad says it's because he trusts *me*, but that's not why." She hesitated. Why not tell him. "He's pretty sure I know he's cheating on my mom," she stopped again and had to force out the last bit, "with her." She was careful not to call her a *lady* as she pointed towards Eve's desk in the hallway.

Mr. Crosby leaned as far forward as his arm would allow for him to look. His brow wrinkled. "Shit, man."

"Yeah, I give my dad a couple of sideways looks and he pees himself." She waited. "I did ask to come here today." She wanted him to know it now because she was sorry.

His gaze became transparent. "I'm glad you came."

He was lying. Her dad had told her sometimes it was easier for inmates to disappear into their Inside life than keep a connection with the world outside. They often asked their families to stop visiting. Meg said, "I know this is weird and I'm sorry."

"That's not your fault." He looked at his feet and cleared his throat. "How do you know? About your dad?" His eyes were wide and it reminded her of the way she must have looked when she found out about Eve.

"I don't know for sure, but her kid is a grade younger than me. He's in 4-H with a friend of mine. And it got from him to me that my dad's been around a bunch. I don't know if that just means *here*," she pointed to the floor, "or at their house, or what."

"That's rough for a kid your age. But your friend might be wrong."

She was glad he hadn't said *for a girl your age*. "I doubt it."

Meg looked out the window toward Eve. All she could make out was a shadow cast on the wall. A month ago a different friend asked about a strange woman eating with Meg's dad at Casa Miguel. She rubbed her stomach where something had started to ache.

"Are you going to tell your mom?"

Meg whipped around. "Hell no, I'm not going to tell her. Hell no. It'd kill her." She wished for a cigarette. "And then what would the Junior League do?" She picked up a pencil off the desk and poked the sharp tip through the knit weave of her sweat pants. She could feel it pricking into her leg. "No way."

"Sounds like good song material."

She eased the lead and laughed. "I don't know how to write music."

"You should try it." He looked toward the window. "Haven't heard anything out there for a minute. Maybe it's over."

And as though to confirm it, her uncle opened the door and both

Meg and Mr. Crosby seemed taken back by it, scared even. Dan eyed Mr. Crosby. When he was satisfied he motioned for Meg to go sit in the other chair. "Everything is under control. Sorry about that, Meg." He smiled then looked to Mr. Crosby. "Mandatory lock down. Officer Percy will take you back to your cell." He nodded at the man in the doorway with the space between his teeth.

The guard walked into the room and bent over the chair with his butt facing Meg. He clipped the zip tie in one small cut then led Mr. Crosby up by the arm. "Come on, we're going back."

"I'm coming." Mr. Crosby said it in a voice of compliance, but he shook his arm a little to loosen the grip.

Meg wondered where exactly they were going back to. She wondered if his cell was decorated the way she'd seen in movies. The cells had looked empty when she'd come in. She walked up behind them. "Do you have any of your band posters in . . ." she started to say *your cell*, but ended with, ". . . here? I could probably get you one." This was a stupid idea but she didn't care. She tried not to look back at her uncle's face. If he wanted to object, he'd have to do it in words, in English words.

The guard slowed, turned, and looked back at Dan. Meg guessed the officer was wondering what her uncle was going to do about her talking like that.

"Or some tapes?" She knew she was so far past the line of what was acceptable that she couldn't have seen it if she'd turned back to look. She was thinking she'd spend her whole savings to bring him a guitar if it could reproduce the look on his face when he'd played. He'd known just who he was and just what he wanted. Meg never felt that.

Mr. Crosby didn't look at her but he did turn his head to speak in her direction. "You just write some music."

Her uncle's breath seemed to burn the moisture off the back of her neck. He wasn't going to let that go. He grabbed her arm and swung her around. "There will be absolutely no contact with him after this!"

It took some mental effort, but she put herself on that train, slow moving, too heavy to stop, impossible for someone else to jump on it. She imagined something valuable was in one of the cars, but she couldn't see which one. She imagined all the cargo doors opened, save the one with the valuable thing. She'd have to get to her destination before she could find out what it was. Soon she'd be away in a place where his opinion didn't mean a squirt of piss. She laughed.

"This is funny?" He turned to the guard. "Get that junkie OUT."

She knew she was asking for trouble, but how bad could it be? Even if he told her parents how she'd behaved, they wouldn't take her car away because no one else wanted to drive Maryanne to school everyday. They couldn't slow her down. Twenty miles out of town, in any direction, was bare freedom.

She tried to move away from her uncle and slide in front of Mr. Crosby to shake his hand. She wanted to talk to him a little longer, wanted to hear how his voice filled out the hollow sounds of the office. One of her hands was outstretched for a handshake, but she couldn't reach him.

The guard pushed Mr. Crosby out the door as he tried to turn around, holding out one of his big red hands as a gesture. The officer, lost in his own gap-toothed thoughts, must have believed he was grabbing for her. He pulled Mr. Crosby a full pace into the hallway by his collar and knocked his feet out from under him. Mr. Crosby's short hair seemed to melt into the brown carpet and for a split second Meg thought it looked like they were all standing on a pool of long curly hair that had sprouted between the time he started to fall and the time he hit the floor. The officer clamped his knee down on Mr. Crosby's chest like a cinderblock on a sack of flour.

Meg lunged for the officer but her uncle grabbed her solidly around the waist. She felt pain in her abdomen where he squeezed her. It didn't hurt any more than cramps, but she wanted to drop to the ground and scream bloody murder that he'd hurt something female in her belly. But she knew screaming for help wouldn't do anything. He was the only authority here. Either way, the officer would still drag Mr. Crosby out by his neck, and she'd never see him again. With that, she opted for another approach that wasn't an approach at all, but an unbuckling. She turned around in the ring of her uncle's grasp and hit him square in the face with her elbow and then her voice, an attack she pointed directly between his eyes. He didn't let go. She fought like she would have if she'd reached the officer. She screamed obscenities, she screamed gibberish, she screamed things she didn't even know she'd hated about him until that moment. And finally, with tears betraying her voice, she screamed things about her father and Eve.

Dan didn't say a word, just half-dragged her, half-carried her over the top of the officer and Mr. Crosby out of the doorway. Eve stood up behind her desk looking like she didn't know thin shit from wild honey. "Is she crazy?"

Meg narrowed her eyes and tried her hardest yet to shake herself free. Her hair caught in Dan's mouth, his arm still around her waist. They were related. They did share DNA, and pressed together, she couldn't forget it. She jerked forward over Eve's desk, eye to eye, her own eyes red and bulging. Eve sat in horror. Meg wanted to spit in her face. "Crazy? You just keep fucking with my father." Meg meant it from the darkest place she'd ever felt in her life. She could literally kill this woman. Right now, without doubt. Everything was wrong.

"That's it." Her uncle grabbed her tighter then pulled her down the stairs into the cold-cement, dry-white hallway with a concrete wall on one side and four stories of cells on the other. All were full and locked down this time. Their inhabitants screamed, too. They stuck their faces through the bars like rancid biscuits bursting from the can. They bit and licked their lips, some pulled out their dicks. A man hollered, "I want your pussy."

She gagged and forced down vomit that rose each time her uncle's arm gouged into her side. She tried to say stop, tried to tell him she couldn't breathe, that he was really hurting her now, but there was no stopping him. They passed through the first gate and she gave up in order to simply swallow what was pooling in her mouth from her throat and the snot sliding down into her lips. He didn't let go. She stumbled through the second gate and back out to the entrance, back to the gate guards and barbed wire and the walkway, and the tracks.

Her uncle and the guards put her on the other side of the fence. He turned loose of her. She made one last swipe for his face and missed, then slumped down fast to the sidewalk on her butt. They closed the gate. She kept her hand on her stomach, she curled her knees to her chest, tried to breathe, and not look at everyone watching her. Each exhale choked up mucus she spit out on the ground. She put her hands on the concrete and came to her knees like someone crawling out of a pool after almost drowning. Finally she stood. She swept loose chunks of hair from her face and straightened to look at him. She had to quit shaking. The back of her hand dried under each eye. He told her to go home and that he would check to make sure she was there in an hour. He said he wasn't going to tell her parents about this.

She stood there, feeling heavy, wanting back in, wondering about David Crosby. What face he had to wear to go back. She made herself stop crying and then forced a little half grin. "Bueno, Le voy a decir a Mama lo sobre Eve y que lo sabices todo el tiempo." She flashed her cruise face, "Buena Suerte." He wouldn't be able to translate it completely, but he'd pick up parts of it that would make him nervous.

No one on the other side of the fence moved, except one Hispanic guard who looked away and scratched behind his ear. She wasn't telling her mother. She searched their faces; her uncle was gone. The rest stood there, easy, with their name badges clipped backwards so no one would see their real faces, the smiles that showed up in pictures with wives and children.

Meg walked to her Bronco, pulling off her tennis shoes on the way. She matter-of-factly stripped off the sweatpants and kicked them into the bushes next to her truck. Her blue panties showed from under the sweatshirt, her legs bare down to white socks. She peeled the socks off, opened the door, leaned over the driver's seat, and grabbed her jeans and an undershirt off the passenger floorboard. With her back to the prison, she slid off her underwear, put her feet into the jeans, pulled them up and buttoned them. All was silent but the train. She tugged off the sweatshirt and bra and put the clean white T-shirt over her head.

The clothes ended up in a pile next to her tire, but not before she retrieved her lip gloss from the sweatpants' pocket. She turned to climb into the truck, ignoring all the guards still standing a hundred feet away, their mouths set to catch flies. She saw now it was the Dallas train, and it took her breath. She slathered the gloss carefully over her mouth, much thicker than usual, and when she pulled out her ponytail holder, her hair fell down freely in the wind, and none of it stuck to her face. There were packages going up those tracks to loved ones in Dallas. There were people who'd left home on those tracks. She hung her head and prayed for the engineer to pull on the light.

●

AMANDA NOWLIN-O'BANION's writing draws—not just on her imagination—but on her myriad experiences of life "off the beaten path." From rural Texas to New York City to the sparkling Alaskan tundra, Amanda has worked as a sailing instructor, served as a jack-of-all-trades in Denali, and taught English inside a maximum security men's prison. She has been pursued by bears, won first prize for her mayhaw jelly at the county fair, and survived to tell about it. Humorous, provocative, and genuine, Amanda's essays, short stories, and other writings reveal the changing landscape of Americana, and the human struggles that come as a result. Her novel-in-progress, *The Greenest Grass*, from which "The Walls, Texas" is excerpted, explores one young woman's struggle as she challenges traditional land inheritance patterns and the labor division of her family's ranch. In 2000, Joyce Carol Oates named Amanda the "¡TEX! Emerging Writer" in fiction, and she was nominated for Best New American Voices 2006. Her work has appeared in the *Dallas Morning News*, *Conversely*, and will appear in the Summer 2006 issue of *SHSR*. Amanda has been an invited guest on National Public Radio affiliate KUHF's program *Front Row*, and at The Blaffer Gallery *Girls Night Out* exhibit. She holds an MFA in creative writing from New York University, and is currently a Ph.D. candidate in literature and creative writing at the University of Houston, where she teaches. Amanda lives in Huntsville, Texas, with her husband, Robert. Special thanks are extended to Robert O'Banion, Debbie and Bill Nowlin, and Ree and Daniel Belhumeur.

Peter Cashwell

THE SNOW CHASER

BACKSTORY: My wife and I have long theorized that Johnny Cash could sing any song, and we've spent many a mile in the car playing the game described in this story, with the same results: he can sing them all but two. One that he sang to great effect in his late career was his version of John Routh's "Field of Diamonds." When I first heard it, the interplay of the simple melody, the sparkling harmonies, and Johnny's dark baritone led me to a visual image—I actually saw deep contrasts of color and shading. I found myself thinking of a clear night sky against a field of snow, and of the different worlds that might lie under that sky. From there, it was only a short trip into the Blue Ridge Mountains to reach this story.

WIND RUSHING THROUGH THE PINE TREES atop the ridge, and I can smell a distant fire somewhere in the cold. The western sky is almost cloudless, the air clear and just below freezing. Somewhere ahead of me—grunting and muttering—is Greylen. Small clods of dirt and twigs fall down the slope, rattling off one another and bouncing from rock to rock. I haven't heard a bird in hours.

"See anything?" I call.

He doesn't answer, and of course I don't really expect him to. Greylen tends to speak only at one volume, slightly too loud when you're indoors and slightly too quiet when you're out in the open. Right now, with the March wind whistling through the cracks in the mountain's face, he makes no more noise than a catamount on the prowl.

Or so I imagined, safe behind the wheel of my Forester, downshifting as I made the turn onto Field in the dim November light and searched for the neighbors' Labrador, which was usually ready to chase me all the way to my driveway. I had never seen a catamount. I'd bet that not a single member of my extended family had, except maybe for Greylen. But he was never one to give a straight answer. If you were to ask him, "Greylen, are there any catamounts around here?" he'd just lean back in his chair, look over your head, and say something cryptic: "I recollect two or three times I went out to the orchard to gather some windfalls, two or three times, and I was out there maybe quarter of an hour, and I knew they was eyes on me." Then he'd shift in his chair and take a drag on his pipe, deepening the wrinkles in his lean face in the process.

Greylen was my wife's cousin, I think four or five generations removed, but no one really knew. The Weakleys were a clan so numerous in Innskeep County that anyone with the name was automatically accorded cousinhood and expected at all family gatherings. Greylen appeared dutifully at every Thanksgiving, Christmas, wedding, and funeral, eating lightly and saying next to nothing. His chief contributions to the celebrations were a few muttered greetings and clouds of sweet tobacco smoke, which I guiltily enjoyed. I hadn't been around anyone who smoked a pipe since my own grandfather had died fifteen years before, and though Greylen's blend had a faint air of molasses about it, the scent's similarity to that produced by Grandpa Polk's pipe had always made me feel affectionate toward Greylen. Not that he seemed to notice.

I had trouble feeling that way about a lot of Corey's family. They never did anything overt, but I was always painfully aware that I was an outsider—a Flatlander, capital F. Perhaps I just imagined it, but sometimes they seemed to harbor a hope that someday she'd move back to the hollows under Walker's Top and forget everything she'd become since leaving to attend college down in the foothills. To that end, they always called her by her birth name, "Cora" or "Cora Marie," even after she'd asked them not to. All except Greylen, that is. He just called her "little girl." It was his name for any of the two dozen women under the age of sixty who might be encountered at a reunion. I was "son," which had bothered me at first, as I told Corey on the drive home from my first Weakley Thanksgiving.

"What's wrong with 'son'?"

"It's just—belittling."

"What?"

"It's like he doesn't believe I'm an adult."

"Well, compared to him, you're not. You're twenty-five, and he's probably three times that."

"I just don't like being treated like I'm ignorant. You remember Dr. Garcek."

Corey turned to look at me. I kept my eyes on the road, but I could see her hair fly around in the corner of my eye. "What does Dr. Garcek have to do with it? I thought he marked you down for using 'y'all' in a poli-sci essay."

"Exactly!" I said. "He said in class one day that it sounded backward. That pissed me off so much I put it in my essay on purpose."

"You are *not* gonna win this contest with me," she said.

"What contest?"

"The 'I Got Treated Like I Was Backward' Contest. I'm from the hollows, hon. My freshman roommate was from Charlotte, and she kept asking me to say the word 'night' because she thought it sounded funny. I've heard every inbreeding joke ever made. And every moonshining joke, too."

"But that's what I mean," I protested. "I'm a Southerner, so every New Yorker and Californian I talk to docks me a couple IQ points just for my accent. I don't like it, but I'm used to it. But I don't think I should have to put up with it from Greylen. He's from the South, too."

"There is no such thing as *the* South," said Corey firmly. And that was all she said until we got home.

The next time we went to Innskeep County, I bristled silently until I realized that Greylen called every man and boy in the family "son." He apparently didn't use it out of disrespect, but just so he could get along without having to learn a lot of proper names.

Corey and I had been married for three years when we happened to visit her parents in the early spring. Her cousin Louise was getting married, and Corey seemed sure that the wedding had been arranged in some haste. "I don't know that a shotgun's involved," she said, stuffing her suitcase with one more pair of warm socks. "But I'll bet somebody stood near Matthew McKellen and whispered the word 'paternity suit' very slowly and clearly."

We drove upwards, back into the winter—cold rain splattered down from time to time, and the scenery wasn't worth discussing. Our car stereo was on the fritz, so we soon fell to playing an old favorite game: trying to find a song Johnny Cash couldn't sing. I still don't recall whether Corey or I had first voiced the opinion that he could sing anything, but we would occasionally test the hypothesis. I sing baritone, though not with anything like the twang and gravel Johnny had, but I'm not a bad mimic. Corey would come up with a song title and I'd do my best to deliver it in Cash style. Usually it sounded pretty good.

"How about 'Alison'? Elvis Costello?" she said as we passed the city limits of Grindstaff, where the grocery store sign read FO D LI N.

"Totally Johnny," I replied. "*Oh, it's so funny to be seein' you after so long, girl. . . .*"

"Yeah, you're right. He gets kind of country anyway."

"You've got to get a little more off the beaten track than that."

"Okay . . . 'I Will Survive.'"

"'*At first I was afraid, I was petrified. . . .*'" I rumbled, and suddenly the song changed from disco camp to a sincere statement of purpose. A man's survival really *had* been in question, and now it really *was* assured. "How the hell does he do that?"

"Authority," said Corey. "Whatever he says, he says with authority."

"Damn straight," I replied, and shifted down as we hit the first long slope into the mountains.

In three years, we'd found exactly two songs Johnny couldn't sing: "I've Never Been to Me," and Cyndi Lauper's "She-Bop."

Nobody mentioned shotguns or litigation at the wedding, of course, and Matthew looked suitably happy to be joining the Weakley clan. I was a bit surprised not to see Greylen around at the reception, though, and mentioned it to Corey's father.

"Greylen? Oh, we won't see him again till April."

"Why not?"

"He's scouting."

"For what?"

"Snow."

On the drive home, I asked Corey about Greylen's absence and she seemed to fall into that zone I knew well, the one between fierce pride in the noble people of the hollows and harsh condemnation of their backward ways. I think the technical term is "conflicted."

"What did Daddy tell you?"

"He said Greylen was out hunting snow."

"You mean chasing snow."

"Okay, chasing. What does that mean, exactly?"

It was dark, but somehow I could tell that she had rolled her eyes—maybe the steering wheel shifted or something. "It means that he spends the last part of March every year wandering around Innskeep County looking for patches of snow."

"Why?"

"To find the last one before it melts."

"He's looking for the last one—"

"He wants to be the one to find the last patch of snow left in the county."

I mulled that one over for a minute. "Does he win something?"

"Bragging rights, from what I hear."

"You've never done it yourself?"

I think the eyes rolled again. "The only person I know who's ever done it is Greylen, and you know how talkative he is. As far as I know, it's just him and some friends all trying to one-up each other."

"So why do they do it?"

Her mountain twang became deliberately sharp. "Well, there ain't much to do up there, you know?"

That was all she said, and all I asked, but the idea kept rattling around in my head. Snow fell in Innskeep County every year, and it wasn't unusual to see bits of it in shady spots days or even weeks after a snowfall. Where Route 88 passed over the ridge in Johnhall Gap, you could look to your right and see nothing but bare limbs waving in the cold sun that fell on Johnhall's Peak. Look to your left, though, and you'd see the north face of Walker's Top, pale blue with shadowed snow. The idea of long-fallen snow in the mountains was completely understandable.

What I didn't understand was the desire to look for a patch of it. Oh, I like snow—well, to be fair, I used to like it more than I do now. When I was a kid, of course, a snowy day was a holiday—the best kind, one that couldn't be planned for, a gift from above. It was gluing myself to the radio to wait for the song to be over so that the announcer could read the list of school closings, then launching myself into the closet to burrow for fallen scarves and mittens. It was clumping up the hill of Austin Road in boots that squeaked against the powder, my Flexible Flyer alternately sliding behind me and bumping my heels. It was launching myself downhill with a muffled *oof* and letting my cheeks go red and raw with the bite of the wind and the occasional stray flake, hauling back hard on the right bar to bend my path away from the curb and the stand of redbuds beyond it. And it was staggering back in, exhausted, to find a toasted-cheese sandwich, bubbling under brown streaks of seasoned salt, and a saucepan of Campbell's Tomato Soup, all waiting for me.

But nowadays? Now snow is just weather. Nicer to look at than rain, certainly, but not fundamentally different. I like the neighborhood after it's snowed, though—all the various patches of lawn, the driveways, the trees, all whited out, all distinctions erased. It's a calm and peaceful picture. But then the markings appear—the tire tracks, the footprints, the scars of shovels—and the mud beneath is revealed. The same mud made by rain, just covered over with white.

Maybe it was different up in the hills. Maybe from up there, snow looked different. Maybe Greylen and his friends saw something in it that made it more important, more desirable. But for the life of me, I couldn't figure out what it was.

When I saw Greylen next, there was no snow anywhere. It was Father's Day, and the Weakleys were gathered at the old John Hall Weakley house for their reunion. The house had been expanded and renovated from its old days when John Hall had built it back in the 1830s. In fact, Corey's dad said it had been the first house in Innskeep County to have both wiring and indoor plumbing, though I didn't know the truth of that claim. The current inhabitants, Calvin and May Weakley, hadn't made any major changes, at least not that I could see from the photos that covered the walls of the front room. It was still a yellow two-story box, tin-roofed and twin-chimneyed, and the long low wing that jutted eastward along the slope behind it had been there since sometime in the days of sepiatone. Okay, the satellite dish was new.

Greylen sat on the porch of the east wing, cocked back in a rocking chair with a pipe in his mouth and a few bits of debris on his plate that turned out to be the remains of Aunt Emma's grape pie. Balancing my own overloaded plate with care, I settled heavily into the rocker next to Greylen's and smiled at him.

"How've you been, Greylen?"

"Can't complain, can't complain," he said after a pause. He had that way of answering even the most inane comments with what seemed like real deliberation. "You and that little girl still gettin' on?"

"Like you said," I replied around a bite. "Can't complain."

I'm sure we must have talked about something else for a while, but whatever it was has slipped away as surely as the meal. A plate of Weakley food is something to treasure, but the shame of it is that each dish obscures the others—at every gathering, there is too much, in too much variety, for an ordinary mind like mine to recapture the particulars. I could bet that my plate that day was overflowing with fried chicken, black-eyed peas, collards, two kinds of cornbread, two kinds of biscuit, baked beans, and Uncle Will's lemon pound cake, but it's only a guess. I have spent too many years bewildered by the choices spread out in Calvin and May's dining room to know now whether Greylen watched me slurping down fresh string beans or Aunt Maria Belle's chicken and pastry. But I do believe it's important that I try to remember.

Eventually, of course, my curiosity got the better of me. "Greylen, Corey was telling me that you chase snow."

He nodded curtly. "Not lately."

"Why not?"

He'd been waiting for that, so he took a second to puff his pipe. "It's June, son."

I snorted appreciatively. "But you were chasing snow back in February?"

"Oh, no. Too early, too early. It's still fallin' up here into March. I've found it in April before. 'Course, that was after a big fall on Saint Patrick's Day."

I'd never heard so many words out of Greylen's mouth at one time, and they didn't stop there. If I'd had a notebook with me, instead of a plastic fork greasy with barbecue sauce, I could have written the definitive treatise on snow chasing, but now only fragments remain. How the object was to find a patch bigger than two hands side by side. How the real chasing began in early March, after one of the early snows was melting away and revealing the likely spots for the last snow's remnants. The basics were clear even to an idiot like me: shelter, height, north. Look for a shady spot at a high elevation on the north side of the hill. But then the nuances came into play. Some high spots were too exposed to wind, and snow might blow away. Some shady spots were so deep in a hollow that meltwater might wash them clean. And if another storm followed the last snow, the whole game changed. A new snowfall started the whole thing over, of course, but if it rained, any spot might go bad in a hurry, unless the rain was blowing in from a different direction than the snow had blown in—that might leave a small patch of snow safe in the lee of a rock or a log. Most unpredictable of all was a late ice storm. It might seal up parcels of snow that could last for quite a while, but it also made finding them difficult—glaring white reflections foiled the chaser's eyes, and slippery rocks and limbs underfoot might send him down the mountain in a hurry, or at least give him a nice set of bruises to take home.

Eventually he paused to draw on his pipe. "That more'n you wanted to know?"

I smiled. It was, of course, far more, but now that I'd heard it, it wasn't enough. And by the time I got back in the car to make the two-hour drive downhill to our house, I'd somehow decided to come up and meet him after the last snow.

"You're what?" said Corey, as we took a big curve on the downhill ride.

"I'm going to come chase snow with Greylen in March."

"Why on earth would you want to do that?"

That was a good question, and I duly noted it aloud, but I didn't answer it at the time. I thought about it at some length, though, there in the passenger seat, and even more over the rest of the summer and fall. Part of it, I eventually decided, was envy. Dixie envy. A Southerner like me is supposed to be close to the land, full of folksy wisdom and arcane knowledge, but of course it isn't so. For all my drawling, like most of my contemporaries, I was a suburban American through and through, better versed in *Andy Griffith Show* reruns and basketball scores than in the way of birds and beasts, and sometimes I envied Corey. For all the chafing she'd done under the grip of her family, that close connection to tradition, to the hollows and hills of Appalachia, gave her a foundation, something she could either stand upon or push against. When I would catch her in the kitchen, belting out an old hymn I'd never heard before, I would sometimes find myself feeling unmoored and weak by comparison. What songs lingered from my own childhood? "The Ballad of Gilligan's Island."

But there was also the fact that Greylen had spoken at such length. There is a certain appeal in obsession. A man speaking about his passion, whatever it may be, tells us that we can find something worthwhile in even the most mundane places. A dark and empty sky still has stars, tiny bits of beauty and light. And if you take the time and trouble to pick out the constellations, there are even stories to be told about them. So maybe there are some bits of purpose even in the front yard, there between the bits of Labrador poop.

Corey's car was already in the driveway. Since she gets out of school about an hour before I get off work, this wasn't so unusual, but when she met me at the door, I knew something was up. She didn't cry, but her hug was a little tighter than usual.

"What's wrong?" I said, muffled against her shoulder.

"Greylen," she replied. "He died yesterday."

The next day we made the drive up to Walker's Top through trees long past their bright colors, now gone brown or bare, and saw Greylen laid to rest in the tiny graveyard behind Grouse Hollow Presbyterian. I looked around for faces I didn't know, and there were only a few—the Weakleys seemed to be the only people there. Where were his snow-chasing buddies?

Calvin and May had of course done what every Southern family knows to do when someone dies: cook. The dining room was once again full, and we all once again loaded up our Chinette plates and balanced them on our knees, perched on folding chairs and trying to keep the grease off our clothes. I was chewing on pound cake, and Corey had found a piece of grape pie—one of her favorites, but only when Uncle Will made it—when May sat down next to me with an enormous slice of coconut cake.

"Thanks for putting all this out for us, Aunt May," said Corey.

"No, thank you for coming all this way," said May.

"Oh, we had to come for Greylen's sake."

"Well, I'm sure he appreciates it. He didn't have many friends, so having the whole family here means a lot."

I put down my fork while she scooped up a big piece of cake. "Actually, Aunt May," I said, trying to drag out the question while she chewed, "I'm a little surprised to hear that. I would have thought some of the people he chased snow with would be here. Or at least might have come to the service."

She chewed thoughtfully, swallowed, and picked up the cup of sweet tea she'd set by her feet so she could wash the cake down properly. "Well, that's true," she said at last. "I honestly don't know them, though. Calvin—come here a second, I got a question."

Calvin didn't know, either. Nor Will, nor Maria Belle, nor Louise, Matthew, or any of the other dozens of Weakleys gathered in John Hall's house. None of the family could name a single snow chaser other than

Greylen. In fact, none of them could say much about the practice of snow chasing—who did it, where they met, how they conducted the contests, who'd won in previous years, where the last patch had been. Nothing.

I soon stepped out of the house and went to sit in one of the porch rockers in front of the east wing. The scent of pipe tobacco was long gone, but the tang of wood smoke filled the evening, and I was able to pick out the stars between the tree limbs. And looking at them, the same stars I could see from Field Street, I didn't feel duped, or foolish. For the first time, I felt like these hollows and hills were a part of me—not something foreign, but just my own flat lawns, folded and wrinkled, but still mine.

"Authority," I said quietly.

To this day I don't know whether Greylen was a true astronomer or not. I do know he was a great storyteller. But whenever it snows on Field Street, and the flakes are caught whirling in the glow of the streetlights, I like to think about the cold dark places on the north side of Walker's Top, and about the patches of white that may linger there, and about the dark shape that guards them on silent paws, with eyes that glitter like diamonds.

•

PETER CASHWELL is a University of North Carolina graduate. Peter's book *The Verb 'To Bird'* was named a Barnes & Noble "Discover Great New Writers" selection in Summer 2003, as well as a Book Sense 76 selection. The book's irreverent tone and eclectic approach to its subject attracted attention from a wide variety of sources. Martha Stewart chatted with Peter on an episode of *Martha Stewart Living Television*. John Hanson Mitchell, editor of *Sanctuary*, the Massachusetts Audubon Society's journal, called the book "[a] fine literary ramble and a good laugh to boot—no mean feat in a genre that perhaps takes itself too seriously." *The Bloomsbury Review* described the book as "[a] delightfully literary and eclectic memoir about the manifold joys of birding," and its author "[a] very literate, observant, insightful storyteller." Peter's work has appeared in *The Comics Journal*, *The Readerville Journal*, and *Woodberry Forest Magazine*, as well as on WVTF public radio. He lives with his wife, Kelly Dalton, and their two sons in Woodberry Forest, Virginia, where he teaches English and speech.

Kyle Duane Hebert

TERMINAL

BACKSTORY: This story is inspired by a Johnny Cash song, "Sunday Morning Coming Down"; though it is based loosely on my father's own battle with cancer. Cash's song is about the emptiness the narrator feels waking up hung over on a Sunday morning and, I believe, the loss he feels over the life he's squandered away. This story tackles the similar theme of life's losses from the point of view of a man dying of cancer.

THE DILAUDID WEARS OFF WHILE HE SLEEPS, and it is the pain that wakes him on this Easter Sunday morning. The pain that says, in case you've forgotten, you're dying of cancer. Like it does most mornings since "Dr. Doom" gave him six months to live—it's now month four—the word terminal arrives in his mind first.

He lies there for a moment, staring at the ceiling trying to decide if he should swallow another capsule and sleep most of the morning off, or get up and deal. Deal it is. He works his eroded frame up off the mattress, sits up with his feet on the floor.

There's so little of him now, and yet the pain keeps getting bigger. He stands slowly and shakily, then turns and checks the sheets. It's a rare night when he doesn't wet the bed or worse these days, but it seems he was fortunate enough the night before to do neither. He ignores the urge to piss, knows nothing will come but that embarrassing trickle until it feels as though his bladder will burst.

On his way to the kitchen he peers into the guest bedroom where his wife now sleeps to avoid the nocturnal disasters, his not often quiet sobs of pain. She's still asleep, and there's no reason to wake her.

In the kitchen he grabs a bowl, fills it with cereal and milk. Grabs a warm beer from the six-pack on the counter. He hardly drank beer before now, but uses it now along with his veritable pharmacy—both prescribed and obtained—to numb the constant pain. He eats a few bites of the cereal before deciding he doesn't want it. Brings the beer out onto the porch where, for a nice change, the paper is actually waiting for him. Most days he has to shuffle out into the yard to fetch it.

The front page features a photo of the cemetery, trees covered in white blossoms. The caption mentions something about a sunrise service being held there this morning and it is only then he realizes, first, that it's Sunday, and second, that it's Easter. He finishes the beer in a few gulps, thumbs through the paper though nothing really interests him. Local news is always boring, and he'll be gone long before this war is ever over.

The pain is only at a low hum, so he decides that another beer is all he'll need for the moment. That and a cigarette. He'd never stopped, didn't see the point now. He lights one, pulls the smoke into his lungs and exhales slowly.

After a second cigarette he goes back inside to dress. Grabs a pair of jeans from the pile on the floor and a shirt. He sniffs the shirt and decides it smells clean enough before pulling it over his head. Checks himself in the mirror, and he looks like a kid wearing his dad's clothes, a skeleton draped in sheets.

On the way out the door he snatches up the last two beers, still held together by the plastic ring. He hopes the Little Store is open this morning. He's got about a two-mile walk ahead of him, both ways, and if at the end of the first half his efforts prove fruitless he might just give up altogether right there. Throw himself into traffic if that's what it takes.

As he walks, a slow rolling shuffle that eases the grating in his hips, a church bell tolls. The sound of it takes him back, though it's to somewhere he's never really been. His parents were religious and his wife, too. He'd gone to enough services in his life to know what went on behind those doors. Seen baptisms and prayer sessions, sipped coffee with a deacon or two in the fellowship hall. In both his parents' church and the one he'd gone to with his wife and their two sons when they were younger, he'd been a target. One of the lost. He'd never really considered their offers of salvation, wasn't something he needed.

He's near the church now. Boys in suits and girls in pink and yellow dresses are crisscrossing the church lawn, eyes to the ground, baskets swinging wildly. There's a few parents trying to subtly hint at the location of an egg or two but not really succeeding.

On the front lawn older couples are gathered, their outfits just grown-up versions of their opposites in the rear. The pastor stands out front beaming, shaking hands. For a brief moment their eyes meet. It is as though the pastor can sense his desire, his need to be in that place rubbing against his tendency to reject everything the pastor stands for. He is now more confused than ever and it's as if the pastor knows this, too.

For a moment he considers going in. He remembers the lyric to an old hymn his mother used to sing, "Just as I am, though tossed about, fighting fears within, without." A little girl, all blonde hair and pink chiffon, runs up beside him. "Can you reach an egg for me?" she asks. "Sure," he says, but before he can, someone, presumably the girl's mother, runs over, says "No honey, not him." Her daughter turns to join the others and the mother delivers a look where every emotion is plain. "You're not welcome here," it says.

He stands on the sidewalk near the church lawn for awhile after everyone else has gone in, and begins to pray. "Lord I wish I was stoned, because then I wouldn't have to feel this... this loneliness, this emptiness." He stops there, full knowing that if the Lord won't answer the prayer, there's a bottle on his nightstand that will.

By the time he reaches the store he's finished both beers. He makes his way back to the cooler to grab another sixer. "Morning Ken," Carl, the storeowner, says as he puts the beer on the counter.

"Morning."

"You walk here?"

"Wife hid the keys. I fall asleep sometimes. Went into a ditch last week."

"The meds or...."

"Both," he says, knowing Carl couldn't say cancer in front of a man dying from it. He'd found hardly anyone could. They'd call it the sickness, or his condition, but never cancer, as if by not saying the word they reduced its power to take him away from them. Carl just nods.

The two of them stand in the quiet store. The sun is just appearing over the tops of the houses across the street and beginning to shine through the big front windows. Someone out front is pumping gas, and the smell drifts in through the door propped open with a broomstick.

"You got any cards?" he asks.

"Playing cards?"

"No. Easter."

"Got a few left. End of the candy aisle."

"Flowers?"

"Two lilies left. Haven't even bloomed yet."

"I'll take them. Be right back," he says and goes to the card rack. The selections are few but he finds one that will do. Up front he pays Carl, grabs the paper sack, turns to leave.

"Take it easy, Ken,"

"Yeah," he says, going out the door.

He takes a different route back home to avoid the church. Doesn't want to feel it pulling on the hollow space inside him.

He reaches his front door sweaty, buzzing from his fourth beer of the morning. The pain has risen from a low hum to a symphony. He'll need the drugs soon. First he finds a pen to write a message in the card. He rereads what he wrote, and can see that even his handwriting has changed into a weakened scrawl, a shaky facsimile of his usually bolder script. The cancer leaves no aspect of his life untouched.

He puts the card and the flowers on the dresser where she can see them when she wakes up. He is so near his own room he has to fight the urge to return to his own bed and spiral down into opioid bliss. He somehow manages and instead returns to the porch with the beer, his smokes, and a paperback thriller.

He's still sitting there when she comes out in a robe and slippers. Kisses him on the mouth, says "Happy Easter."

The hole he felt earlier, the longing to sit on a pew in that church is burnt up by the flame of her kiss. He hadn't known what to write in the card, bought the damn thing so he didn't *have* to know what to write, but it had not been enough. *Thanks for all you've been doing for me* is what he scribbled down, which still wasn't exactly right, but he could see in her eyes that she knew what he meant.

He knows she is frightened lately. Knows there are days when she could just punch him in frustration at his reluctance to discuss anything with her. His cancer, his death, his funeral, he'll speak of none of it. But now she comes around and sits on his barely perceptible lap. Her weight is almost too much, he feels its crush on his bones. He can smell the shampoo in her hair, the sleep smell of her skin. "Happy Easter," he says back.

He doesn't feel so alone now. In this moment he can pretend he has back all the yesterdays he squandered. He can pretend the moment their love first faded and then disappeared has yet to occur and that he won't let it this time.

●

KYLE DUANE HEBERT lives and writes in Lexington, Kentucky. His fiction has appeared in *The Glut*, *Sexy Stranger*, and *Mitochondria's First Anthology of Rarities and Loose Ends*. He is also the fiction editor for *Nougat*. His first manuscript for a novel is sitting on an editor's desk waiting to be read.

Emily Reardon

BEAT BACK THE DROWNING TIDES

BACKSTORY: The song "Drive On" brings to light our mysterious will as humans to do things that go against our natural inclinations, the ability of the mind to overcome the instincts of self-preservation and self-love, and to compel the body to act in ways that can be damaging to us. The fact that we are able to put a cause or idea from the outside world before our own desires and safety makes it seem as though we are born with self-sacrifice in our veins. This will strikes me as a big part of what makes our world and our own lives at once so baffling and so admirable.

T*ERI? SHERRY?* MOLLY FLICKED HER ZIPPO and sucked on a Red, trying to recall which name she'd said. She stared at the forest of his back hair. *Nice and sound, snoring like a pig.* The blue dawn light already fingered the sky. She pulled on her jeans and coat, looked around the room. *Why do they never have any taste? And the worst, always that black leather sofa as though it's some totem of manhood, their furniture like their fucking balls.* She rolled her eyes and dropped her butt on his clean, black kitchen tile and crushed it with her boot. *"Don't we all wish we was from Texas?"* She had smiled like she knew what he meant. Molly had never been there, but she figured that was the kind of macho asshole thing a Texan would do—put out a butt on some bastard's clean floor. She muttered in Southern, running her tongue along her teeth, *Maybe I do.*

She jabbed and cracked at the lock but it wouldn't budge. Dead bolt. *Why dead? Oh goddamn it, he's up.*

"Hey there. . . ." from the bedroom. *Searching—doesn't remember the name either.*

"Cherry," she provided.

He walked out, brows knit at this, but said, clapping his hands together and doing a gross little knee-dip, "Yes! Cherry, honey, you're leaving already? We were sure up late to be leaving so early."

Molly breathed out, "Yeah, I've got a busy day," but had to bite down and look away to avoid his appraisal. *Sloppy watering mouth.* "Lock's stuck."

He put a beefy hand to the door. With half-fake suspicion, "Well, when am I gonna see you again?" *Oh shit, not going to let me out?* She felt sweat burst out on her face.

"Uh, sometime soon, I guess."

"Alright." He lifted and twisted the bolt, and Molly heard it click. "When?" as she slipped into the hall, her eyes on him low.

"Actually. It's not such a good idea." *Jesus, quite a stare. Why every time do I have to go through this? As though I'm breaking their goddamn hearts.* "I actually have a boyfriend. So. . . ."

A little air sailed through his nose in disbelief and he shook his head. "Little whore." And a slam of the door. *Finally.*

The dry, freezing air on her hot cheeks. *Feels good. Oh, thank God. Well, that was quite a pick, lady.* She oriented herself and headed home, smoking and feeling the freedom of the gray empty streets mix with her self-disgust. *Lunch with Karen. She'll know because I'll probably look like hell.* She climbed up to the third floor, entered her studio, dropped her purse by the door and fell on to the bed. She raised herself a little to set the alarm for eleven and then she sank and sank. *Joseph Campbell and the necessity of sorrow, self-sacrifice. That man's greediness, his need. Loneliness, putting it onto me, the desire like a wave he's lost in, couldn't paw his way out if he wanted. . . .* And then sleep—dreamless, wordless.

Molly opened her eyes to the midday light. *Uhm. Head pounding. Shit, must be late. No—Saturday. Oh God.* The night before rushed through her. Leaving Maureen after dinner, would go home and finish *The Mythic Image* or maybe some Baldwin. But she'd felt good, didn't have to get up, would have one more on the way. The two of them, the only ones left in the bar toward three. He'd walked her home. A little gross. But could talk about Virginia Woolf. *God only knows what he said. He probably just mentioned her and I jumped. Jesus. Pathetic.*

Out of the shower, she turned on the radio. *Can't deal with NPR.* She flipped around, heard the DJ say Johnny Cash, so she left it. "Drive On" came on. *Vietnam. O'Brien talks about the insanity, the terror, but also, somehow a love for it. When that guy shot the little baby water buffalo, tortured it because his friend died. Or maybe not because his friend died. Maybe just did. How "normal," non-war life can never live up to that intensity.* She lit up a smoke, put on red lipstick, and stood smoking, looking at herself in the mirror. As if she was tough. Johnny sang in the voice of a vet, how he was a walking miracle from Vietnam, told himself how it didn't mean nothin', told himself to drive on.

She hit the street walking fast. *Late as usual.* When she pictures herself with Karen she sees them lying on the beach silently, letting the waves' rhythm sink into them before fall. Or at the zoo, laughing with some joy she'd be tempted to describe as untainted, at the humanness of an orangutan. *Is it that my life is truly this desolate piece of shit right now or is it that the mind is great at editing? Maybe I was always restless, but all I remember is the good?*

Karen was sitting at a table near the front, reading what looked to be a novel. As Molly bustled into the opposite chair, she slowly drew her eyes up and placed the bookmark tight in the binding. "Hey, flyface. Rough night?"

Molly removed her sunglasses. *Karen looks perfect as usual.* "Yeah, I guess."

Karen looked Molly over, eyebrows raised but with no particular look on her face. "Meet the man of your dreams?"

"Well. If that's what you call an overweight fifty-year-old greasy detective from Oklahoma." Molly couldn't help smiling at this description, despite her total lack of desire to tell Karen about the night.

"Oh, Jesus," Karen half-laughed. "Sounds disgusting." Then, "I have no idea why you do it to yourself." *Of course you don't, Miss Safe Little Boyfriend.* Karen's boyfriend, Ralph, was perfect. A nice-looking feminist, bookish painter who adored her and was always fun to be around and was supposedly great in bed on top of it.

"Neither do I." Molly sighed genuinely. *Why* do *I do it?* Molly tried to think while the waitress came over. She heard Karen order the shaved parmesan salad with walnuts and she heard herself say, "Whatever the soup of the day is." When the waitress went away, Molly spoke slowly. "It seems—necessary. Like a sacrifice." She gained momentum. "You know, like Joseph Campbell says—that we have to give ourselves up to a degree, be willing to suffer in order to connect with others." *Is this total bullshit?* "I'm relieving their loneliness by being weak. So I understand them more, the good and the bad of people."

"You really want to know these losers you pick up in bars and then hope you never see again?"

"Oh God, I don't know. But I know I understand more about men's desire than most men do."

Karen sighed seriously and frowned. *Is she intrigued or annoyed? Oh God, I shouldn't have gotten into this.* Karen shook her head as though trying to clear it. "Well, I don't know either. But frankly, that sounds like bullshit to me. Sounds like you're lonely and get drunk and want attention from whoever's there to give it. I don't mean to be mean. But your life isn't some goddamn philosophical proof to be worked out by endangering yourself."

Molly rolled her eyes. *Jesus Christ.* The waitress came and placed the dishes before them, saying to Molly, "It's cream of vegetable." Molly looked up into the dull brown eyes. "Thanks," she smiled. *Perfect. I love the cream of vegetable here.* She waited to speak while they both had their first tastes of food. The soup in her throat made her think of sinking into a hot bath. *That's what I'll do tonight. Bring a bottle of wine into the tub and finish Campbell.* "I'm not endangering myself," she said quietly. Suddenly she couldn't wait to be in the tub with the wine. *Maybe even this afternoon.*

"Yes, actually you are. You know you are." Sometimes Karen's hypochondriac arsenal of fears was funny and sometimes it wasn't. "You don't know these men. They could lock you in their basements, sell you into slavery. I just read an article about a man in Russia who had six women locked in his basement for ten years. He made them work for him and raped them on a daily basis before finally one of them escaped. TEN YEARS!" Karen made a face of dread.

Molly pictured herself locked in a cold basement being raped in front of other women by some crazy Russian. *Ugh God. Why does that shit happen?* "Well," dryly, "I know that these things happen. But this is Manhattan, and I've been known to be a decent judge of character. Even when I'm drunk." She put down her spoon and looked up to where the ceiling met the bright yellow wall. "Besides. It don't mean nothin'."

Karen rolled her eyes, annoyed. "What are you, some kind of cowgirl now?"

Molly ignored her and looked around the room, humming the Cash song. Then she raised herself up straight in her chair and said, "Anyway, we don't have to spend the day analyzing my life and loves. What book are you reading?"

"Oh, an essay by this poet Anne Carson who Ralph's all in love with lately. She's pretty good though. I like her a lot, too."

"Yeah, I think I've heard of her. What's the essay about?"

"Well it's kind of about her doing the Camino de Santiago, you know that pilgrimage in Spain? She does it with her boyfriend, whom she refers to as her Cid. It's interesting because she starts talking about shame and these women who hide in holes in these stone walls along the path, I guess out of some Catholic ritual of shaming themselves. Anyway, they depend on food from the pilgrims to survive. Listen to this." Karen pulled out the book and turned right to the page she meant to read from. *Oh God, usually I love this stuff, but I'm just not in the mood right now to hear about women's shame.* Karen read: "'Shame is the presence of someone right up against me. Hot because her eyes are closer to me than my own honor. She is a woman in a pit in a wall with a stone as hot as the midday sun in her hands: listen the footsteps go fading down the street.' (Apparently most of the pilgrims just walk by without giving any food.) 'She is my Cid cut open by a word from me, him weeping within me. Kinds of water drown us.' Ugh. Anyway, I just love the idea of the heat of shame, and somehow letting someone in beneath your honor."

Molly thought about the heat of her face this morning in that man's apartment. *But why should I be ashamed. Isn't the key that I* let *them use me?* "I don't know. I guess I like the idea, too." Karen looked directly at her very kindly, but sadly. *Oh God, now I feel like crying. I love Karen. But I've got to explain it somehow.* "But what is honor worth in anything? I mean what about letting someone see beneath your honor, which I guess means to let someone see your weakness, your badness, sinfulness, whatever you want to call it. And then forgiving them for seeing it. And letting yourself see others' badness and forgiving them that, too?"

"Well that's awfully nice of you." Karen said, signaling to the waitress for the check at the same time.

Oh God. Am I having lunch with my mother here? "We weren't talking about me; we were talking about an idea. Besides, it's better than always protecting yourself and being around only one kind of people and never letting yourself get hurt."

Karen stopped digging through her purse and looked directly at Molly, not kindly this time. "Is that what you think I do? You think I'm not living fully just because I don't go out and fuck everyone I can for some stupid philosophy of. . . . I don't even know what. Self-sacrifice?"

Molly realized she'd been holding her whole body tense during the whole exchange and she could feel her throat constrict as her voice rose. *Enough, enough of this stupid conversation.* "Fine. Maybe it all means nothing but for some reason I do it. It's what I do right now, as awful as that sounds. And it's what I'm drawn to. I don't like it either. But for God's sake I don't know why you're so worried. It's just fucking." The waitress had been standing there waiting for her to finish.

"Here's the check. Thank you, ladies." She smiled sympathetically at Molly and again Molly felt like she might cry.

Karen looked down and said, "I'm sorry. Let's not talk about it anymore. There's supposedly this great Egon Schiele exhibit at the Neue Gallery. Do you want to go see it? I just love him."

Molly was exhausted but she didn't really have anything to do. *It's a little early for vino. Maybe I'll head home to the tub after the museum.* "Yeah, that sounds good. Neue's a pretty small museum, isn't it?"

Karen smiled. "Yeah. No more than an hour."

"Perfect." They paid and Molly left an unusually big tip. When Karen looked at her like she was crazy, Molly just shook her head and waved her hand. "I don't know why. I just liked her."

They walked out and cut over to Central Park on 85th. It was one of the spring days when all of the trees lining the blocks are in bloom, and so you get feathered with petals whenever there's a breeze. The day had gotten pretty warm, and it lifted their moods. *Oh thank God we're out of that restaurant. It's beautiful. Makes me feel like a little kid or something. Or that when I was a kid isn't as far back as it usually seems.*

As they crossed into the park, Molly said, "I don't know his work. I only know a poem about him. He died of the Spanish flu, didn't he?"

"Yeah. I think so, I guess I don't know much about his life, only seen his work. But I think you'll like it." They walked on in silence for a while. The further they got into the park, the lighter Molly felt. She wasn't really thinking about anything in particular when she realized her eyes were resting on a big butt on a bicycle seat. *That is one big butt to be in flaming red biker's pants. But I guess the rest of him isn't fat. Only has a big butt.* She suddenly realized that she had been looking at him for a long time and that the guy was moving like a turtle. She poked Karen's arm and she whispered loudly, "Look at how slow that guy's going."

Karen burst out laughing. "Yeah, I was looking at him, too. But it's a nice spanking new outfit he's got, shoes and all to go out riding so slowly. He looks exhausted." They continued watching him. "But he's not even going uphill."

Molly snorted. "I didn't even know it was possible to go so slow on a bike without it tipping over." They were laughing when they noticed he was making a slow loop and heading back toward them. So they straightened their faces. Still coming about one mile an hour, they saw his face approach. He looked like the nicest guy in the world and he exhaustedly exhaled a "hello" as he passed them. Molly and Karen burst into laughter again when he had gone. "Poor guy."

"Well, you've got to start somewhere," Karen said.

Oh, nice to feel comfortable with Karen again. I hate it when she's all judgmental. "It reminds me of this Johnny Cash song I heard on the radio this morning. Do you know the song 'Drive On?'"

"No, I don't think so."

"It's about the guys in Vietnam who, when they lost one of their buddies, when one of them would get shot, they'd just tell each other to drive on, that it didn't mean anything. In order to keep themselves going. When of course it meant everything."

"Oh lord, that's depressing. Oh. So that's what you meant when you said that today."

Molly felt herself flush when she realized she'd said that to Karen, referring to her own stupid little situation. *As though it's fucking Vietnam.* "Yeah. Anyway, that guy's driving on. Hell or high water." Karen laughed. And Molly relaxed.

They got to the museum and it wasn't crowded at all. *Nice museum. I like this Viennese style of modernism.* They went in and went right up to the exhibit. The first painting was a gorgeous grayish tree bent like a hand in the wind. Molly got a chill. *Oh, this is going to be good. I love going to museums with Karen. Perfect place. Don't have to talk.* They went into the next room, which was full of portraits of women. *Fragile, I want to call them. Or the lines are fragile, the colors. What is it?* In the next room, there were two portraits of women, legs spread touching themselves. Molly noticed herself flush pink, her hair stand on end.

In what, defensiveness? Anger? Why do I care? They probably loved being painted like that. They went on and there were more trees, and finally a self-portrait. *Young, good-looking. Probably a total pig.*

"Hey." Karen startled her as she was locking eyes with Egon. "Want to get a coffee or something? They have a gorgeous café here."

"Yeah, sure. I love this style of design." *Oh lord. I'll just say I loved it all. Why am I such a prude sometimes? Me, of all dang people.*

Karen ordered a coffee, Molly a red wine. *Ugh. Why do I feel stressed right now?* "I guess you can't smoke in here," she said, looking around.

Karen was looking directly at her. "What did you think? Aren't the paintings just amazing?"

"Yeah! I loved that tree when we first went in."

"Yeah, me, too. And I love all the portraits."

"Yeah. He was obviously a little bit of a pig though." *I'd kill to smoke a cigarette right now.*

"Oh, do you mean the women with their crotches open for all to see? Well, all artists are pigs. They always have these young naked women around. What do you want them to do? Except Ralph. And maybe the Impressionists. They mostly stuck to fields and hay."

"Yeah, I think I'd go out with Van Gogh if I had to choose."

"Oh lord, well, he was a little crazy. But I see what you mean." Karen smiled. "Anyway, Ralph and I are going to a party in Brooklyn tonight. Some artist acquaintance of his or something. But he said he's been to the guy's loft and it's amazing and that the roof has great views of the city. So I think it will be fun."

Hmm. All the way to Brooklyn. "Um. I don't know. I think I might just stay home, pop in the bath. I was up pretty late last night."

"Alright, well, give me a call if you change your mind. I think we're heading over around eight."

"Okay. Well, should we get the check?" Molly raised her hand to the waiter.

Out on the street, Karen said, "Well, I think I'm going to do some Upper East Side shopping since I find myself here. And I know that's not your cup of tea. So call me later if you want to go."

"Okay. I will. And we should get together next week sometime if not. There are a million movies out right now I want to see."

"Alright, lady. See you soon." Karen walked away bouncily. *Light as can be. Well, what now. So nice out. The bath isn't sounding all that great anymore.* Molly lit a smoke and walked back into the park. About halfway through, she saw their man on the bike again. *Still at it. Still going slow.* She smiled. *Drive on. Well, Saturday evening. I think one or two beers won't kill me. And then I'll go home to my lovely bed.*

Molly bought a copy of the *Times* and walked into Joe's lounge, which was more of a dive than a lounge. But cheapo beer. Molly sat at the end of the bar near the window. The late day rays slid beautifully in onto the wood of the bar and illuminated her smoke. *Poor Johnny Cash. The poor guys in Vietnam.* She sighed. *Poor everyone.* Some man who'd been sitting in the dark of the back of the bar came up to put some songs on the jukebox. "I Walk the Line" came on.

"Hey, you mind if I sit here with you in the sun?"

Not bad. "No. No one's sitting there."

He waited a couple of minutes. "You like the Man in Black here?"

"Yeah. As a matter of fact, I was just thinking about him."

"You don't say." He smiled a little sarcastically, a little flirtatiously as he looked directly into her eyes. *Well, at least he's not staring at my chest like a fool.* "My name's Jack." He put out his hand. Molly bit her lip for a second, then put out her hand. "I'm Cherry. Nice to meet you." *Drive on.*

•

EMILY REARDON received her MFA from New York University. Most recently, she has had her poems published in *NYArts Magazine*, *The Comstock Review*, and *Southern Poetry Review*. Emily has also been a guest editor for *NYArts Magazine*, and she recently finished a stint as the first Writer-in-Residence for the Lower Manhattan Cultural Council. She lives and writes in New York City.

Vernell Hackett

THE GIRL FROM BOULDER RIDGE

BACKSTORY: This story is loosely based on Johnny Cash's "Tennessee Flat Top Box," which he recorded in 1961 and his daughter Rosanne recorded in 1987 on her *Kings' Record Shop* album. When I was a kid this was one of my favorite songs on the radio. I was intrigued with the kid and his guitar and I was thrilled when he made it to the Hit Parade!

I WASN'T FORBIDDEN TO GO THERE, it was just an understood rule of the house that as a teenage girl, I shouldn't go to the County Line Club because something might happen.

I didn't know exactly what that "something" might be; I was just going to the club to listen to music. Well, truth be told, I went mostly to look at the kid playing guitar. He didn't look old enough to be there, but he was with the band so that made the difference with him. I was the underage teenager who snuck in through the back door because a friend of mine waitressed there and the owner kind of overlooked me *if* I sat quietly at a side table and was as invisible as Roger Rabbit.

This kid, his name was Sammy, was something else. Tall, dark hair, crooked smile that just lit up his face when and if he smiled, which seemed only to happen when he hit just the right lick on that shiny red guitar. He couldn't have been much older than me, maybe eighteen, and the rest of the men in the band were older guys, at least in their thirties, but he could play the hell out of that guitar. Even someone like me, who knew very little about music, could hear that.

I knew beyond a doubt that the majority of the women in the club came to just look at Sammy. He was, without question, one of the most gorgeous guys I had ever seen. Yet it went beyond looks...there was something about his attitude, the way he carried himself, the way he looked right through you from the stage, yet made you feel that he was looking into your very soul. I read in one of the fan magazines that it was called stage presence, or charisma, and that stars like Elvis and Chuck Berry and Patsy Cline had it. I couldn't imagine any of them having more stage presence than Sammy...when someone you didn't know could make you feel like they were reading your entire soul with one look, well, that was pretty powerful charisma.

I know my folks must have suspected where I was going every weekend, even though I used the excuse of football games or parties at friend's homes. And my sudden interest in Johnny Cash, Hank Williams, and Jim Reeves instead of the rock and roll I usually listened to was also a dead giveaway. Yeah, they knew, but for some reason they had resigned themselves to letting my newfound fascination run its course. Maybe they figured I was only a few months away from legally walking into County Line, so why create controversy in the family.

I can't tell you when it happened, but one night I realized that Sammy was watching me. At first I thought I was imagining the glances coming my way. But no, he was watching me almost as intently as I usually watched him. The hair on my neck stood straight up when I realized what was going on but I talked it down right away, figuring he just noticed me because I was about his age. The feeling came back when, at break, Sammy gently wiped off his guitar, put it on its special stand, and headed straight for me.

"Hi."

I knew he was speaking to me but I could barely catch my breath when he offered the one syllable greeting.

"Anyone sitting here?" The question had an obvious answer; I was always there by myself.

I managed to shake my head so he pulled out the chair and sat down.

"I'm Sammy," he said, offering me his hand, the one that so lovingly caressed his guitar.

"I'm Cheyenne. . . . Hi." I shook his outstretched hand and quickly let go, a move that brought a slow smile to his face.

"You're here a lot," he continued, making another obvious statement; I had been here every weekend for three months now.

"Yeah, I like . . . uh, the music," I replied, thinking to myself that there was no way I could ever admit to coming here to see him.

My friend the waitress came by and gave me an obvious stare. Sammy asked for a Coke and indicated she should fill my glass as well. With a slight toss of her head, which wasn't lost on me, she walked away to fill the order. I knew she wouldn't tell my folks, but I knew I would be in for a round of questions tomorrow.

"So are you from around here?" Sammy questioned.

"Yeah, I live off Farm Route 1155," I answered. "What about you?"

"Well, I come from over around Parsons Bend," he replied. "Got me a job pickin' with this band, so my grandpa lets me come over here with them to play. He don't like it too much, me playin' in a beer joint, but he lets me 'cause we need the money."

"That's pretty far to come," I said, understanding then why I hadn't recognized him as one of the local kids. "What does your mom think about it?"

His face clouded for a minute and I was instantly sorry I had asked that question.

"My mom and dad were killed a couple years ago in a car wreck," he said. "I better get back onstage," he added, nodding toward the rest of the guys making their way toward the front of the room. "Maybe I'll see you again."

Thousands of thoughts ran through my mind the rest of the night as I sat and watched him. Now I knew why he was so intense and why he didn't smile. I knew why the blues numbers seemed to be his favorite even though the band favored country music; I knew why he played so passionately on all the sad songs.

Sammy started coming to my table during all the breaks. We'd sit and talk—well, he did most of the talking. He told me he had started playing guitar after his parents were killed. "I could make it say all the bad things I was feelin' inside," he said."I don't know if I'll ever get over losin' them but music has helped me get through it."

One night he asked me about my dreams and plans. I told him I guessed I'd be in Boulder Ridge forever, just like my older sister. She got married right out of high school and already had two kids. I didn't think she would ever realize her dream of being a fancy magazine editor.

"Well, I'm not staying around here," he told me. "I'm gonna play music and to get a record deal I'm gonna have to go to Memphis or Nashville or maybe even New York. Music will be my ticket to see the world, and it will be my ticket to makin' enough money to support my grandparents so they won't have to ever work that farm again."

I told him he was definitely good enough to get a record deal and he just looked at me in a way that made my heart jump. "I'm sure gonna try," he said.

A few weeks later, when Sammy sat down at my table, he was more excited than I'd ever seen him. With a country-and-western music magazine in his hand, he showed me an ad that invited unknown singers to come to an audition in Austin.

"I have to go," he said.

"How are you gonna get there?" I asked. Austin was more than 100 miles away and I knew his grandpa would never let him drive that far.

"I'll catch the bus or I'll hitchhike," he said defensively. "It don't matter just as long as I get there."

Sure enough, Sammy got a bus ticket and went to Austin for the auditions. I wasn't surprised; I knew if he didn't get there he would just have died inside. I waited anxiously for his return. Half of my heart wanted him to be discovered; the other half wanted him to stay right there at the club.

I was almost afraid to go in the club that Friday, but there he was onstage. When he saw me he waved and grinned, and at break he walked over to the table and sat down. By now my friend knew just to bring him a Coke and leave us alone.

"Well, how did it go?" I asked.

"The guy said he liked me and he wanted me to come to Nashville to record a couple songs, but I had to pay him $500," Sammy answered. "I didn't have $500 and another guy did so he went to Nashville."

"I'm sorry," I said, putting my hand on his. "I'm really sorry."

Suddenly I realized I was practically holding his hand and started to pull mine away when he turned his over and held onto mine. My heart stopped as he looked intently into my eyes.

"I'll make it," he said. "I just have to. It's the only thing in this whole world that I care anything about... except my grandparents and you."

My breathing came to a halt and all I could do was look at him as his words burned into my heart and mind. I couldn't even think about what he might mean by that statement and I sure wasn't going to ask.

"If I do make it," he continued, "you can come out with me once I get things going." The grip on his hand tightened around mine and he leaned forward, asking in a voice just above a whisper, "Would you want to do that?"

I nodded, still unable to catch my breath enough to speak, and he gave me one of those smiles. "I'd like that."

The next few weeks were uneventful compared to that night, except that Sammy and I celebrated my eighteenth birthday by actually going to the burger place down the street before the music got underway at the club. I guess you could say it was our first official date. We shared one more thing that evening...he walked me to my car and he kissed me goodnight. It was our first kiss. I didn't remember driving home but I did arrive there safe and sound.

As weeks turned into months, the excitement of the trip to Austin faded away but the dream was still alive. Sammy wrote a song for me called "Girl from Boulder Ridge." Finally I got up enough nerve to introduce him to my family and they actually liked him, though they weren't too thrilled that he was playing music in a bar.

"He's good," my dad admitted after they had come to see him one Saturday, "but he'll never make any money singing in bars. You better talk some sense into him if you want any stability in your future."

I just smiled; I knew I would never be able to talk any sense into Sammy when it came to his music. He was determined to become a star and he wanted me to be there by his side. It sounded glamorous and exciting and I was ready to go with him whenever he asked.

A few Saturday nights later I went into the bar and my friend motioned me over. "Sammy's not here," she whispered. "There's some other guy that's setting up his guitar."

I whirled around and stared, sure she was wrong. She wasn't.

"Do you know, does anyone know...." I couldn't finish the sentence.

"No," she said. "I asked the band leader and he said Sammy just didn't show up for a show and his grandparents told him Sammy had left to go to Nashville."

Once again my heart stopped. I couldn't believe he would leave without telling me. I couldn't believe all the things he'd said to me had been lies.

Weeks went by, then months. I couldn't eat and I wasn't getting much sleep. I thought about what Sammy was doing in Nashville; if he had found anyone who would listen to his songs. Maybe he was playing at some club and there was another girl who had caught his eye. The only thing that helped me get through the nights was the country music I had come to love. One night I was in my room, trying to read but mostly thinking about Sammy, when I heard a voice on the radio that caught my attention. It was new and different and achingly familiar.

The singer and the song played through, and the deejay said, "Folks, that is a new kid out of Texas named Sammy Blanchard. It's his first record, and we think it's gonna be a hit. You folks call in and let us know what you think.

"I'll tell you what I think," the deejay continued. "He can play a mean guitar and he's only eighteen. I think this kid will hit the big time if he keeps at it."

Time kept ticking by and I had the radio on every minute of the day. I would hear Sammy's record but he didn't get in touch. Since I couldn't see him, hearing his voice and his pickin' were as good as it got. I finally reconciled myself to the fact that he wasn't gonna come back for me and that he'd never meant it when he told me he would.

A few months later some friends had persuaded me to go to a movie with them. My folks were listening to the Grand Ole Opry from Nashville. I stuck my head in the living room to tell them we might stop for burgers after the movie when I heard the Grand Ole Opry announcer say, "Folks, we've got a special treat for you tonight. Sammy Blanchard is making his Grand Ole Opry debut and I want you to make him feel welcome."

I froze in my tracks. Sammy sang his hit song and then he said, "I'm gonna sing a song I just cut for my album that should be out in another couple of months. It's about a special person and I hope she's listening."

When he hit the first note I knew it was "Girl from Boulder Ridge." When he finished singing the crowd went wild. The announcer could hardly make his voice heard over the applause so he could talk to Sammy.

"Well, that was historic," the announcer told Sammy. "I don't think anyone has received that many standing ovations since Hank came on and sang 'Lovesick Blues.' You're quite a singer. Now you said that last song was for someone special—do you want to send a message to her if she's listening?"

"I sure do," Sammy replied.

"She must be pretty important," the deejay said.

"That she is," Sammy agreed as I sat down abruptly, not quite believing what I was hearing. "Cheyenne, if you're listening, I want you to know I still want you out here with me and I'll be seeing you soon."

•

VERNELL HACKETT is a freelance journalist in Nashville, Tennessee, who has covered the Nashville music scene for a number of magazines, including *Country Weekly*, *Classic Country & Western Music Magazine*, *The Home Services Guide*, *Bluegrass Unlimited*, *American Cowboy*, *Billboard Magazine*, *Country Song Roundup*, *Working Cowboy*, and *Venues Today*. A native of Riesel, Texas, Vernell moved to Nashville in 1973 to write articles about country music. She has interviewed many country, bluegrass, western, and Christian artists, including Johnny Cash, Garth Brooks, Michael W. Smith, Dolly Parton, Brad Paisley, Don Edwards, Del McCoury, Willie Nelson, George Strait, Nitty Gritty Dirt Band, Merle Haggard, Michael Martin Murphey, Waddie Mitchell, Reba McEntire, Trisha Yearwood, Stephen Curtis Chapman, Amy Grant, Larry Stephenson, LeAnn Rimes, Alan Jackson, Montgomery Gentry, and Hanna McEuen. Vernell helped establish *American Songwriter* magazine in 1984, which she edited until 2004. She graduated from Sam Houston State University in Huntsville, Texas, with a BS degree in journalism. Vernell has written about a variety of subjects during her career, including music, art and entertainment, travel, pets, food, legislation, characters, home décor, crafts, history, video, and business.

Adam-Troy Castro

THE TRAIN STOPS

BACKSTORY: Johnny Cash's prison songs often deal with the aftermath of unforgivable crimes. The most famous of these, "Folsom Prison Blues," deals with a murderer who will never again know the world outside prison, and who must bear the nightly passage of the trains that symbolize a freedom he will never know. But is that torment limited to this world, alone? Are there prisoners, down below, who also hear distant trains pursue a journey forever denied to those who have lost their own chances of redemption? This one's for the Man in Black!

THE TRACKS CARVED A PATH THROUGH the most populous regions of Hell.

They rose from the starless murk, passed through a tunnel torn through the mountains of Dis, then crossed over the valley of pain itself, in a pair of parallel lines so direct that the trains that ran upon them barely seemed touched by the suffering of all the souls enduring Eternity here.

And then, unlike anything else in this loveless place, they moved on, their whistles trailing behind them like cold apologies.

There is a station, just across from the wall of Murderers, but the trains themselves rarely stop.

Ed Johnson waited.

It was all they'd left him.

In life he had been an impatient man, who had hoarded time more jealously than any of his handful of other blessings. Everything he'd ever wanted, he'd wanted now: not thirty minutes from now, not five. Now. Waiting had made dark clouds pass over eyes already the color of slate.

He had never spoken any words that anybody would ever want to quote in a book—his greatest source of contempt, in life, being anybody who cottoned to those mysterious artifacts of print and paper—but some of the things he'd said had defined him as well as anything possibly could.

Can you hurry it up awready?

And

Get a move on, will ya?

And his favorite:

I ain't got all day!

He had hoarded the seconds and resented anybody who had stolen them from him and he made his displeasure known in ways ranging from irritation to rage, all on the pretext, obvious to him, that he was being kept from better things he had to do.

All of this made him an asshole, not necessarily a sinner.

But a sinner he was, and for his punishment he had nothing to do but wait.

His cell was a tiny box, to his senses about the size of a phone booth, except too short to stand up in and too narrow to lie down in. The walls were sometimes so cold he was wracked with shivers, and sometimes so hot that his flesh blackened and peeled, but never for long in either case. Neither was allowed to become routine, the bursts of extreme cold or heat being merely cruel punctuation to an existence that was otherwise a long dull imprisonment. There was no door, as he would never be allowed out. There was no guard, as there was nothing he could do to escape. There was one narrow slit of a window, at eye-level, perfectly positioned for a man who from now until the end of eternity would never have anything to do but look...but most of the time there was nothing to see but darkness.

Except when the trains passed, carrying their light with them.

He hated the trains.

He cursed them and he screamed at them and he begged them to stop and take him with them, and when the last of the sound they made trailed off in the distance he slumped against the pitiless wall again, hating himself as much as he hated them.

Hating the stupid face of the boy in the checkered shirt.

Ed still didn't know what color the boy had been. It didn't matter, of course, the penalties were the same, but as long as you have to be sent to Death Row for killing a man you might as well know whether the bastard's black or not. The kid had a complexion like light coffee that might have been just the result of too much time in the sun or might have been the Mexican footprint of someone in his immediate family history. The family might have provided a clue, but only the mother showed up in court, and while she looked white enough, the absent father could have been any shade on the spectrum. Ed had never settled the matter to his satisfaction because nobody had ever brought it up and he wasn't about to ask, being just smart enough to know that asking might have added a bullshit hate-crimes charge to all the sixteen other species of shit being dumped on his ass. Ed didn't need to deal with that on top of everything else. Not that he was entirely a stranger to that aspect of things; he'd had a lot of time to contemplate what he'd done, during his seventeen years waiting for the appeals to run out, and the more he thunk on it the more he figured the kid's precise shade of mocha might have had a large part of what made seeing him die so appealing. But that hadn't been it, not really. The fact was that, whatever color he'd been, the kid had just annoyed the shit out of him. He'd opened the register as ordered and he'd gotten down on the floor as ordered and he'd pressed his stupid nose against the floor tile as ordered and he'd cooperated with Ed in every way as ordered, and he'd done every candyass thing he possibly could do to save himself, but he'd also cried, trying his best to suck it up but not quite managing, that moist sniveling sniff of his escaping despite all of Ed's stern warnings to shut the hell up. And maybe, okay, maybe it made sense for the kid to be so scared, him eighteen and already a father, and Ed standing there pressing a barrel to the back of his head, blowing a gasket because there was only $22.50 in the cash drawer. But he could have said "please" without whimpering like that. He could have been a man and said, "I'm sorry, mister, but that's all there is." That would have been reasonable. He didn't have to make like a girl and be such a pain in the ass that, for the duration of one nerve impulse, Ed would be willing to pull the trigger, just to watch him die.

It was all the kid's fault, is what it was. It was the kid's fault that Ed had found himself a murderer instead of a robber, a most-wanted fugitive instead of a criminal who could blow town and be forgotten about, a death-penalty defendant instead of a piece-of-shit case that got bargained down to manslaughter. It was the kid's fault that Ed's parents had needed to mortgage the house to pay for his defense, and the kid's fault that Ed's brother stopped talking to him midway through the trial, and the kid's fault Ed had needed to put on an ugly tie every day and sit there listening to the cops and the forensic guys and the kid's family talk their shit for hours on end. It was the kid's fault that Ed had spent seventeen years rotting in a cell far removed from Gen Pop, waiting for everybody to stop discussing whether he should be put out of his misery or not.

It was the kid's fault that by the time they finally strapped Ed down, and started dabbing his arm with the cotton swab, Ed was so bored and depressed and ready to get on with the next thing that when they asked him if he had any last words to offer, he knew exactly what he wanted to say.

He said, *Can you hurry it up awready?*

And

Get a move on, will ya?

And his favorite:

I ain't got all day!

After all, he didn't know what was coming next, but was sure it had to be more interesting than this.

Most of the time the trains went right on by, providing vivid reminder that there were people who did not have to stay in this place, and a brief shining lift that left purple after-images burned into Ed's retinas. He had no way to tell time, so he had no way of knowing how often they came. As far as he could tell, the intervals between them ranged between hours and years, but they might have been running like clockwork for all he knew, the subjective time between them varying only according to how heavily his imprisonment weighed upon his back.

Less often, one stopped.

Moments like that were the only thing to look forward to, and he always drew close to his narrow window, his sensation-starved mind eager to take in anything his eyes could feed it. At such moments the train, idling at its platform, was less a streak of light than an artifact with heft and weight and detail. He saw the long narrow cars, each glimmering with a soft inner radiance, each giving off an ethereal vapor that might have been steam and might have been the fumes released by the burning of a fuel he could not even begin to imagine. He saw the rows of windows, streaming even more light into the surrounding darkness, and he saw the shapes of people, mingling inside. At this distance he couldn't make out anything but their outlines, which were most of the time just ovals cast by what must have been the heads of travelers peering out at the landscape that included him. The first few times trains stopped, Ed had screamed at them, in a hoarse voice he had trouble recognizing as his own. *Hey!* he'd cried. *I'm over here! Can you hear me? Don't just sit there! Help me!* But those oval blobs never gave any sign that they heard him, or, if they heard him, that they cared. Behind them, the shapes of other people sharing the cars with them moved to and fro, on their own mysterious errands. He didn't know if the insides of these trains were anything like the trains he'd been on in life, but in his mind they were better: the seats all lush and luxurious, the people all at peace, the music rich and coming from every direction at once. He knew nobody riding the train could possibly want for anything. The powers running the line would see to it that their every need was met, from cups of coffee to exotic cigars.

Sometimes women passed by those windows, their shapes just distinct enough to imply how beautiful they must have been, and at such times Ed slammed his fist against the walls of his cell and cursed them, just for being there while he was over here. It wouldn't have been so bad if he could just see their faces. Even that much would have been a comfort. Even a glimpse would have given him something to hold on to, in the long dark time between the passage of trains.

He no longer wondered why some trains stopped. He had, in the beginning. But he had made up his mind that wondering was a waste of time. He was sure he would never get any answers.

In this, as in most things, he happened to be dead wrong.

He hadn't slept since his arrival, but his mind went where it wanted to, and sometimes he dreamed.

Mostly he dreamed of that moment he'd wanted to see that stupid kid die, watching it again and again the same way he'd once watched his favorite movies, seeing it play out again and again, with every detail unchanged.

Sometimes he dreamed of other things.

He dreamed of the two or three women who had been kind to him, and who had loved him, and who had been driven away less with his cruelty than with his dulled, dissatisfied apathy. He dreamed of sunny days on the highway, that year he'd worked on the road crew, his muscles aching and the sweat pouring down his back in sheets. He dreamed of being able to go into any store any time he wanted and being able to walk out with a newspaper, or a sandwich, or a beer. He dreamed of the fights he had won and the fights he had lost, each one leaving him bloodied and scarred but able to stagger home at the end of the day. He dreamed of once thinking he'd be famous someday, which had more or less come to pass, even if he'd imagined himself fronting a platinum-record band instead. That had been as close as he'd ever come to an ambition, though (typically enough). He'd lost patience and hurled the damn thing in a corner the first time anybody tried to show him how to use a guitar.

Once in a great while he dreamed of that cool lake, behind the house where his family had lived the two years things had gone well: the way the water had felt so good splashing against his skin on a steaming August day, and the way his mother had laughed when he and his brother Mike took turns dunking each other's heads beneath the surface. It was a good memory, but even that didn't make him feel all that much better, as it always came with the realization that those moments had been the happiest he'd ever know, and that everything else had been a study in just how much wreckage he could make of every chance he'd ever been handed. Still, it was the closest thing he had to a comfort, and he held on to those memories with ferocity that dwarfed any anger he had shown in life. *You can't take this away from me, bastards.*

But as much as he tried to remain in that moment, all his dreams became litanies of the things that had been said about him, both leading up to and following the terrible thing he had done.

In cold blood.

No damn good.

Broke your mother's heart.

Murdering trash.

Malice aforethought.

And in all these dreams he was the invisible presence who floated above the drama and ached to say that he hadn't ever planned to hurt anybody at all, not for a moment. He had just needed some money, that's all. He was sick and tired of having to wait *always wait* for all the things he wanted, and had found himself a little behind, and he had nobody willing to help him and he had never considered hurting anybody, not even once, and had the bad luck to look down on the back of a stupid kid's head and just for one moment wanted to see him die.

That's all it was, his dream-self kept saying.

That's all.

That's all it was.

He was allowed to continue imagining that this was as bad as things were ever going to be allowed to be, until the time the train stopped for him.

He had been standing at the window, as always, peering out into the darkness, as always, trying to perceive detail in that blackness, as always. And then he heard a whistle blowing, somewhere in the far distance, and pressed himself closer to that narrow opening, already straining to make out detail in the shape about to coalesce out of the murk. Then the train pulled up to the station, as bustling as ever, the forms silhouetted in its windows still moving amongst themselves with a freedom that made him long for some other sight, any other sight, that would give him something else to look at if he allowed the pain to make him turn away. As always, he ached to join them, and as always, he hated them more than he'd ever hated anything before.

But this time was different. This time he was able to see one of the cars come into focus, its doors opening and a single bent figure stepping down onto the platform. He was able to see that figure, backlit by the radiance enveloping the train, look up, hesitate, descend three more steps to a ground Ed could not see, and then, after another moment of palpable reluctance, start making his way toward Ed's cell.

Ed had not felt his own heartbeat since his arrival in this place. He had assumed that he no longer had one. But the sudden shift in his routine hit him like an invisible fist, clenching tight around whatever he still had in his chest. He wanted to scream at his shadowy visitor, curse him, tell him that there was nothing he could say that Ed would ever want to hear. But either the dark forces that ruled this prison, or the paralysis born of fear, robbed him of voice, and left him unable to do anything but watch as the figure made its way across the plain that separated the tracks from the places where people like Ed were kept.

Ed would have thought it took forever, for the figure to arrive, had he not already had a taste of forever. But it was still a long time, rendered worse by all the times the figure seemed to disappear into one patch of darkness or another. At times, the figure emerged into a patch of relative light, no longer coming straight at him but instead detouring to the right or left, as if avoiding obstacles that only he could see.

Ed was in agony. He thought

Can you hurry it up awready?

And

Get a move on, will ya?

And his favorite:

I ain't got all day!

Then the figure appeared again, this time only a few arm-lengths away.

It was a man unfamiliar to him, tall and wiry, his skin pale, head topped with wisps of thin white hair, his eyes sad but shining. He was bent in the way that so many are bent by age, but he moved without pain. When he grimaced with apparent distaste at something spotted on the ground before him, he revealed a perfect set of teeth, that to Ed's eyes seemed to possess the same radiance as the train he had left.

He was dressed the way he must have dressed in life, in jeans and a red flannel shirt, a set of black bifocals hanging from his neck on chains.

Ed still didn't know him. Still following the path visible only to him, the man turned right and passed out of Ed's line of vision.

For one terrible moment, maybe the single worst in all the bad moments Ed had known since the poison stopped his heart, Ed thought he was sure who the man was. It was the stupid kid, the one from the store. Yes, he didn't look anything like the kid, wasn't even the same color as the kid, and looked about six decades older than the kid had ever lived to be. But he was here, clearly pursuing some kind of unfinished business, and nobody Ed could think of had any unfinished business with him except for that stupid kid he had killed.

Then the man came around. His ancient face, framed by the slit in Ed's wall, was lined with the furrows life leaves in everybody who makes it to an age neither Ed nor his victim had ever known.

Ed thought he recognized the man now, even if there was no earthly, or unearthly, reason for him to be here. "Grandpa?"

The visitor shook his head. "Try again."

For a second Ed was fresh out of ideas. And then the answer hit him, sharp as a knife in a chest, bringing neither relief nor understanding. *"Mikey?"*

The old man nodded, looking away, this one moment of recognition apparently too much for him. Maybe he was ashamed, though there was no way of knowing whether it was of himself, or his brother.

Between that last fight during the trial, and that day seventeen years later when Ed finally walked the fifty yards he'd been waiting so long to walk, there had not been a word.

But Mikey was here now, looking chastened and a whole lot older, his eyes downcast, his face drawn, his chin trembling as he fought for something, anything, worth saying. "Is it bad, Eddie? Is it really as bad as they say?"

Ed's throat felt like a sack lined with razors. "What do you think?"

"—I don't—"

"It's Hell, you stupid asshole. It's every bit as bad as they say. And I'm not about to lie to you and say it isn't, and you're not about to give me a ride out of here. So why are you wasting my time?"

The old man nodded without surprise, that probably being the only answer he'd expected or thought he deserved. He swallowed, looked away, seemed to come to a decision, and faced Ed again, his eyes hard and cold. "You weren't the only one who had to live with it, Eddie. Dad became an old man overnight. Mom never smiled again. Neither one of them ever looked at me again without seeing you. I lost fifteen years to drink, and went through a coming attraction of this place just dragging myself out of the hole. And that's without once mentioning the poor man's family. Did you ever think of them, even once? Were you ever sorry? Or even here, have you been too busy thinking of this as something the world just did to you out of meanness?"

Ed had long hungered for the sound of another human voice, but this was more than he could take: insult to injury, he thought. He had wanted a kind word, not this. And though he knew he should have backed down, and said anything that could have persuaded the decrepit old bastard to turn to talk of happier things, the assault on his character, combined with the weight of all his tormented years, made him angrier than he'd ever been. "That the point of this visit? Telling me off?"

The old man looked wounded. "No, Eddie. I just needed to see you one last time."

The silence grew heavy, and the eye contact more labored, until the old man averted his eyes, murmured a soft platitude about praying for him, and turned away, threatening to skip the final goodbye.

Were Ed able to force his body through the slit, and wrap his hands around the sanctimonious old man's throat, he would have—but for the first time, in their brief conversation, he also felt something else mixed in with all the resentment and hurt: a sense of all the empty eons to come, pressing down on top of him. For the first time he didn't want it to be over. And so his tone became pleading: "No, wait! I'm sorry! I don't want that to be all of it! Tell me you'll come back!"

The old man, who had only taken a couple of steps, now turned around and regarded his brother with the kind of pity that cuts deeper than any knife. "I can't tell you that, Eddie. One visit is all I get."

Forever loomed. "And y-you're... okay with that?"

There was no triumph in the old man's voice. "I won't have to be okay with that. I'm not the first person who ever had to leave somebody he loved in this place. And the conductor's already told me the same thing he must have told Mom and Dad, years ago... that the first blessing I'll receive, when I get to where I'm going, is being able to forget you were ever born."

Then he turned around and walked away, responding to none of the screams Ed hurled at his receding back.

The trains kept coming, of course. They changed designs, from the locomotives that had lit up the sky in the time after Ed's arrival, to the sleek bullets of the years that followed, to shapes that grew more and more unfamiliar to him, including some that his eyes insisted on seeing as starships. They all roared as they passed by, rendering themselves fully audible to each and every one of the Damned. The imprisoned had nothing else to do but note the light carving a path through the darkness.

Some screamed. Some wept. Some begged. Some hurled curses. Others closed their eyes, shutting out the light as they could not shut out the sound.

But the trains kept coming.

And they remained the cruelest torment, for those imprisoned along the way.

●

A Johnny Cash LP was the first album **ADAM-TROY CASTRO** ever owned, to go along with a portable turntable significantly smaller than the diameter of the record. He played Cash's renditions of "Don't Think Twice, It's All Right," and "The Long Black Veil" on an almost daily basis till both record and turntable were worn out. Adam went on to become a writer of science fiction, fantasy, and horror, whose career output to date includes eighty short stories and four novels. His work has been nominated once for the Stoker Award, twice for the Hugo, and five times for the Nebula. His work for BenBella includes previous essays for the King Kong, Superman, Harry Potter, and *Alias* volumes. His other media criticism includes regular DVD and movie reviews for www.scifiweekly.com, and bi-monthly book reviews for *SCIFI* magazine. His most current career info, along with a regular assortment of rants and artwork, appears on his Web site, www.sff.net/people/adam-troy. His latest book, also for BenBella, is *"My Ox is Broken!": Detours, Roadblocks, Fast Forwards, and Other Great Moments from TV's* The Amazing Race. Adam Troy lives in Miami with his long-suffering wife, Judi, and a rotating collection of cats that includes Uma Furman and Meow Farrow.

Bob Batchelor

DOES IT EVER END?

BACKSTORY: Two of my favorite things in the world are Johnny Cash and basketball. Living in California, about halfway between San Francisco and Wine Country, I played hoops with a bunch of guys three mornings a week at a local gym. Pulling into the parking lot one day at about 5:30 A.M., I saw a woman sitting in her car in the space next to me. Two seconds later, a young guy in a sports car pulled up. She jumped into his car, leaving hers behind, and they sped off, obviously not going inside for a workout. My internal writer's alarm went off—who were they and why did they meet so secretly? The scene immediately reminded me of a modern day Johnny Cash song, like "The Sound of Laughter" or an updated "Long Black Veil." That morning while working up a sweat on the court, the following story developed. Over the years, I could never get the scene out of my head. The resulting story blends together a lot of what I had seen and heard during the boom years of dot.com mania with this clandestine meeting on a cold, drizzling Northern California morning.

JACK AND CHLOE TURNED THEIR ONE-TIME affair into a routine. It was simple.

Every Tuesday, Wednesday, and Thursday at about 5:35 in the

morning they met at the Novato Fitness Center. Chloe parked her shiny red convertible, the one with the V-8 that her husband insisted she have—you know, just in case she needed to go zero to sixty in less than six seconds—and climbed into Jack's midnight blue sedan, the heater blasting hot air at her passenger side seat, just like she liked it. From there, they drove the six-tenths of a mile to his apartment. Well, you know the rest.

About an hour later, give or take a handful of minutes, they pulled back into the parking lot, surveyed the occasional sweaty soccer mom leaving the gym in a heap of soiled terrycloth, and disengaged.

No one seemed to look twice and certainly no one cared. Or so it seemed.

Frank, Chloe's dupe—err... husband—sleeping soundly in their pretty little home in their pretty little cul-de-sac no more than three miles away, had a recurring nightmare, the same one that haunted him for the last several years. The dream returned whenever Frank felt the chaotic strain of stress pull on his senses due to the enormous pressure he placed on himself.

The adult Frank—the one with the $3,500 mortgage payment and the sixty-five-hour-a-week job writing speeches for alternatively glamorous or vilified high-tech CEOs (often depending on that week's stock market intrigues)—suddenly found himself back on campus, a blotchy, much older version of the dapper young achiever he had been at the University of Pittsburgh. Smack dab in the middle of Benedum Hall, the school's largest auditorium, Frank walked in to discover that the final was about to take place and he didn't even know what class it was, though he vaguely thought it might be something math-related.

Frank's initial panic intensified as he looked around and saw all the smiling faces of the young frat rats in hooded sweatshirts and dirty baseball hats who didn't seem the least bit worried about the impending exam. On his left, a cadre of geekier kids pored over loose-leaf notebook pages and traded monosyllabic grunts. Not only did his newfound peers look prepared, they were confident.

Suddenly, it dawned on him, without passing this particular exam, Frank wouldn't graduate with his class and would have to fork over another couple grand to pay for a summer-school course. A dull thud at the base of Frank's skull let him know that this wasn't going to be pleasant.

The professor entered the cavernous room. A flurry of activity ensued, students grabbing for bluebooks and checking and re-checking their pens. Frank sat there stupefied, but did recognize the prof—a German classicist and star recruit brought in from Harvard to beef up the Philosophy Department. A hush fell over the auditorium.

"For those of you who studied, this exam will be a breeze," the professor gushed with a heavy guttural-laden accent. "Outline the first twenty-three chapters of the *Iliad*, providing three plot points for each and a one sentence overview."

Then, with a thin smile, "Begin now."

Beating himself up for not studying, and furthermore, never even showing up to this class for an entire semester, Frank stewed silently, wondering where he had left his bluebook and if someone would let him borrow a pencil.

Jack had a goofy smile and seemed kind of aloof. In fact, when Chloe first saw him (eight months earlier when she was hired as a senior consultant at Venture Consulting), he had his back to her.

That day, Ellen, Chloe's new boss, led her around the floor on an initial meet-and-greet tour. They stopped at the entrance to each cube, where Ellen delivered a few quick bullets of information about Chloe to each of her new "teammates." A whirlwind of faces and forgotten names ended back in the bullpen area where Ellen's immediate team occupied eight or ten spaces.

"That's Jack," Ellen said, pointing in the direction of the lone male in the bullpen who sat with his back facing them. No one could see what he was doing and his wide shoulders blocked out the laptop in front of him, but the sound of tapping keys gave him away.

"Don't mind him, he's in the middle of a big, ultra hush-hush project," Ellen told Chloe. Then, loudly clearing her throat, "Jack, meet our new teammate, Chloe."

He barely turned, kind of giving her a quick wave over his shoulder. Chloe's first impression was that this guy was cute, but had the personality of a cucumber.

A few hours later, she was at her welcome-to-the-company lunch out with Ellen—a late forties, kind of librarian-looking woman, but jazzed up in expensive suits—and the team of smart, Gen X women she put together. She listened to them dish on Jack and detail flirtatious interactions with him in the lunchroom or in the couple minutes preceding team meetings. Ellen simply "loved" Jack, thought he was gorgeous, and liked a little male eye candy in the overly female office.

After the initial burst of gossip and storytelling ended, Ellen took center stage again and gingerly scanned the room to see if anyone else from Venture was there. In hushed tones, she drew the group in and let them in on a secret.

"Keep this quiet," she said, "but I found out that Jack was married several years ago, right after graduate school, but his wife left him after a year."

"No way" was the general consensus among the shocked women. At least one let out an audible gasp.

"Supposedly, one day she just hit him with a bombshell, announcing that she considered this her starter marriage, and she was running off to live with an old boyfriend from college," Ellen continued. "Jack was devastated and basically dropped off the face of the earth for a while."

Chloe wondered what a starter marriage was, but didn't want her boss of only about six hours to think she wasn't hip. Luckily, one of the others asked.

"You're asking me? Isn't that the trend among you and your age group—to try out a marriage for a year or so, then divorce if it doesn't seem to work?" the boss answered.

"Sounds like another ridiculous Hollywood influence that has filtered down to the masses," Chloe said, after pondering whether to chime in for a number of seconds. A roar of laughter and Ellen's broad smile told Chloe that she was going to fit in fine with this group.

"Well, whether it's a passing fad or another nail in the coffin of Western civilization, it nearly killed Jack, the poor baby, he needs a whole lot of TLC," Ellen said. Another round of laughter ensued.

Frank's main speechwriting gig was for Tony Montaro. Montaro made billions of dollars by writing a little piece of software that attached itself to e-mail and served as a kind of certified mail for the electronic age. All of a sudden, no one had to wonder whether an e-mail was received or not. When the message hit the receiver's inbox, another little message zapped through cyberspace, letting the sender know it landed.

Starting a grassroots marketing campaign by giving the product away to a couple hundred people, then watching it spread to thousands, then tens of thousands of others, Montaro landed on the cover of *Fortune* magazine and a writer profiled him for *The Wall Street Journal*. Corporate America gobbled it up, virtually revolutionizing human resources. A year or so later, Montaro took the company public, cashing in a small percentage of the millions of shares he held.

Frank met Montaro at a software industry function, introduced by another founder/CEO tech guy, who proclaimed that Frank's handiwork with speeches "could turn a monkey into a guru, if he could get the damn thing into a three-piece tux." The software mogul and the plain-spoken kid from hardscrabble Western Pennsylvania bonded almost instantly despite the twenty or so years that separated them.

Slugging down whiskey and waters, the main topic of conversation was a big heavyweight bout the older man recently attended (the once-unbeatable Mike Tyson got the crap kicked out of him by some unknown British slugger in four rounds). Shortly thereafter, the topic turned to fighting in general. Montaro, despite the almost universal past all these guys shared as computer geeks and engineering nerds, viewed himself as kind of a tough guy. There were whispers around Silicon Valley about Montaro's infamous sparring sessions with world-class fighters from all over the world. Over time, this persona increased exponentially—in direct correlation with his net worth.

Frank shared his stories about the brawls he witnessed and participated in as a college student, which seemed to get more dramatic as time passed. However much exaggeration took place though, the scar across Frank's nose from his last battle—on the losing end of a broken beer bottle, pushing the tuft of skin all the way under his right eye until he reached up and re-jiggered it back into place—lent credibility to the younger man's tales.

"The blood spurted straight out at a high arc about two feet in the air," Frank explained, while Montaro laughed. "I couldn't see very well and every time I turned my head, all these people standing around got sprayed. The girls were flipping out as blood sprayed on them."

"Then, you just reached up and pushed what was left of your nose back in place?" Montaro asked.

"Yep, luckily, I was just drunk enough to numb the pain," Frank said.

Montaro hired trainers to craft his aging muscles and chefs to painstakingly plan his caloric intake to support the weight work. In the gym, he dabbled in a number of martial arts and trained in Brazilian grappling, where one uses an opponent's aggression as a weapon to defeat him—usually by breaking a wrist or popping a shoulder out of socket. Montaro also hired a small team of bodyguards, particularly after a handful of threatening, anonymous letters showed up at his private office overlooking the Golden Gate Bridge.

None of the men employed to protect Montaro were criminals, but one could say that each had a slightly checkered past. Through Montaro, Frank met Steve Mogar, the defacto leader of the protection team, a former Special Forces grunt who wasn't quite sure what to do now that he was deprogrammed. It was through one of Steve's backdoor connections (which they didn't discuss in detail) that Frank got the gun.

Venture Consulting occupied the top three floors of the Bank of America Tower in San Francisco's Financial District. The company spared no expense to impress its big-time software clients, particularly when they visited the offices for day-long brainstorming sessions.

As project leader for the KnowledgeBase account team, Chloe orchestrated every detail, right down to which muffins and pastries would be on the breakfast trays that lined one long row of desks in their large conference room looking out over the Golden Gate and north into Marin County. Alcatraz was just a dot below, but that always gave their business partners something to talk about at the various breaks in the day's schedule. Chloe also prepared Ellen for the client's arrival, writing out her "talking points" and delivering gossipy tidbits on the ranking execs from KnowledgeBase.

Getting a call from reception, Chloe got word that the client was running late, thus the meeting would begin about half an hour behind. As she turned to tell Ellen, both women looked up as Jack walked into the room, carrying his laptop and precariously balancing a giant coffee mug on the keyboard.

"Chloe, I've asked Jack to sit in for at least half the day," Ellen said, quickly switching from her chatty voice to that of stern female executive. "We'll need his expertise on database taxonomy."

"Looking forward to it," Jack said, smiling, and gave Chloe a little wink. "The meeting…and the free breakfast." He took a seat at the opposite corner from Ellen and plugged his laptop into the network connectors running up from holes in the dark brown boardroom table.

Jack looked at the printed nametags on each side of his seat and saw that Chloe would be in the next space over. A last-minute addition to the meeting, he'd have the unceremonious duty of wearing a handwritten one. The people from KnowledgeBase would probably figure that he was some kind of intern or low-ranking grunt.

With time to spare before the client arrived, Chloe sat down next to Jack, wondering how she would put up with such a boring task for an entire day. She secretly nicknamed him "Mr. Cucumber" for his bland personality and wondered how such a great-looking guy could be so utterly devoid.

She peeled the paper off an oversized blueberry muffin and pulled a chunk of the top off. Chloe smelled its sweet, sugary aroma and felt her stomach gurgle a little. My nerves must be getting the best of me, she thought. Then, Chloe turned slightly away from Jack, slowly enough that he wouldn't notice, and washed the first bite down with coffee.

"Damn, I dread these meetings," Jack said both to Chloe and no one in general. "But, with you running it, I know it will at least be somewhat productive." He smiled and averted his eyes.

"Thanks. . . . I think," Chloe said.

She feared getting pulled into a conversation with Jack and started scanning the agenda in front of her, hoping that some detail would jump out and force her to attend to it. She spun a little more, hoping he would get the hint. Other members of the team started filing into the room, including several of Ellen's fellow managers.

Standing, Chloe smiled at each person and motioned them to the pastry tray and coffee. Out of the corner of her eye, she sensed Jack fiddling with something, but didn't want to look down, in case he saw her. When she sat back down, Chloe felt something on her leg, just a couple inches above her knee. Quickly turning to Jack, he moved his index finger to his lips, giving her the universal quiet sign.

Chloe looked at her pant leg and saw that Jack had affixed a sticker there. It read, "Property of ____" and where the blank was, Jack filled in his initials, "JD." It must have been a shipping sticker from the desk.

"Now you're mine," Jack whispered.

Just then, Bill Nesbitt, Chloe's counterpart on the client team, walked into the conference room and waved to Ellen. As Chloe rose to greet him, she forgot about the sticker for a second and it stuck there on her leg. Then, remembering, she reached down as discreetly as possible, pulled it off, and stuck it on her laptop, below the keyboard.

After exchanging pleasantries, Chloe sat down and looked at Jack. "That's our little secret," he said, pointing to the sticker. "You can keep that as long as you want."

For the first time, Chloe's heart melted as she looked into Jack's green eyes and watched him transform from bland to beautiful. She sipped at her coffee in hopes of clearing the giant lump in her throat and silently prayed that no one would call on her to clarify anything for a few minutes.

Under the table, out of reach of the office's prying eyes, his knee brushed hers. Chloe moved it so that they would continue touching. The fire in her chest burned.

Frank soon found himself in Montaro's inner circle, surrounded by a posse of moneygrubbers that he liked to call cling-ons. The boss's secretary called to request his services and Frank loaded up his laptop, tape recorder, and notepads and raced to Montaro's personal compound nestled in the hills outside San Rafael, about a twenty-minute drive directly north of the city. When he arrived, Frank usually found that it wasn't a speechwriting gig Montaro wanted, but to trade stories or work out together in his gym.

Occasionally, Frank and Montaro put on heavy gloves and went at it in the ring. With oversized headgear, the sparing sessions never turned ugly, though pride forced each man to expend what he had. Montaro, lean and ripped, could still wheel and deal in the ring.

Frank found himself slowly getting back into fighting shape and thought that he had better start training on his own if he hoped to keep pace with his most profitable client. Writing gigs like this one don't come around all that often, Frank thought, especially with the fringe benefits Montaro offered. I'd better start using that gym membership Chloe signed us up for when we moved. He made a mental note to stop by and check out the weightlifting equipment and see if they had any speed bags there.

Frank sat on a long wooden bench outside one of the sparring rings and plunged his left hand deep into a steel bucket filled with water and ice, watching Montaro receive instruction from the guy who coached the U.S. fighters at the 2000 Olympics. The last two knuckles on Frank's hand ached, despite the extra tape the trainers applied. He busted up his hand in the first real fight he ever had in eighth grade. The class bully called a girl he secretly loved a whore and Frank finally stood up to him. No one knew he had quietly been training for just such an event. The bloodbath that ensued shocked everyone who saw it because Frank thoroughly punished the bully. He won his secret crush's heart, which played to his budding romantic side. No one messed with him again for years.

Although he enjoyed working out with Montaro, Frank realized that the financial gain from writing speeches for him could potentially change his and Chloe's lives. Montaro paid well and promised to introduce Frank to his CEO buddies, an ever-growing list, considering that many middle-aged white guys wanted to hang out with Montaro and his hard-charging cronies.

The upside to more work always came back to paying down the mortgage on their house and taking some of the pressure off his wife. Venture Consulting worked her like a dog. They talked about starting a family, but who could afford to in Northern California? Childcare alone would kill them. Despite the pain shooting through the knuckle on his ring finger, Frank smiled at the thought of having children, and the financial gains he made from his new boss that might make that possible.

At the end of his session, Montaro leaned over the ropes, looking at Frank. "How's that hand holding up, champ?" he asked. "Am I going to have to take it easy on you next time?"

"It's good, Tony," Frank said. "The damn thing has been sore so long that I hardly even notice it anymore. I'll be okay in a day or two." Montaro laughed, which led to a chorus of catcalls from his workout partners.

Frank pulled his hand out of the icy water, sending a chill up his arm to the base of his skull. Looking down at the pinkish white flesh, Frank shook it a little, wondering if his wedding ring would fit over the swollen digit.

Jack and Chloe started going out to lunch a couple times a week, just to get out of the office and blow off some steam. The attraction was obvious, but neither strayed from within the bounds of office flirtation. At meetings, often during the endless strings of PowerPoint decks filled with tiny, unreadable fonts and brightly colored pie charts, Jack caught Chloe staring at him. When she realized that he returned her gaze, Chloe turned away red-faced.

Their favorite lunch hangout was an old-fashioned diner, remarkably different than most of the places around the Financial District. It specialized in meat and potato kinds of meals, which meant that no one from the office would be caught dead there. Jack and Chloe's teammates concentrated on carb-friendly establishments, while the older partners went to expensive restaurants where they covertly downed martinis to steel them for the afternoon's work.

One day over matching plates of fried chicken and mashed potatoes, as they discussed weekend plans or some other totally innocuous subject, Chloe told Jack how impressed she was with his easygoing personality, which stood in such stark contrast to her own. "You know," she said, brushing her hair back from her face, "that's one of the things I really love about you."

Jack's smile betrayed his emotions. He looked into her eyes. Had she just basically told him that she loved him, he wondered?

"Ugh, I can't believe I just let that slip out," Chloe said, her face turning crimson. She put her right hand over her eyes, trying to cover her whole face.

Jack reached across the table and moved her hand away. As she dropped it, he saw the smile on her face and felt waves of warmth cascade over him. He took her hand in his, stammered for a second, and said, "I love you, too, Chloe."

He knew by the look on her face that life could not get better than it was at that very instant. Chloe was so beautiful that it looked like she had permanent backlighting. For the first time since his wife left, Jack looked forward to something—anything that put him in close proximity to this amazing woman—yet he had never even kissed those perfect pink lips or held her through the night as they slept wrapped together.

The waitress approached. "Can I get you two lovebirds any dessert today?" she asked. They looked at her and giggled; now someone else shared their secret.

"Umm, no thanks," Jack answered. As she cleared the table, they locked legs underneath—her knees clutched between his own—and held each other's hands tightly, as if doing so could freeze this moment in time and enable them to stay together forever.

It didn't take a rocket scientist to pick up the edge in Chloe's voice each night. Frank heard it loud and clear, particularly when she questioned the time he spent at Montaro's lair and the puffy spots under his eyes from the most recent sparring match.

What does she want from me, Frank wondered, trying to concentrate on the sidewalk ahead. I'm just trying to solidify things for us on the tail of a rich computer geek with a typically oversized ego. When I'm not working enough, she's unhappy. Now that I have a steady client—a bit on the odd side, but steady, nonetheless—she's still not satisfied.

He faintly caught the sight of his breath in the chilled morning air.

The thin cotton gloves Frank wore to protect his hands from the cold scratched his eyelids and burned a bit as he wiped at the beads of sweat rolling down his forehead.

The first step in his workout plan—if he was going to catch up to Montaro—was to put in a couple miles of roadwork. Frank didn't pump off jabs, like Sylvester Stallone did in the *Rocky* movies as he canvassed the streets of South Philly, but he did attempt to visualize various scenarios that he would face in the ring. Chloe, however, kept slipping in and throwing off his concentration.

Slowing just a bit to check his stopwatch securely tied to his left hand, Frank plodded along, being extra careful not to trip on the uneven pavement. He'd never again run the six-minute miles he could nail like clockwork in high school and college, but his time was still respectable. He tugged on his sleeve to keep out the chill and thought about his breathing pattern.

I've got so much energy to burn this morning, rather than end the route at home, I'll duck into the gym and hit the heavy bag for a couple rounds, then jump some rope, Frank thought. He knew the place would be practically empty. Few noble souls dragged themselves out of bed into the pitch darkness to work out. The ones there passed from exercise machine to machine quietly, like ghosts, an occasional nod or faint smile the only thing that proved they weren't sleepwalking.

Frank retreated into his own dreamlike state, feeling the way his hands molded into the heavy leather covering the punching bag with each syncopated thud. He heard the sound of his breathing, but it seemed filtered through some faraway speakers. Frank bobbed his head, ducking imaginary jabs, and fired successive left hooks into the ribcage of his fake opponent. Sweat pooled on the floor beneath him.

Taking a short breather, Frank drank from a small paper cup and gazed out the thick, dark glass that lined most of the exterior walls. Using his discarded sweatshirt as a towel, he mopped his forehead and neck. Out of the corner of his eye, Frank noticed a car speed into the parking lot, coming to an abrupt stop near the back of the parking lot. He saw a woman emerge from the passenger's side. She quickly walked around the back of the vehicle and went to the driver's door, leaning in to give a last kiss.

Her familiarity caught Frank off guard. Is that Chloe? Frank felt a ball well up in his throat and drop like cement into his stomach.

After several long seconds, the two broke apart and the blue car sped away. Then he saw it and couldn't believe he had practically been looking at it for the last half-hour without noticing. The red Mustang, her dream car, stood there, not more than twenty-five yards away. He watched Chloe climb in, adjust the rearview mirror, than slowly pull away.

Frank swallowed the spit welling up in his mouth through the lump in the back of his throat. He fought off the dizzy ringing in his ears. Frank felt blood pulsing at his temples and inflame the sore patches on his face, left over from the snap of Montaro's gloves.

In the future, when Frank replayed this moment in his mind, he didn't even have to visualize it—he could taste it. More importantly, however, he questioned his actions that morning and came to believe that he should have run out into the parking lot and confronted Chloe right then and there. He imagined the yelling match that would have broken out between he and Chloe and the fight with the fucking guy in the car, who wouldn't have stood a snowball's chance in hell of keeping Frank from kicking his ass.

The memory that slipped from Frank's thoughts as time passed was the sensation of utter panic he had felt and the strength it took just to keep standing there, watching his worst nightmare unfold right before his eyes. There really wasn't time to think in that brief moment or lay out some elaborate plan. Fate, gut instinct, or something akin to blind fear kept Frank cemented to that one spot in the gym. It really made no sense to second-guess himself.

"Do you know who I am?" Frank spit out the question between clenched teeth.

"I have a pretty good idea," Jack said. "I recognize you from the picture on Chloe's desk."

"Don't say her name again, goddamn it. You have no right to say her name," Frank said, pushing the barrel of the gun a bit harder into his temple. He was tied down, on his knees, execution-style, completely at Frank's whim.

It didn't take much in the way of James Bond moves for Frank to follow the man home after one of his trysts with Chloe, particularly after stumbling upon their meeting place. What surprised Frank was in all that time, weeks really, leading up to this very moment, he never came up with what he considered a good plan.

"What's your name?" Frank asked. "I want to know the name of the man who's fucking my wife."

"Jack," he replied. His eyes were pinched closed. He bowed his head slightly and slumped his shoulders, like he already knew that the end was near.

"Let's hear it then, Jack. Why are you sticking your dick in my wife? My wife, get it Jack? My wife. . . . " Frank said, moving the gun away.

"Look, I'm sorry. I . . . I mean we . . . didn't want this to happen. Please, whatever you want, I'll never see her again. Just don't shoot me. It isn't worth it."

"Well, this is certainly an interesting turn of events," Frank said. "This morning you were having sex with another man's wife, now you're begging for your life like some little bitch. You don't deserve to live."

"If it's any consolation, know that I love her," Jack said. "I love Chloe."

"Well, buddy, I've got some bad news for you. Chloe's dead. My decision now seems to be whether or not to kill you, too."

Letting the news settle in, Frank stuck the gun into Jack's cheek, watching tears roll down onto the barrel. Jack fought back sobs.

"Go ahead, pull the trigger. Pull it. I don't care now."

Frank moved the gun around and put it directly between Jack's eyes. "How romantic. How stupidly romantic," he said.

"Actually, I'm not going to kill you," Frank calmly stated. "After today, you'll never see me again, unless you decide to go to the police, then I will put a bullet between your eyes. I'm not going to kill you, because you'll have to go through the rest of your life knowing that you caused her death. Her blood is on your hands, live with that."

Placing the gun on the dining room table, Frank picked up the ether-stained rag he had used to knock Jack unconscious and held it firmly over the man's nose and mouth. He let Jack fight back just a little, as Mogar, the Special Ops vet, instructed him to, knowing that the more Jack struggled, the faster the drug would work. Then the kicking stopped.

Frank cut the ropes binding the man's hands and feet and put them in a knapsack, along with the rag and gun. He slowly opened the door and looked up and down the hall, seeing no one. He slipped out, and walked briskly to the fire door. A few minutes later, Frank was on the road.

Days later, as daylight crept up on the horizon in front of him, Frank replayed the scenario in his mind, wondering if he should have just pulled the trigger. The question would haunt him forever.

Although they had been married for only five years, Frank and Chloe were together for more than ten. She grew to become his best friend, in addition to his lover and soul mate. Now, all that was gone. He could not imagine life without her, but he could also not conceive of moving ahead with a partner who wasn't faithful.

As he drove on, headed home to Pennsylvania, the land of his people for generations, Frank wondered what Jack's first move was once he woke up. Did he call the police? Did he frantically dial Chloe's cell phone, knowing that there would be no answer and praying against all hope that she would somehow pick up? Frank chuckled and a thin smile formed on his tired face.

Looking back, he could never have killed Chloe, not the woman who meant so much to him for so long. She may have destroyed his dreams, but he wouldn't take her life. Instead, he simply walked out the door.

The timing couldn't have worked out better. One of her biggest projects went south that afternoon, forcing her to fly to Tampa last minute in an attempt to salvage the work. Before she left, Chloe darted around the apartment, literally throwing clothes into her suitcase. She mumbled to herself, checking off an invisible list of items in her mind. Chloe barely noticed Frank hovering around, but he tried to stay out of her direct line of sight. The final word Chloe would ever speak to him was a hurried "good-bye," followed by a peck on the cheek.

Frank waited until the scheduled takeoff time then called her cellphone carrier and cancelled the policy, putting her out of reach for the time being. Then, he packed the few belongings that meant something to him and his laptop and put his plan into action.

Jack's immediate pain and suffering would be enough. Even if the ruse lasted only for a few hours, Frank realized in that space of time, those hollow moments while he contemplated Chloe's death, he had gutted the man's soul.

•

BOB BATCHELOR is an award-winning writer and historian. He teaches public relations in the School of Mass Communications at the University of South Florida. A noted expert on American popular culture, he is the author or editor of the books: *The 1900s* (Greenwood Press, 2002), a history of the first decade of the twentieth century from a popular culture perspective; editor of *Basketball in America: From the Playgrounds to Jordan's Game and Beyond* (Haworth Press, 2005); co-author of a study on the development of consumer culture and marketing: *Kotex, Kleenex, Huggies: Kimberly-Clark and the Consumer Revolution in American Business* (The Ohio State University Press, 2004), and co-author of *The 1980s* (Greenwood Press, 2006). His fiction has appeared in *The Pebble Lake Review*. Bob has published more than 500 articles and essays in magazines, Web sites, and reference works, including the *Dictionary of American istory, Inside Business* magazine, and *The American Prospect Online*. His essays have appeared in newspapers in California, Tennessee, and Delaware. Bob graduated from the University of Pittsburgh with degrees in history, philosophy, and political science. He received an MA in history from Kent State University. He has taught history and nonfiction writing at Cleveland State University and Neumann College. Visit him online at www.bobbatchelor.com.

NONFICTION

Leigh H. Edwards

WALKIN' CONTRADICTION: JOHNNY CASH AND AMERICAN AMBIVALENCE

FROM ROCKABILLY BADASS TO COUNTRY MUSIC elder statesman, Johnny Cash embodied paradoxes. No single Johnny Cash existed. Full of inconsistencies, Cash always changed, whether he played the drugged rock star trashing hotel rooms or the devout Christian touring with Billy Graham. He was the "Man in Black": a progressive voice for the disenfranchised and the Southern patriarch performing at Nixon's White House. Cash embodied the rebel outlaw hillbilly thug and later symbolized the establishment. At the heart of all these ambiguities lies Cash's appeal.

Let me begin my inquiry into Cash's iconography, then, with this simple observation: popular culture images of Cash consistently and obsessively refer to him as a contradiction. For the most famous example, we need look no further than Kris Kristofferson's tribute song, "The Pilgrim; Chapter 33," which dubs Cash a "walkin' contradiction."[1] There, Cash the man becomes a mythological figure because he is the trouble-maker, the stoned musician, and the preacher-prophet. Merging fact and fiction, Cash becomes the lonely, empathetic, fallen pilgrim

[1] Kris Kristofferson. "The Pilgrim; Chapter 33." *Silver Tongued Devil & I.* Resaca Music Publishing Company, 1971.

searching for redemption. Kristofferson's lyrics point to the dual roles Cash plays, both the sacred and the profane. This depiction is typical in that it fetishizes Cash for being a paradox and locates the nature of his appeal. The question I wish to explore is: what is the allure of this image of Cash as a walking contradiction?

My argument is that a key part of Cash's appeal lies in the way his cultural persona is itself explicitly contradictory, in the pull of cultural ambivalence. He brings disparate or even opposed cultural ideas into close, symbiotic relationship with each other. His iconic image in fact depends on his ability to stage the idea of irresolvable ambivalence—to illuminate how that model of ambivalence, what we might call a "both/and" idea, is an important paradigm for U.S. popular music and for American identity.

Cash embodied the tensions in the American character without resolving them. And in so doing, he encouraged listeners to engage with our most fundamental national paradoxes, from the contradictions of a free democracy founded on slavery to the whipsaw between individual rights and national identity. He once said to an audience, "I thank God for freedoms we've got in this country. I cherish them and treasure them—even the right to burn the flag." As some booed, he went on, "We also got the right to bear arms, and if you burn my flag, I'll shoot you. But I'll shoot you with a lot of love, like a good American."[2] At times, Cash sounded like both sides of the Toby Keith/Dixie Chicks debate over the role of patriotism and social protest in popular music. But what Cash does is to ironize and to push adamantly on contradictions, to question false logics and false oppositions, in this case involving paradoxes of "natural rights," where one person's idea of individual freedom can take away another's. His comment is not simply perverse; rather, it speaks to American tautologies.

Cash represents key social tensions in their intricacy, framing them as troubling, true, and distinctively American—and related to the social role of popular music in the United States. Popular music becomes a way to allow audiences to engage emotionally with such issues. Here, what Stuart Hall would call the "emotional realism" of the music does not lead listeners into passive consumption, but into active contemplation of the vexed complications that make up the American character.[3]

---

[2] Fine, Jason, ed. *Cash: By the Editors of Rolling Stone*. New York: Crown, 2004, 43.

[3] Hall, Stuart and Whannel, Paddy. *The Popular Arts*. London: Hutchinson, 1964, 269–83.

Kristofferson dubbed Cash Abe Lincoln with a "dark, wild streak," and music journalists incessantly compare him to Walt Whitman in order to make sense of him as a large, democratic, national figure that can contain multitudes.[4]

Cash illuminates key issues at the crossroads of American studies and popular music studies, not only because he is an exemplary case study, but also because he offers this conceptual model of irresolvable contradictions. In this essay, I analyze how the trope of contradiction permeates the social construction of Johnny Cash. His life and work illuminate other important questions in popular music studies and in popular culture more generally, such as: the complex position of popular music in U.S. culture, popular culture's ability to question traditional binaries (like sacred versus profane), and the changing models of *authenticity*. While I focus my discussion on those issues, I also attend to how constructions of masculinity and race play into versions of authenticity, key topics in the study of popular music and of country music specifically.[5]

Using literary analysis techniques, I unpack an array of representations of Cash, attempting to address aspects of production, the work itself, its reception, and its socio-historical context. Critic Joli Jensen, in her analysis of Patsy Cline's multifaceted image, notes that the popular image of any artist is the result of the interplay of the media, the audience, and the work itself. All three of what Jensen terms these "levels of explanation" must be examined together, because there is no "true" or "real" version of the artist, only complex layers of representation.[6] Here, I address elements of Cash's own self-presentation (from his two autobiographies to his music, liner notes, interviews, and the marketing of his iconographic Man in Black image) and how others have depicted him (in biographies, documentaries, music journalism,

---

[4] Mansfield, Brian. *Ring of Fire: A Tribute to Johnny Cash.* Nashville: Rutledge Hill Press, 2003, 12.

[5] See, for example, Barbara Ching, *What I Do Best: Hard Country Music and Contemporary Culture* (New York: Oxford UP, 2001); Joli Jensen, *The Nashville Sound: Authenticity, Commercialization, and Country Music* (Nashville: Country Music Foundation/Vanderbilt University Press, 1998); Richard Peterson, *Creating Country Music: Fabricating Authenticity* (Chicago: University of Chicago Press, 1997); Michael T. Bertrand, *Race, Rock and Elvis* (Urbana: University of Illinois Press, 2000); Cecelia Tichi, ed., *Reading Country Music: Steel Guitars, Opry Stars, and Honky-Tonk Bars* (Durham: Duke University P,ress 1998); Kristine M. McCusker and Diane Pecknold, *A Boy Named Sue: Gender and Country Music* (Jackson: University of Mississippi Press, 2004).

[6] Jensen details how Cline's image illuminates country music's constructions of femininity. Jensen, "Patsy Cline's Crossovers," *A Boy Named Sue* 107–131.

producer Rick Rubin's marketing of him for the American Records label, Mark Romanek's video for "Hurt," and the *Walk the Line* biopic).

All of these elements, fact and fiction, go into creating Cash's cultural image, so it is necessary to analyze them together. As I trace these paradoxical images, I argue that Cash's legacy is most importantly about his ability to slip out of boxes or categories, to make us look at contradictions without papering over them, to express radical ambiguity that insists on painful complexity.

Issues and Contexts

Scholars such as Cecelia Tichi have called for more American studies and cultural studies attention to country music as a genre precisely because of such formative links between these "folk poetry" discourses and American thought.[7] Cultural ambivalence and contradiction are key issues in American thought, whether the contradictions stem from capitalism and class struggle or the legacy of race slavery. While Cash's model of "both/and" is not a radical critique of dominant U.S. culture, it is not simply a model of liberal pluralism either, because it does not offer up some false consensus culture. Rather, his corpus incorporates a struggle over meaning as part of his identity construction, as a model for authenticity, because it insists on presenting the contradictions themselves and eschews easy resolution. His texts participate in and illuminate the dominant culture's anxieties, but they remain stubborn and disjunctive. As such, his work is an apt case study for how popular culture is a site of negotiation and struggle and is not simply a playground for escapism or for only corporate agendas (here, I side with critics who argue that while corporations produce commercial culture, thus market forces control popular culture; they can not completely control the range of meanings consumers might derive from that culture, however limited that audience agency is).[8] Cash is, of course, not

---

[7] Tichi, Cecelia. *High Lonesome: The American Culture of Country Music*. Chapel Hill: University of North Carolina Press, 1994, 1.

[8] For accounts of this kind of cultural studies model of popular culture as a site of negotiation and struggle, see Stuart Hall, *Stuart Hall: Cultural Dialogues in Cultural Studies*, ed. David Morley and Kuan-Hsing Chen (London: Routledge, 1996); John Storey, *Inventing Popular Culture* (Oxford: Blackwell, 2003) 48–62. For discussions of how popular music exceeds the logic of the marketplace, see Bertrand in *A Boy Named Sue* 63; Barry Shank, *Dissonant Identities: The Rock 'n' Roll Scene in Austin, Texas* (Hanover: Wesleyan University Press, 1994) 251.

unique in addressing American ambivalences through popular music, but he is distinctive and yields insights particular to his work.[9]

Likewise, Cash is useful as a case study for complexity in this popular music genre. As Barbara Ching has detailed, country music features its own internal critiques of authenticity, and critics must listen for the complexity of those critiques, rather than simplicity in the genre, otherwise they are in danger of insisting on what Jensen calls "purity by proxity," an act of trying to make the genre transparently stand-in for traditional virtues.

Cash's death in September 2003 prompted an intense emotional response from legions of musicians and fans worldwide. Such large-scale affective investment in a popular artist itself occasions a need to inquire into his impact and legacy.[10] As Kristine M. McCusker and Diane Pecknold note, his popularity is so widespread, we have to account for his appeal beyond niche markets, beyond a country audience. Insofar as the market is a measure of popularity, Cash has sold more than fifty million albums, and he was the bestselling artist internationally with his prison albums in 1969 (he outsold the Beatles that year, selling 6.5 million albums). He recorded more than 1,500 songs, fourteen number-one hits, and won numerous awards, including eleven Grammys, and he was inducted into both the Rock and Roll and the Country Music Hall of Fame. His albums surged in popularity just after his death, with sales doubling.[11] The Oscar award-winning biopic *Walk the Line*

---

[9] Critic Greil Marcus, in his landmark study, detailed how key rock 'n' roll artists like Elvis articulate the equivocations of American democracy, between separation and community, rebellion and conformity, and how they consequently fight over the mythology that is American identity. Cultural theorist Barry Shank has argued eloquently for how Bob Dylan, in the sixties, embodied the countervailing search for both autonomy and authenticity in American culture. Music historian Bill C. Malone has beautifully detailed the Southern and working-class polarities that have shaped country music's appeal. But as Shank notes, each artist is specific in how they engage with American problems in distinct socio-historical contexts. See Greil Marcus, *Mystery Train: Images of America in Rock 'n' Roll Music* (New York: Plume, 1997); Bill C. Malone, *Don't Get Above Your Raisin': Country Music and the Southern Working Class* (Urbana: University of Illinois Press); Malone, *Southern Music/American Music: New Perspectives on the South* (Lexington: University Press of Kentucky, 1979); Malone, *Singing Cowboys and Musical Mountaineers: Southern Culture and the Roots of Country Music* (Athens: University of Georgia Press, 2003); Barry Shank, "'That Wild Mercury Sound': Bob Dylan and the Illusion of American Culture," *Boundary 2* 29:1 (2002): 97–123.

[10] Noting the intensity of Cash's effect on some audiences, Marty Stuart says that while on tour with Cash, "I saw everything from a little boy coming backstage in Kansas and asking him to pull his tooth to a prisoner's mom getting down on her hands and knees, wrapping her arms around his calves, and begging him to get her boy off of death row" (Mansfield 64).

[11] "Johnny Cash Album Sales Soar," *Launch Radio Networks*, 18 Nov 2003 http://launch.yahoo.com/read/news.asp?contentID=214647.

(2005), which has earned more than $120 million at the box office to date, sparked yet another round of renewed interest in him, landing his second autobiography on the bestseller list and prompting yet more biographies.[12]

I have suggested that Cash helps explicate popular music's role in society in the sense that his music gives audiences a way to engage with contradictions in American thought and identity. In so doing, he also provides us with models for thinking about how popular culture can question traditional categorical binaries (tradition versus social change, establishment versus anti-authoritarian, conservative versus progressive, patriot versus traitor, morally righteous versus fallen, pure versus impure). Cash's work exposes the problems with such rigid categories, whether political or musical.

In addition, Cash is an exemplar for thinking about popular music's long-running love affair with the idea of authenticity, that hotly contested, endlessly debunked fantasy of what is genuine. Theorists have long argued that authenticity is a constructed set of ideas and values that reflect particular socio-historical contexts of production and reception. Audiences and record companies might deem an artist or their music *authentic* because they seem to convey honesty, truth, and an organic relationship to their roots or fan base. Country music has always been framed as a genre of sincerity.[13] But one person's "authentic" favorite singer-songwriter is another person's *manufactured* bubble-gum pop star. The idea of authenticity involves a complex set of beliefs about taste, values, identity, and models of artistic creation. It is an arbitrary, constantly changing idea. And it is our job to unpack what it means in each specific instance—and what such ideas reflect about U.S. culture.

I would argue that a large part of what counts as authenticity regarding Cash is precisely this image of a walking contradiction. While he changed his persona over the years, this theme is a touchstone in marketing across the arc of his career, ranging from his early Sun Records

---

[12] Chief among them is the authorized biography, Steve Turner's *The Man Called Cash: The Life, Love and Faith of an American Legend* (Nashville: Thomas Nelson, 2004) and Michael Streissguth's account of the Folsom concert, *Johnny Cash at Folsom Prison: The Making of a Masterpiece* (Cambridge, MA: Da Capo Press, 2004). Various others include: Stephen Miller, *Johnny Cash: The Life of an American Icon* (London: Omnibus Press, 2003); Garth Campbell, *Johnny Cash: He Walked the Line, 1932–2003* (London: John Blake, 2003); Dave Urbanski, *The Man Comes Around: The Spiritual Journey of Johnny Cash* (Lake Mary, FL: Relevant Books, 2003).

[13] See, for example, Barry Shank's critical cultural studies ethnography of identity constructions involving ideas of "sincerity" in Austin music scenes. Shank, *Dissonant Identities.*

rockabilly years with producer Sam Phillips (1955–58), to his long stint with Columbia (1958–1986), which covered his 1960s drug years, to his wildly popular prison recordings in the late 1960s, to his early 1970s superstardom, and to Nashville's abandonment of him as a solo artist in the 1980s when Columbia shockingly dropped him from their label. It also pervades his 1980s and 1990s work with supergroup The Highwaymen (with Willie Nelson, Waylon Jennings, and Kris Kristofferson), Mercury's half-hearted attempt to revive his solo career (1986–1992), and his career resurgence with American Records (1993 until his death in 2003, with posthumous releases still appearing).

Responding to his performance, as well as his image, critics consistently refer to Cash and various parts of his musical oeuvre, such as his prison recordings, as "authentic." Undoubtedly, ineffable aspects of his musical performance are essential to his authenticity effect, a certain kind of constructed idea of genuineness, and it is important to note how his musical and performance elements also involve a sense of contradiction. Cash's distinctive bass-baritone voice, a deep-sonic tonic, is a vital ingredient of his appeal. It is in part through what theorist Roland Barthes calls the grain of the voice, the embodiment through voice that exceeds words and language, that Cash achieves his emotional effects on audiences.[14] Often described as a bad singer who could not maintain his pitch and had very little range, Cash nevertheless mastered the art of conveying sincerity and suffering through his singing. One music critic describes the musicality of Cash's voice as follows:

> Earthy-deep, ominous sometimes, resonant [in terms of loudness or power], virile, untrained, unconventional.... Cash has a blue tonality, does not sustain his notes, does not sing by the scale or sing sharps, and he slides into his flats... is constantly blending the tone... and decorates his melody according to his own interpretation.[15]

Musicologist Denise Von Glahn observes that Cash's sound is unique in part because the depth of his voice leaves more room for overtones. When other sounds are layered on top of it, the result is a singular, fuller, richer sound that ultimately signifies power. Simultaneously his voice has a flattened, direct, folk-like character. It possesses little vi-

---

[14] Barthes, Roland. *The Responsibility of Forms: Critical Essays on Music, Art, and Representation.* Trans. Richard Howard. Oxford: Blackwell, 1986.

[15] Quoted in Urbanski xiv.

brato, a quality long associated with vocal training and synonymous with the high arts. His voice is raw and grainy. She notes that Cash's unpolished sound coupled with his defiant insistence on being heard fits nicely with his image of speaking for the disenfranchised or the "common man."[16]

Cash's voice cuts through other sounds but also blends in on his recordings and performances. Cash's longtime producer, Jack Clement, dubbed him "Captain Decibel," because his voice picked up remarkably well on sound recording equipment. Clement notes:

> He's got the most amazing recording voice that I know of, in terms of getting on the tape. There's what you call apparent level, and then there's actual level. He has this apparent level that just gets on the tape. It's a commodity. You just can't hardly cover it up. It's almost impossible to drown him out. You can put in lots of drums, horns, a roomful of guitars and everything else—he still cuts through. It's powerful. There's few voices I've ever heard like that.[17]

Von Glahn points out that this effect would be due to the fundamental pitch of his voice and how the partials vibrate.[18] Yet at the same time, elaborating on how Cash turned his imperfect voice into a highly effective emotive vehicle, Clement notes how Cash blended in:

> I wouldn't call him a great musician. I'd call him a great musical entity. He was a musical force and a great singer. People believed what he was saying. Most people don't understand that the voice is like an instrument and has to blend in with the other instruments. Somehow Cash understood that. Mostly because he didn't care. He would just sing. Somehow it worked. [19]

Likewise important are Cash's compelling abilities as a performer who delivers a sense of emotional rawness and *truth*. The simplicity of his music, the often-noted struggles he and his first band, The Tennessee Two, had with playing their instruments on the early Sun Records, also contributes to this sincerity effect. But the simplicity is deceptive. As musician Guy Clark points out: "'I Walk the Line,' it just sounds

---

[16] Von Glahn, Denise. Personal Interview, 22 March 2006.

[17] Mansfield 38.

[18] Von Glahn, Denise. Personal Interview, 22 March 2006.

[19] Turner 234.

like the simplest thing in the world, but it's really not. It's really a fairly difficult song to play and sing at the same time. To actually play it on a guitar and sing it is kind of like patting your head and rubbing your stomach."[20]

Thus, there are clear musical and performance elements contributing to Cash's authenticity effect. But I would argue that it is his cultural image that synthesizes the different components of Cash's performance; his effect vitally depends on his themes and iconography. And I would argue that what is most iconographic in him is this trope of engaging with and embodying larger cultural contradictions, between good and bad, light and dark, God and drugs, faithfulness and cheating. As music critic Anthony DeCurtis notes, Cash was both "Saturday night and Sunday morning," a dynamic that contributed to his world-wide success as well as country music's fluctuating rejection and embrace of him.[21]

Cash's paradoxical cultural image, like his constant mixing of musical styles, kept people guessing about who the *true* Cash was. He had to keep admitting that he never did hard time, because his songs and image made people think he had. Wildly disparate groups tried to claim him as their own, from fans of traditional country to indie rockers. In one notable example, MTV reports of his death genuflected to him as "the first punk" because of his projected attitude, citing his notorious amphetamine addiction in the 1950s and 1960s and his pioneering work in the area of rock stars trashing hotel rooms. As June Carter Cash said: "He's always been a sneerer."[22] Cash was perhaps the original rock 'n' roll hell raiser.

Indeed, in its form and content, Cash's body of work imagines him as a border crosser, a category-breaker who merges musical styles, political stances, and social identities. His musical genres include gospel, folk, rockabilly, rock, blues, bluegrass, and country. His mix of cultural forms includes popular music, oral narrative, popular literary genres including autobiographies and historical novels, Appalachian and other folk cultures, film, documentary, and music videos. He constantly bucked efforts to categorize him politically, and his stances varied from social protester and outsider populist critiques of institutions such as prisons to support for U.S. nationalism. In his work, Cash also positions himself

---

[20] Mansfield 40.

[21] "Controversy: Johnny Cash vs. Music Row." CMT, 11 September 2004.

[22] Quoted in Dawidoff 186.

as an iconoclast who problematizes identity categories, from the progressive advocate of American Indian land rights and Vietnam protests to the conservative, flag-waving patriot. He famously sang about shooting a man in Reno for the sole purpose of watching him die, and he less famously wrote a novel about St. Paul and religious faith, *Man in White* (1986).

Projections of Identity

Looking at how the trope of contradiction appears in Cash's own self-presentation, we can see key recurring themes. In addition to musical genre category busting, tensions involving the commercialization of country music and the commodification of celebrity, and country music's well-documented anti-modern critique and nostalgia for an agrarian past, Cash's work and career also comment forcefully on key issues like identity politics, the relationship between music and politics (such as his commentary on competing definitions of American patriotism), and formulations of Southern white masculinity and authority.

On the issue of gender constructions, Cash for some embodied masculine authority as the patriarch of country music's "First Family," since he married into the Carter family. Musician Bono of U2, who recorded with Cash, declaimed: "We're all sissies in comparison to Johnny Cash."[23] Yet for others, his work sometimes questioned traditional gender role identities and socialization (critic Teresa Ortega has claimed Cash as a lesbian icon because he allows fans to identify with "troubled and suffering masculinity").[24] This troubled masculinity is appropriate coming from an artist who started out in rockabilly, that formative style that hailed the mixing of country and rhythm and blues that resulted in rock. Critics Mary Bufwack and Robert Oermann have shown how rockabilly stars violated gender taboos, taking on feminized behaviors (such as hip-shaking, sob-raking performances). Michael Bertrand has shown how "culturally schizophrenic" Hillbilly Cats crossed both racial and gender taboos. In his study of Elvis, Bertrand details how the integration of "white" hillbilly music and "black" rhythm and blues in the 1950s and 1960s South implied racial integration and was seen as

---

[23] Quoted in Fine 208.

[24] Teresa Ortega, "'My name is Sue! How do you do?': Johnny Cash as Lesbian Icon." *South Atlantic Quarterly* 94 (Winter 1995): 267.

dangerous in the context of desegregation and the Civil Rights movement, but also how the rockabilly stars identified with outsider aspects of black masculinity, drawing on identification between black and white Southern working class cultures.[25] That kind of troubled and troubling racial identification and appropriation emerges from the kind of love and theft critics such as Eric Lott read in earlier blackface minstrelsy.[26] In an artist such as Cash, who later spoke explicitly to social movements targeting racial inequity, like Civil Rights, the complex identifications and appropriations that comprise his racialized gender performances consistently place his performance and stable identity categories under question.

In his own self-presentation, Cash insists on irreducible complexity. He goes so far as to create a model of identity as multiple.[27] Perhaps most famously, he created the "Man in Black" narrative persona in his 1971 song as a conscious construction to speak for the poor and the disenfranchised.[28] He also imagines numerous selves in his two autobiographies, *Man in Black* (1975) and *Cash: The Autobiography* (1997). There, he uses different names for the different "Cashes" he played in different social contexts. He stages a struggle between "Johnny Cash" the hell-raising, hotel-trashing, pill-popping worldwide star and "John R. Cash," a more subdued, adult persona. To some family and friends, he remained the "J. R. Cash" from his childhood. In an interview with her father, Tara Cash once asked him, "Did you ever have an imaginary friend?" and he replied, "Yes. Sometimes I am two people. Johnny is the nice one. Cash causes all the trouble. They fight."

Cash discussed slipping in and out of character, whether in public or private dimensions of performance. In his second autobiography, when describing himself as operating with "various names" and "various levels," he characterizes himself as "complicated," and endorses Kristofferson's walking contradiction line as well as daughter Rosanne Cash's depiction: "He believes what he says, but that don't make him a saint."

---

[25] Bertrand, *A Boy Named Sue*, 62, 64.

[26] Lott, Eric. *Love and Theft: Blackface Minstrelsy and the American Working Class*. New York: Oxford University Press, 1993.

[27] Pamela Fox addresses female country stars' construction of complex identity that negotiates class and gender-coded notions of authenticity, and she notes identity switching in female autobiographies of stars like Dolly Parton, Loretta Lynn, and Reba McEntire. Fox, "Recycled Trash: Gender and Authenticity in Country Music Autobiography" *American Quarterly* 50.2 (June 1998): 234–266; 235.

[28] John R. Cash, "Man in Black," *House of Cash*, 1971.

Cash elaborates: "I do believe what I say. There are levels of honesty, though."[29] He describes navigating his performance of identity:

> I prefer to meet people before my shows, not after. When I walk off that stage I'm no longer the character I was in the songs I sang—the stories have been told, their messages imparted—but often it's a while before I'm J. R. again. When I meet people, it's important for both of us that I'm J. R.[30]

His comments register how authenticity is always a constructed idea that depends on the context, since he and his audience both need to be aware of his narrative persona, "Johnny Cash," as a character he slips on and then gradually sheds.

Locating his appeal in "his vast love and his vast acceptance of paradox," Rosanne Cash argues: "His heart was so expansive and his mind so finely tuned that he could contain both darkness and light, love and trouble, fear and faith, wholeness and shatteredness, old-school and postmodern, and sacred and the silly, God and the Void."[31] On the topic of juggling his private and public lives, the deep context for his identity construction, she suggests that Cash was only comfortable when he could keep his competing impulses in productive tension:

> It's weird. He's so comfortable living this public life for forty years that it's part of his private life. Real life tends to be disappointing for him a lot. I see him trying to get away from it. His impulses for healing and spirituality are constantly being pulled on by his impulses of self-destruction. They're the same thing. One is a warped attempt to do the other. The constant travel, the spiritual seeking, the drugs. It's too much to sit still and be on this planet.[32]

Her formulation is striking for how she sees Cash's opposing poles as versions of the same in his identity construction, the sacred and the profane as mirror images of each other. Implicitly, in her telling, as in many others, this tortured imbrication of healing and self-destruction, grace and pain—and the restless, seeking energy it produces—defines both Cash and the culture that produced him.

---

[29] Cash, Johnny with Carr, Patrick. *Cash: The Autobiography.* New York: HarperCollins Publishers Inc., 1997, 9.

[30] Cash, *Cash* 146.

[31] Fine 13–14.

[32] Turner 194.

In terms of his own specific thematic paradoxes, a trio of his favorite themes, famously marketed on his three-disc boxed set, *Love, God, Murder* (Sony 2000), provide further examples of his equivocations. Moving back and forth across his lyrics, thematic content, autobiographical narratives, marketing, and public persona, we can find convolution on these topics. Cash sang about marital fidelity (to his first wife), but his most enduring love story stems from infidelity (the *Walk the Line* biopic turns on this equivocation, making epic drama from the painful struggles involved in how he fell in love and got involved with June Carter when both were married to other people). As Merle Haggard said, the song was "kind of ludicrous for him to sing," because Cash "never walked any line."[33]

Concerning religion, Cash was a devout Christian who took Bible classes, became an ordained minister (with the Christian International School of Theology), made a film about Christ called *The Gospel Road* (1973), and evangelized on the Billy Graham crusades. Yet he often avoided organized religion himself, slammed religious hypocrisy, and encouraged his children to follow their own beliefs. The liner notes to his *God* disc market his religious paradoxes. Cash writes: "At times, I'm a voice crying in the wilderness, but at times I'm right on the money and I know what I'm singing about." In liner notes for the same disc, musician Bono writes: "Johnny Cash is a righteous dude... but it's the 'outlaw' in him we love." On the question of murder, Cash was famous for singing murder ballads, which contributed to his outlaw image, but, again, he never did time (apart from a few nights in jail from drug busts) and his concern was with redemption; he felt a kinship with prisoners due to what he termed his own religious fight between dark and light within himself, what some journalists attributed to the legacy of his father's alcoholism (though Cash himself downplayed its impact on him).[34]

Depictions of Contradiction

In others' depictions, the sheer wealth of reference to Cash as a contradiction is staggering, but so is the sense that Cash is something to

[33] Quoted in Fine 24.

[34] Turner 225–235.

be fought over and defended. A particularly spectacular example of responses to Cash's political complexity is the protest at the 2004 Republican National Convention in New York. When Convention organizers held a reception honoring Lamar Alexander and Cash at Sotheby's to coincide with the Cash memorabilia auction there (which earned more than four million, triple what was expected), student Erin Siegal organized a protest, replete with 600 fans wearing black, pompadours, and guitars, who insisted that Cash's populist message could not be co-opted by the Republican party.[35] What does "Johnny Cash" symbolize to people, why would both the Left and the Right want to claim him, and why does he need defending? As the story made national news and Republican organizers defended their right to celebrate Cash, Cash's family responded to the controversy only by saying that he did not have an official party affiliation.[36] While I would side with the protestors, what I think is interesting is that Cash's cultural image allows for enough contradiction for both sides to believe they can claim him.

Equally noteworthy is how often accounts make him a metonymy for America. In Steve Turner's authorized biography published after Cash's death, Kris Kristofferson's foreword enshrines him as "a true American hero, who rose from a beginning as humble as Abraham Lincoln's to become a friend and an inspiration to prisoners and presidents."[37] Kristofferson often argued that Cash's "face ought to be up on Mount Rushmore," a line journalists repeat incessantly.[38] Turner explains Cash's life as one "clouded by pain" (tons of physical suffering and medical problems plus guilt over his brother Jack's tragic death as a teen, his father's mistreatment, his infidelities, and drug abuse) and "colored by grace" (Cash interpreted all his trials and tribulations along the lines of Job).[39]

Music journalist Brian Mansfield, in his compilation book of quotations about Cash, discusses Cash's mythology in ways that are typical in the sense that he posits the essence of Cash's social presence as an icon as irresolvable American paradox. Mansfield writes, "Perhaps no other

---

[35] Gray, Madison J. "3-Day Johnny Cash Auction in New York Rakes in Nearly $4 Million," *The Associated Press State & Local Wire*, 16 September 2004.

[36] "Row over 'Political' Cash Tribute," BBC, 28 August 2004 http://news.bbc.co.uk/2/hi/entertainment/3608956.stm.

[37] Turner ix.

[38] Mansfield 12.

[39] Turner 226–27.

singer in American popular music has crossed as many boundaries as Johnny Cash." He goes on to locate the source of the singer's appeal along these lines:

> Cash was seen as a poet, patriot, preacher, and protestor. He absorbed the images the way black absorbs light. He was all those things—and, by being the sum of them, he became something entirely different. Cash, with his overpowering presence, was large enough to encompass such paradoxes.... Did he contradict himself? Very well then, as Walt Whitman might have said of him, he contradicted himself. He was large. He contained multitudes. He was, after all, Johnny Cash.[40]

Sweeping, democratic American figures like Whitman are the ones that can sustain profoundly equivocating rhetorics. Likewise, writer Nicholas Dawidoff, in his 1997 book on country music, frames Cash in terms of warring personality traits that mirror America.[41] Dawidoff argues that Cash is as much a "piece of Americana" as the objects Cash collected, like "John Wayne's pistol, Frederick Remington's cowboy sculptures, Buddy Holly's motorcycle, and Al Capone's chair."[42] Cash as American folk hero becomes a national collectible. The link critics make between Cash and his country is both thematic and musical. Dawidoff argues that Cash's voice is a metonymy for a certain version of the South: "Lodged somewhere between talk and music, his singing is flat and artless and grim, the way the white poverty-stricken South was flat, artless, and grim."[43]

In yet another posthumous tribute book that interprets Cash through the cultural vocabulary of contradiction, Mikal Gilmore, in the *Rolling Stone* book *Cash*, cites the mid-1980s concert for a conservative audience at Nassau Coliseum in Uniondale, New York, where Cash upheld your right to burn the flag and his right to shoot you for it. Gilmore accounts for this stance by saying Cash:

> was a complicated patriot, and those complications—like the contradictions of the nation itself—never ceased.... It was a statement full of extraordinary twists and turns, genuine pride and dark-humored irony—

---

[40] Mansfield 5–7.

[41] Dawidoff, Nicholas. *In the Country of Country: A Journey to the Roots of American Music*. New York: Vintage, 1998, 169–199.

[42] Dawidoff 169.

[43] Dawidoff 182.

> and only Cash could get away with weaving such disparate stances and affectionate sarcasm together. . . . Cash looked at America the same way he looked at himself: with forthright regrets and unrelenting hope.[44]

Here, Cash explicitly becomes a model for America, and what makes him gripping is his emotional realism and his troubling of binary oppositions.

Gilmore, like others, underscores key moments in Cash's personal and artistic history that embody polar opposites. Gilmore cites Cash's 1969 session and collaboration with Bob Dylan on "Girl From the North Country" for Dylan's *Nashville Skyline* album. This musical meeting of the minds brought together icons of country and rock, melding the supposedly conservative, nostalgic values of the country genre with rock's revolutionary, avant-garde critiques in a collaboration that was somewhat shocking to some audiences at the time. More importantly, from the point of view of American controversies, Gilmore notes Cash's stance on Vietnam and his 1970 visit to Nixon's White House as examples of his complexity.

Indeed, if we look at Cash's oeuvre as a whole, the Vietnam/Nixon issue is a particularly good example of how Cash bucked categorization. Cash supported the office of the president, but also the student protestors against the Vietnam War. He famously supported the students' right to protest in his song "What Is Truth?" (1970) (one of the songs he sang for the Nixon performance).[45] Similarly, his lyrics decry the pile-up of dead soldiers in Vietnam. Invited to the White House, Cash refused to play Nixon's requests: Merle Haggard's "Okie from Muskogee" and Guy Drake's "Welfare Cadillac." He reportedly refused the Drake song berating welfare recipients because he thought it was racist, and headlines gleefully cried that Cash had snubbed Nixon.

Yet in later lyrics and comments, Cash playfully avoids resolving the tension between his patriotism and his social protests. He makes fun of efforts to spot his inconsistencies, ducks any attempt to script him into consistent political positions, and insists on his ability to fashion his own complicated stances. An early version of one of his songs references the Nixon White House incident in order to lampoon standard accounts of it. Satirizing press efforts to pin him down as well as all

---

[44] Fine 43.

[45] John R. Cash, "What is Truth?," copyright John R. Cash, published by Songs of Cash, ASCAP, 1970.

the false mythologies that circulate about him, he jokes that he's never been to prison, knows little about trains, doesn't know why he wears black, and would be happy in a mansion or a shack. He says he will let false stories about him stand, but he'll set reporters straight about the fact that he loves his wife.[46] Cash the speaker expresses his weariness at all the same old questions, all the efforts to defrock his authenticity, criticize his mixture of wealth and folksiness, or his own identity constructions. An early draft of the song references the Nixon White House incident and resists the narrative that he made a forceful critique of Nixon by not playing the requested songs. While the published version of the song omits these lyrics, the original lines seem perverse, contrary to his other public stances on the issue of social protest, counter to his Man in Black outsider persona.

In what seems like an apolitical retreat that deflects any truth claims about him, Cash's lyrics use the White House event as an occasion to critique the process of turning him into an icon. More than that, however, they critique any effort to hold Cash to a resolved, coherent narrative about his life experiences, musical tastes, or how he has expressed his politics. In his autobiography, he similarly performs a double move—he both articulates his politics and insists that no one else can inscribe those politics for him:

> The issue wasn't the songs' messages, which at the time were lightning rods for antihippie and antiblack sentiment, but the fact that I didn't know them and couldn't learn them or rehearse them with the band before we had to leave for Washington. The request had come in too late. If it hadn't, then the issue might have *become* the messages, but fortunately I didn't have to deal with that.[47]

He goes on the record but then again he does not; he resists reporters' accounts but leaves ambivalence in his own version, precisely on the issue of how others are going to frame his actions and beliefs—he claims he did not have to go on record with his politics at the White House, but he leaves open the possibility that he might have. He thus asserts the power to construct himself, and he will do so through paradoxes.

Many reporters have unsuccessfully tried to fashion a clean story for Cash, the same one *Walk the Line* (2005) dramatizes—a redemption

---

[46] John R. Cash, "I'll Say It's True," *House of Cash*, BMI, 1979.

[47] Cash, *Cash* 286. Fine 102.

narrative where he moves from rebel youth druggie to dramatic recovery through the help of God and June Carter. While Cash approved the film's script and sometimes supported this kind of narrative, at other times he did not. Noting how Cash delighted in thwarting reporters, an early biographer, Christopher S. Wren, notes, Cash "has never been able to explain himself," and the star's deflection of easy answers or story arcs "usually sends reporters frustrated to their typewriters."[48] Cash more often kept his own vacillations active. His second autobiography, for example, notes his multiple drug relapses over the years alongside his deep religious faith.

Some journalists actually go so far as to label inauthentic any portrait of Cash that is not about contradiction. In a *New York Times* editorial criticizing the *Walk the Line* film for downplaying Cash's religious faith, Robert Levine notes the new Broadway show based on Cash's music, *Ring of Fire* (2006), itself downplays Cash's bad behavior. Hitting the common note about Cash as contradiction, Levine says perhaps "Cash's life is simply too big for one movie" and "different fans could remember him in different ways." He goes on to argue:

> But he was far too complex a figure to be claimed by either side in the culture wars. Although he was guided by faith, he never cared much for organized religion; he had a sense of himself as deeply flawed, but not beyond hope of redemption. Those contradictions, as much as the compelling story of *Walk the Line*, are what make him fascinating.[49]

Apparently, Cash's projected identity is in the eye of the beholder. But *Walk the Line* and similar biographical narratives do not so much ignore Cash's paradoxes as try to find explanations for them that are ultimately unsatisfying because his ambiguities foil closure.

It is important to note that Cash and his record companies have used this idea of contradiction for marketing, raking in millions of dollars. There is obvious manipulation involved in the idea that he can play to both sides of the aisle. Indeed, the image of him as a category-breaker has been one of the most successful marketing tools producer Rick Rubin and the American Records label have used for him, both before and

---

[48] Wren, Christopher S. *Winners Got Scars Too: The Life of Johnny Cash*. New York: Ballantine, 1971, 6.

[49] Levine, Robert. "Cash Film's Missing Ingredient: Religion," *The New York Times*, 4 March 2006 http://www.nytimes.com/2006/03/04/movies/MoviesFeatures/04cash.html.

after his death. This image of Cash as an artist able to combine distinct cultural traditions into new forms has contributed to his cultural impact and longevity. Claiming him as a murder ballad forefather of the rap artists in his stable, Rubin produced four critically acclaimed albums and a posthumous box set (*Unearthed*), with extant recordings still to be released. Rubin explicitly resurrected the old rebellious Cash from the dusty respectability of his 1980s image, merging the drug-addicted wild man and the respectable father of country music into one paradoxical, Southern gothic image, with stark covers of, for example, Cash in a black longcoat, flanked by a pair of ominous dogs. The *Unearthed* boxed set includes an album of gospel songs alongside his covers of bands like Nine Inch Nails and U2.

But Cash's engagement with contradiction exceeds the logic of the market, because it is deeper than a simple commodity practice. As in his flag comment, he draws out the absurdities and problems inherent in U.S. paradoxes. If he is authentic because he is paradoxical, then Johnny Cash does the cultural work of putting long-running socio-political and cultural contradictions in U.S. culture on the table, putting ideological contradictions on display without resolving them. Cash can both embody the generative energy of cultural mixing, this idea of a Whitmanian figure containing multitudes, as well as the sense of ambivalence and complication some of his boundary crossings provoke.

•

LEIGH H. EDWARDS is assistant professor of English at Florida State University. Her research on U.S. literature and popular culture has appeared in journals such as *Narrative*, *The Journal of Popular Culture*, *Feminist Media Studies*, and *Film and History*. She is currently completing a book on Cash titled *Johnny Cash and American Ambivalence*. Other research in media studies includes a book manuscript, *Reality TV's Family Values: Narrative, Ideology, and New Domestic Forms*. Recent publications include: "Dangerous Minds: The Woman Professor on Television," in *Geek Chic: Smart Women in Popular Culture* (2007), edited by Sherrie A. Inness; "Chasing the Real: Reality Television and Documentary Forms," in *Docufictions: Essays on the Intersection of Documentary and Fictional Filmmaking* (2006), edited by Gary D. Rhodes and John Parris Springer; and "'What a Girl Wants': Gender Norming on Reality Game Shows" (2004) in *Feminist Media Studies*. She has forthcoming articles on PBS's *Frontier House* and frontier mythology, and on interracial romance narratives. A staff writer for *PopMatters*, an international magazine of cultural criticism published online at popmatters.com, she reviews television and film. She has also published a poem on Cash, "Johnny Cash Ode," in *Xconnect: Writers of the Information Age, Volume VII* (Xconnect, print annual, 2005) and in the online journal issue, *CrossConnect* 23 (September 2005). An eighth-generation Floridian, she earned her B.A. from Duke University and her M.A. and Ph.D. from the University of Pennsylvania as a National Mellon Fellow.

Don Cusic

JOHNNY CASH AND C. S. LEWIS

THERE HAVE ONLY BEEN A FEW figures in American Christianity who have occupied the role of *secular* Christians. By that, I mean someone who is a public person not connected to a religious organization, church, or group as a pastor, spokesman, or as an otherwise employed *professional* Christian. This public person must be someone who stands outside the religious world—the Christian sub-culture—and articulates Christianity to both non-believers and believers. Both C. S. Lewis and Johnny Cash have fulfilled that role for American Christianity.

C. S. Lewis has fit the role since the latter half of the twentieth century. He was a university professor, serving first at Oxford, then at Cambridge, a scholar of sixteenth-century literature who rose to the top of his profession. Johnny Cash also rose to the top of his profession as an entertainer, singing songs that became hit recordings, heard on radio, television, and in live concerts.

Lewis was well-known and respected amongst his peers, but his fame in the world-at-large was such that he could walk the streets in relative obscurity and eat a meal in a restaurant without being constantly asked for an autograph. Johnny Cash's fame was such that he could *not* walk the streets in relative obscurity, and if he ventured out in public he was usually besieged by autograph seekers. While Lewis was a public figure during his life, he was not a celebrity; Johnny Cash was both a public figure *and* a celebrity.

On the surface, the two men could not be more different—one a British University professor, the other an American country music singer. Lewis grew up in Northern Ireland, Cash grew up in northeast Arkansas. Lewis spent his professional life in the academic world of universities; Cash went through the School of Hard Knocks and spent his professional life in the world of show business.

There are a few superficial similarities: both served in the Armed Forces—Lewis with the British Army in World War I and Cash with the U.S. Air Force during the Cold War. Both met and married women who became part of their professional as well as personal lives and are essential to understanding them; Joy Davidson for Lewis and June Carter for Johnny Cash.

What binds these two together is their Christian faith and, beyond that, their writings about their faith. Ironically, one of Lewis's most famous books, *Mere Christianity*, and the songs of Johnny Cash both achieved their initial fame when they were heard on the radio.

Johnny Cash and C. S. Lewis lived in two different worlds—the music business and academe—which are, literally, worlds apart. There are different sets of rules that govern each world. For country music it is the fight for fortune and fame through hit recordings and the creation of stars. In academe it is the fight for promotion and tenure through teaching and the publication of academic articles. Success is defined in country music in terms of celebrity with the public at large; in academe *success* tends to be defined by the respect from those within your profession. This leads to an inherent contradiction; if academics achieve public celebrity in the world at large they are likely to receive the scorn of their peers who deem such worldly success a betrayal of academic rigor, discipline, and principles. There might also be a hint of jealousy involved, as well.

There is an inherent snobbishness amongst academics. Most simply don't believe the world-at-large is capable of understanding their research and writings because, frankly, academics feel they're smarter than people in the general populace who are not academics.

This was a dilemma that C. S. Lewis faced. Yes, he was a respected scholar within the worlds of Oxford and Cambridge, but many of his books, *The Chronicles of Narnia*, *The Screwtape Letters*, and others, were popular with the general reading public. This tended to lower Lewis in the eyes of his academic rivals.

There is a contrary view residing within the world of country music, which is, basically, the music of the white working class. These are folks who have traditionally considered themselves "poor but proud," lacking in "book learning," but filled with "common sense." This leads to anti-intellectualism within the world of country music, a brazen stand against the notion of education in favor of intuition and instinct guiding a person's life.

In short, just as many in the academic world tend to look down their noses at country music, many of those in country music tend to distrust those in the academic world, feeling that academics don't really live on the same planet as the working-class folks. Also, the working-class is often confronted with what seems to be hare-brained ideas emanating from professors employed by institutions of higher education.

And yet the worlds of academe and country music each have a certain appeal for one another. Many in the academic world seem to find country music exotic and a source of interesting study; those in country music see the academic world as one of prestige and respect and hold it somewhat in awe.

American Christianity has its own set of rules and contradictions. At the dawn of the twenty-first century it seems that American Christianity is divided into two large camps: the *fundamentalists*, who by and large attend independent or non-denominational churches, and the established churches of mainstream denominations such as the Methodists, Episcopalians, and Catholics. There are countless contradictions and exceptions to that statement; for example, the Southern Baptists tend to be fundamentalists within a denomination, while the Catholic versus Protestant division, which is certainly still alive, has been blurred by the fact that there are fundamentalists within the Catholic Church.

In general, American Christianity holds the common beliefs of Jesus as the son of God, the Holy Spirit as the voice or messenger of God, and the Bible as the word of God. Having said that, these common beliefs ignite countless arguments concerning intensity of belief, interpretation of faith, and the role of religion in everyday life. Those arguments will not be pursued here. However, it is generally accepted that the fundamentalists, as they are generally referred to (or, in some cases, *right-wing fundamentalists*) are quite intense in their faith and fairly narrow in their beliefs.

What makes this particularly relevant in this article is that both C. S. Lewis, who was an Anglican (or Episcopal in American terms) and attended a mainstream church with a liturgy, and Johnny Cash, have been embraced by fundamentalists. Although Cash, who was a Baptist (although he attended several different fundamentalist churches), has generally not been embraced as warmly as Lewis.

In fundamentalist churches, religious emotionalism tends to be valued more than intellectual heft in presenting the faith. There is even a strong strain of anti-intellectualism in fundamentalist churches, with the opposition to the teaching of evolution a prime example. The emotionalism of Protestant fundamentalism also manifests itself in the music played in churches.

While the Anglican Church sings old hymns—often difficult to hum—the American independent churches tend to use contemporary music, rock, pop, and country, to get their message across. C. S. Lewis never really liked music in church. For Johnny Cash, music was a key to his religion. As he noted in his autobiography, *Man in Black*, "To me, songs were the telephone to heaven, and I tied up the line quite a bit" (28).

C. S. Lewis was, in many ways, a typical British academic. He wore tweed coats and smoked a pipe. His great pleasures were intellectual—where truth is pursued in probing questions, not in pre-selected definitive answers—and he found his great comforts to be reading books or having a pint of ale in a pub with friends. Throughout most of his life, his conversations with friends were on academic subjects—mythology, literature, philosophy—and they all enjoyed mental games. Ironically, in some ways, Lewis was the antithesis of the American Protestant fundamentalists who now embrace him.

Johnny Cash was a typical country artist, but with an un-typical career. He wrote and recorded songs, hoping each would be played on the radio. He toured, performing in a variety of venues for audiences, and life on the road was a normal way of life. Cash dressed in stage clothes and his great comforts were musical—jamming with friends and swapping songs. His conversations were often about music and the music business. Although he seemed to do everything possible to destroy his career, at the time of his death he was voted the Greatest Country Music Artist in the history of the genre by CMT (Country Music Television). As for his religion, although his lifestyle during his early career led him away from the church, the basic Bible-belt beliefs of fundamentalist faith never left him.

Although it looks like the worlds of Johnny Cash and C. S. Lewis are worlds apart, upon closer examination there are numerous similarities between the two, primarily their Christian faith, which was expressed in autobiographies that documented their spiritual journeys, creative works (songs and fiction) that center on their faith, and a public life where they exhibited their Christianity to all the world.

The book by C. S. Lewis which became *Mere Christianity*, a definitive work on Christianity from Lewis's perspective, began as three separate sets of lectures: the first "The Case for Christianity," broadcast over the BBC in 1943; the second "Christian Behaviour," broadcast in 1943; and then "Beyond Personality," broadcast in 1945. In the preface to his book, Lewis writes, "I was not writing to expound something I could call 'my religion,' but to expound mere Christianity" (7).

Neither Lewis nor Cash trained as theologians, and yet millions heard or read theology from each of them. In his autobiography, *Man in Black*, Cash writes, "Telling others is part of our faith all right, but the way we live it speaks louder than we can say it. The gospel of Christ must always be an open door with a welcome sign for all" (33). He adds, about his life, "I was working toward what I was put in this world to do: entertain people; be something worthwhile to them; be an example; be a good influence; stand strong; don't compromise" (244).

C. S. Lewis confronted his Christian faith and presented it to the world in letters, conversations, articles, and books, attempting to explain his faith to a mostly unbelieving world. In a world of intellectuals, the faith of Lewis baffled those who felt they had no need for Christianity or any other religion. In the population at large, many people also rationalized an *I'm okay, you're okay* type of personal belief, which dimmed the appeal of Christianity.

In *Mere Christianity* Lewis confronted this attitude, noting:

> Christianity tells people to repent and promises them forgiveness. It therefore has nothing (as far as I know) to say to people who do not know they have done anything to repent of and who do not feel that they need any forgiveness. It is after you have realised that there is a real Moral Law, and a Power behind the law, and that you have broken that law and put yourself wrong with that Power—it is after all this, and not a moment sooner, that Christianity begins to talk. When you know you are sick, you will listen to the doctor (38–39).

Cash echoed this sentiment, stating about his early musical career, which was filled with drugs and the perks of stardom—easy sex and worshipful fans:

> To repent and reform all the way to righteousness requires a man to first recognize and admit he has been all wrong. To make such a change as I needed, and to be able to say, "I'm going to be right from now on," I was also required to say, "I've been all wrong up to now." And I didn't care to admit that (109).

Johnny Cash hit bottom because of his addiction to drugs; his personal life was in shambles and his professional life was in trouble. Ultimately, Cash pulled himself out of this abyss and gained valuable insight when he did. Cash states:

> The hard times, the torture and misery I put myself through made me know pain and gave me tolerance and compassion for other people's problems and understanding of their many differences and shortcomings. But the greatest lesson I learned was—God is love (19).

Lewis also had compassion for those who fell short of the demands of life, stating, "A Christian is not a man who never goes wrong, but a man who is enabled to repent and pick himself up and begin over again after each stumble—because the Christ-life is inside him, repairing him all the time" (64). Cash echoed this sentiment in his autobiography, stating:

> God is love and God is forgiving. He'll forgive you seventy times seven and seventy times that. He is long-suffering, patient, compassionate, and He understands even before you try to explain your weaknesses and shortcomings to Him. When you stand with Him, you must renew the stand daily; you must daily be on guard. The hounds of hell are not going to stop snapping at your heels. The devil and his demons aren't going to give up on you as long as they can find a vulnerable spot once in awhile (179).

Lewis could have been profiling the life of Johnny Cash when he wrote, "The better stuff a creature is made of—the cleverer and stronger and freer it is—then the better it will be if it goes right, but also the worse it will be if it goes wrong" (53). Lewis added:

> Fallen man is not simply an imperfect creature who needs improvement: he is a rebel who must lay down his arms. Laying down your arms, surrendering, saying you are sorry, realising that you have been on the wrong track and getting ready to start life over again from the ground floor—that is the only way out of a "hole" (59).

Cash himself states:

> The truth falls hard and heavy: If you're going to be a Christian, you're going to change. You're going to lose some old friends, not because you want to, but because you need to. You can't compromise some things. You have to draw the line daily—the line between what you were and what you're trying to be now—or you lose even their respect (21).

C. S. Lewis believed strongly that a Christian should be a member of a church, that an essential element of the Christian life was fellowship with other believers. Not only does this help the believer strengthen and sustain his own faith, this fellowship serves as a beacon of light, a magnet of the faith for non-believers outside the faith. "Men are mirrors, or 'carriers' of Christ to other men," writes Lewis.

> Sometimes unconscious carriers. This "good infection" can be carried by those who have not got it themselves. People who were not Christians themselves helped me to Christianity. But usually it is those who know Him that bring Him to others. That is why the Church, the whole body of Christians showing Him to one another, is so important (163).

This view is affirmed by Cash, who stopped going to church when his life became one of making numerous personal appearances, traveling constantly, and living full-time in the world of show business. In his autobiography, Cash confesses:

> My policy of aloneness and severed fellowship from other committed Christians would weaken me spiritually. Not that missing church necessarily meant missing God. It was just that Jesus never meant for us to try and make it on your own. There is something so important in worshiping together with other believers. And missing it would leave me vulnerable and easy prey for all the temptations and destructive vices that the backstage of the entertainment world has to offer (87).

Comparing songs to books is, in a sense, like comparing apples and oranges. A song has to capture what it is going to say in about three minutes; a book has much more room to make its point. A song is heard; a book is read. Having said that, let's compare the beliefs Cash expressed in some of the songs he wrote—his primary outlet—with what Lewis wrote in *Mere Christianity*.

In his book, Lewis addresses the hypocrisy in Christians as well as the failure of Christians to live a fully Christian life, stating, "[W]e have failed to practice ourselves the kind of behaviour we expect from other people," and, "[A] great many things have gone wrong with the world that God made and that God insists, and insists very loudly, on our putting them right again" (20, 45).

There is a segment of American Christianity that promotes a housebroken Jesus, a kind-hearted, smiling, easygoing Savior who is everybody's best friend, or at least the best friend of anyone who calls on Him. But there is another side to God and Jesus, as anyone who has witnessed a violent storm or a human terror can attest. In *Mere Christianity* Lewis writes, "God is the only comfort, He is also the supreme terror; the thing we most need and the thing we most want to hide from. He is our only possible ally, and we have made ourselves His enemies" (38).

Cash addressed this topic in several songs toward the end of his life. He painted a vocal picture of a God who makes harsh decisions about the actions of believers and non-believers alike. This version of Cash's God doled out justice and blame in deliberate doses.

In the end, for both Lewis and Cash, Christianity is a forward-looking religion, a religion that looks toward better days in earthly lives as well as the life after a life on Earth. In his book Lewis states, "Hope . . . means that a continual looking forward to the eternal world is not (as some modern people think) a form of escapism or wishful thinking, but one of the things a Christian is meant to do" (118). Cash also took this thoughtful approach to Christianity in his writing, presenting a glorious Heaven open to all.

C. S. Lewis sums up Christianity this way: "We are told that Christ was killed for us, that His death has washed out our sins, and that by dying He disabled death itself. That is the formula. That is Christianity. That is what has to be believed" (58). Cash held similar beliefs, singing of the redemptive powers of Christ's death.

Few men live past their time; few names and lives are remembered through the ages. Two of those rare beings are Johnny Cash and C. S. Lewis. In terms of a great life lived, filled with words and deeds which impact millions of people as well as an impact that lasts past their time on earth, it is more important that God believes in a person rather than if that person believes in God. By that I mean there are only a few chosen for this role while most are not; some are called for a life above and beyond what most mortals live. Johnny Cash and C. S. Lewis were two humans who were so called.

The message is clear: God certainly believed in both C. S. Lewis and Johnny Cash.

•

DON CUSIC is the author of fourteen books, including *Johnny Cash: The Songs*. As an author, teacher, historian, musician, songwriter, and executive, Cusic has been actively involved in the music business since 1973. He is currently professor of music business at Belmont University in Nashville. In addition to the book on Cash, Cusic is the author of the biography *Eddy Arnold: I'll Hold You In My Heart*; an encyclopedia of cowboys, *Cowboys and the Wild West: An A–Z Guide from the Chisholm Trail to the Silver Screen*; *The Sound of Light: A History of Gospel and Christian Music*; *The Cowboy Way: The Amazing True Adventures of Riders in the Sky*; *Music in the Market*, *Poet of the Common Man: Merle Haggard Lyrics*; *Willie Nelson: Lyrics 1959–1994*; and *Hank Williams: The Complete Lyrics*.

Works Cited

Cash, Johnny. *Man in Black: His Own Story in His Own Words*. Grand Rapids, MI: Zondervan Publishing House, 1975.

Cusic, Don. *Johnny Cash: The Songs*. New York: Thunder's Mouth Press, 2004.

Lewis, C. S. *Mere Christianity*. New York: Macmillan Publishing Co., Inc. 1943, 1945, 1952, 1960, 1978.

Laurel Snyder

NOTHIN' SHORT OF DYIN' HALF AS LONESOME AS THE SOUND

THE LAST TIME I SAW JOHNNY CASH was the first time I saw Johnny Cash—and he didn't look good, but he sounded like home. I lived in Iowa then, in the middle of the cornfields, where country music was the only music that felt right. I took a trip to Nashville, a much-needed vacation.

This all happened in 2002, which was not an especially good year in my life—full as it was with too much drinking, bad boyfriends, the end of my life as a full-time student, and the worst winter the Midwest had seen in decades—but it had nice moments.

I worked in a diner—a real greasy spoon—and the morning shift was full of what we waitresses called "The Porridge Club." Older farmers, now farmless, in Carharts and John Deere hats, who talked about the price of soy and sow-bellies, ate oatmeal with extra sugar, drank black coffee, and listened to Johnny Cash. Some of them thought I was cute, and some of them thought I was crazy, but every morning I woke up with The Porridge Club, just as every night I closed the bar down with the punk-rock kids who (like me) depended on twenty-five-cent draft beers for a good time, and who, incidentally, also loved Johnny Cash.

The punk kids loved Cash so much so that they'd plug the juke box—fifty cents a song—and forgo two whole drinks, just to wallow in the gravel of that low, low voice. Despite the fact that country music was, they told me, "fucking stupid."

But back to the diner, where I listened each morning, with ears bred on Bob Dylan and Leonard Cohen, to talk of sow-bellies and country music. I had the ears of an East Coaster, who up until that time had only enjoyed fiddles and banjos for the kitsch-factor, or maybe with a sense of false nostalgia for an era I'd never really known. But now here I was living amid farms and farmers, surrounded on all sides by green in spring and summer, gold in fall, and white in winter. Surrounded also by people who lived without healthcare, who lived *with* rampant alcoholism, in blue jeans bought at Sears.

There wasn't any kitsch in the diner at 7 A.M., in the bacon grease or the cholesterol levels that accompanied the bacon grease, in the trucks that needed a jump start on a daily basis, or in the worn pictures of children now grown and gone. There wasn't any kitsch in the lives of these men who joined me every day, but as a soundtrack for those years, country was all there could be. I had to redefine this music for myself if I wanted to live where I was living. If I wanted to be who I'd become.

I can't pretend I ever really related to those men, since I was (and still basically am) me. I don't know how to understand myself if I can't be honest—if I can't paint my own caricature clearly. As a writer, it's unfair to describe others if I can't describe myself—then and now.

Who am I? I'm an overeducated woman, who buys organic milk and drives a foreign car. I pay too much for haircuts and don't change my own oil. And while I was poorer in 2002 than I am today, I was basically the same girl back then, just a few years younger and a few pounds slimmer. I still smoked.

It wasn't as if I'd fallen on truly hard times, gotten knocked up, or searched for a husband to take me away from the roofers and farmers I served. Or looking among the roofers and farmers for a way *out* of the diner. Sometimes I felt like that, like *that* girl, but it was never true. I was always playing a role. And even if that had been the case, I'd still have been me: Jewish, raised in Baltimore by two teachers, a reader of academic poetry. Even if I'd ever become *that* girl, I'd have eventually outgrown her, and whatever poor diner patron she'd managed to sucker. I can't lie—I was never authentic. My tight jeans were always a costume.

And as such—in all my privileged glory, I cringed to hear The Porridge Club discuss politics—blacks, guns, liberals, and hippies. I hated the way they stared at my ass. One man had a swastika carved into his arm, but he was nice to me, so I just bit my tongue and brought him his bacon. These men were different from me, a new experience. They would have scared my grandmother.

To say that I understood The Porridge Club in any substantial way would be false. I may be occasionally ridiculous, or petty, or pretentious, but I try not to lie. Whatever our differences, the fact remained: I *was* a waitress, and I *was* broke. As such, I was not beyond sharing an experience. For those years I was financially dependent on the kindness of all kinds of strangers, on their one-dollar tips. Just like them, I didn't have healthcare or job security. I shopped at Sears, too. Who was I to judge?

All of this to say that I realize I never knew Cash like The Porridge Club knew Cash, or like the punk-rock kids. All this to say that I understand it would be dishonest to pretend I was ever "one of them," since my own poverty felt temporary to me. I had to believe it would end—and real despair requires a sense of permanence in hardship. But still, for those years I drank nightly, woke with the sun to put the coffee on, shook off my whiskey, counted my pennies, and spent a great deal of my time with men who lived that way, and would forever. So it was.

So it was that I lived and listened. We'd all sit and sip our coffee, listening to the words of "Sunday Morning Coming Down," echoing through the diner. So it was that I'd listen and think. Until one morning, coming down myself, coming down hard, after a particularly rough night and a worse day-before, left by a man I should never have met in the first place. *Left*, as in, *driven away from*. As in, *abandoned for the open road and countless other women. Driven* in all senses of the word. By a guy who—when he drove his cab on the nightshift, sometimes let the drunken girls kiss him on the way home from the college bars and frat parties. By a guy I forgave regularly for kissing the drunken girls who climbed into his cab. That morning, after he finally left me for good, I was no longer thinking. Instead I was feeling, and maybe humming, and for the first time I really *got* the music. I got it on the *inside*.

Of course, the man who left now lives deep in my past, where most of the regrettable pieces of my life reside, and I'm a happy person again. But that feeling of *getting it on the inside* lasted. Over the years that followed, country music became an important part of my life. Even now, it ripples through each day. I've become an occasional music critic, writing specifically for publications that cover country music, and in fact, the first essay I ever published was about loving the steel guitar, hearing the steel guitar as poetry.

I began line dancing without irony. I met the *man who became my husband* at a country rock show, where he was working the soundboard. He still plays bass in such a band, and together we visit Nashville, Knoxville, and Austin. Together we live in the south, where country music is all around us.

But years before we were married, and years after the morning I was left by that other—lesser, regrettable—man, we went to Tennessee, the *man who would become my husband* and I, to attend the American Music Association's annual conference and awards ceremony. I took a few days off from my life at the diner, which was coming to an end anyway, as I rose out of that bleak phase of my life. There I saw Johnny Cash perform, with June and other members of the Cash-Carter clan. He looked like hell, but sounded like heaven to me.

We were there because we could be, because we needed a vacation, and we'd heard the music was going to be good. We'd come to see the Bottle Rockets and Grey DeLisle. A rumor circulated around town that Emmylou Harris would play an unannounced set. I even ran into Emmylou in the bathroom, where she looked as beautiful as she ever does, but oddly out of place, drying her hands on a paper towel with her silver hair gleaming under the fluorescent lights.

But nobody had said we'd get to see Johnny Cash. Nothing could have prepared me for such an experience. In my mind, Johnny Cash was a myth. He was a voice that came out of the radio, a vestigial limb from a more brutal, more honest era. The possibility of seeing Johnny was something that had just never occurred to me—like the possibility of seeing a caveman or a Founding Father. Cash was the stuff of PBS documentaries, not a real-live human being.

Suddenly though, he appeared onstage in the flesh. Fleshy... too much sad and tired flesh. Looking like a truck so old that you give up on it, park it under a tree, and plant flowers in the engine cavity. But he was singing, like a truck with flowers in the engine, rolling down the interstate at seventy miles per hour.

Cash sang with June, and then suddenly a handful of other family members, too. I think Carlene was there, and some faces I didn't know, and everyone sang. I stood fixated on Johnny Cash, who—true to myth—sounded like Johnny Cash, sounded like the radio on a frozen morning in Iowa when the windows are steaming up and the oatmeal is bubbling on the stove at the back of the diner. His voice rang out unchanged and unwavering, despite his body, which I could tell was dying, and his labored breath.

They sang, he and June, later joined onstage by the whole family. The crowd joined in. The whole family, including Emmylou, Buddy Miller, Rodney Crowell, Kris Kristofferson, and all the many, many people who, with their varying degrees of fame and success, could not believe it anymore than me. They were singing with Johnny Cash. Singing with Johnny Cash. Fucking Johnny Cash. The whole room singing.

Bear in mind that this happened at an awards ceremony. So we were all sitting oddly upright and sober, at formal round tables, on stiff and expensive folding chairs. It was a strange place to experience a legend. There were ugly centerpieces and nametags, many men wore suits, while others had on the traditional country uniform of blue jeans and cowboy hats. We all sat with strangers.

My table was full of hipsters, indie musicians representing the new voices of acoustic country music who, in their vintage western-wear finery, wept openly. People all over the room were weeping at Johnny—at seeing him and hearing him. His low voice rising from a face so bloated and old, a face about to fold in on itself. June was a disaster too, straggly and smiling. If you'd seen her at a bus stop without knowing who she was, you'd have looked the other way.

But the love between them was another constant. Johnny loved his fat, tuneless wife, and when I saw that, I thought of The Porridge Club, of Iowa farmwives, of the man who'd left me, and the man beside me, and I started crying, too. Crying and singing with Johnny. I stood up. Everyone did.

Living in Iowa, waking up with the farmers and going to bed with the punk-rock kids from the bar, my days both began and ended with Johnny Cash. I didn't think about it much back then, but when I returned from Nashville, I couldn't shake the idea.

It was clear why The Porridge Club loved Johnny Cash as they did, since it was the music of their era—of Sun records and A.M. radio, girls who set their hair in rollers and kissed, and then pretended to be virgins. But suddenly it seemed important to me to figure out why the punk-rock kids loved him, too. I felt like it was something to understand.

Why did the green-haired and tattooed grill cook I worked with—who later lost his leg to blood poisoning and an amputation—love Johnny so much, despite his disdain for all my other CDs, John Prine, Buck

Owens, and Marty Robbins among them? We fought daily over what to listen to when we closed the diner down. He hated country music, hated banjos and fiddles, hated anything the least bit folksy, hated religion and gospel— "fuckin self-righteous fuckers," he would say—but Johnny Cash didn't count. He was the only bridge we ever found, my grill cook and I.

It wasn't just that the punk-rock kids didn't *like* country music. They *hated* country music. They loved to hate it, took pleasure in their hatred, smiled as they spat at it, and laughed at it, at me, once I came to love it so. Their universal mantra: *Fucking redneck bullshit.... Fucking dumbass hicks.* They teased me for my line-dancing, but there was something about Johnny that was different. What was it?

Despair, lack of healthcare, whiskey...there was just something about Johnny Cash, something deeper and sadder and harder, with a little bit of a death rattle, and a little bit of faith. Prison inmates love Johnny Cash, and veterans of foreign wars do, too, as they attempt to snap along with missing fingers. Men love Johnny Cash as they leave the women they love, and women love Johnny Cash, before and after they've been left. There was just something about Johnny Cash that rose above the genre distinctions. When he sang it, he meant it, and that meant a lot. To the farmers and the punk-rock kids, and when I was down, to me, too.

Despair isn't just a cliché, an over-the-top stereotype—poverty and lack of education and fear of illness and the desire for something good. Despair is God and the devil, in hand-to-hand combat. Despair is frustration and acceptance and the inevitable belief in both. Despair. It's a condition, a way of life. Most of us end up there at some point.

Despite what I thought I knew from my years in Iowa, I'm pretty sure I don't really understand Johnny Cash. I'm just too comfortable at most moments to come anywhere close. But his music and his life have been powerful enough to show me, as a foreign tragedy might, just how little I comprehend of what it is I'm drawn to. I may not ever know Johnny Cash, but I'm pretty damn sure that there's something huge in him I'll never quite get. I choose to believe in that—in the greatness of the thing I can't quite grasp.

The truth is that I've never fallen into a ring of fire, but in his gospel and his heresy, Johnny Cash makes me wish I could—makes the ring of fire enviable. Maybe The Porridge Club, and the punk kids, too, sense that envy and feel envied. Maybe that's important. What else can I say?

That ring of fire looks good from where I'm standing, however far off I may be.

•

LAUREL SNYDER is the editor of *Half/Life: Jew-ish Tales from Interfaith Homes* (Soft Skull Press 2006), and the author of *Daphne and Jim: A choose your own adventure biography in verse* (Burnside Review Press) and a forthcoming book for children, *Inside the Slidy Diner* (Tricycle Press). She also edits the award-winning Webzine Killingthebuddha.com, and her country music writing has appeared in *No Depression*, *Harp*, *Paste*, and the *UTNE Reader*. She lives in Atlanta, and is online at JewishyIrishy.com.

Alison Stine

RING OF FIRE: LOVE AND LONGING

I WAS TRYING NOT TO TAKE THE world at face value.

But everything was breaking. My computer, my car keys, the ceiling fan, the front door. I was twenty-five and living in rural Pennsylvania, in love with one man who lied to me, and another one who didn't. I had a bad feeling I couldn't shake. I felt jumpy, like a stretched wire. I kicked the front door when the lock stuck, when it refused to open in, blistered with humidity. I said aloud, *What do you want from me?* I might have aimed at the sky.

It was August. A heat index of 100. Five or more minutes waiting to cross the street because of truck traffic, watching the tar bubbles on the asphalt rise. I could not throw myself into work, my writing, because it was too hot to work. I would have braided my hair into chains. I would have worn a red handkerchief on top across my chest, that and only that. I would have driven all night to him. Or to him. I would have.

What calms me has always been walking, playing music and walking, listening to music, but sometimes even that won't work. Sometimes, like that day, I cannot find the right song from the hundreds of songs. There are too many. There are iPods and downloads and mixed CDs and samples that bring too much music to us, all kinds, all choices and keys and degrees of newness and different-ness and sameness and moods.

Then I realized, not one of the new ones, one of the old: Johnny Cash.

Only Johnny would calm me. Only Johnny understood right then, that moment, whatever that moment was. In my case: the dying corn, crossing the railroad tracks, the storm. How? Because he was there. He wasn't there, but he could have been easily, how easily, substituting the fields for the fields, the storm for the storm. The heartache for the heartache.

It was that real.

Everyone has that friend, the one you call at three in the morning and expect to come, the one that will come, the one that doesn't mind if you're crying and drunk and rolling on the floor, that doesn't yell at you, that doesn't judge, that drops her plans, that picks up a bottle in a brown sack, and the buzzer rings and she's there.

I have been that person. I have dropped my plans. I have woken up at once. I have come, to him and to him. But sometimes even that person needs someone else. I needed him to come, Johnny, the Man in Black. I needed someone to come, crystallize from the fields, become leather, become flesh. And he did not.

The dream was a city. The dream was a stage. The dream was windows and leaving them behind. There were two windows together in a corner of my childhood bedroom on the second floor. Kneeling between them, I could see the neighbor's peaked roof, and stars beyond. There was not a trellis, but an old TV tower rusted to the side of the house, spackled with ivy. I could climb it, slip in and out of my window. No one would know.

I did climb it. No one knew.

The dream changed as I grew: became hill, became country. Strike that, reverse it. It changed again, became mountain, became woods. Became more specific. On the mountain, we sat on the porch and drank wine in jelly jars, my friends and I, and someone was up on the deck, and I wanted to be the one up on the deck. The moon cracked open. We danced on the rug.

People did this, I thought to myself. People built houses, built decks just to lie on summer nights. That's enough. That's fine. I wasn't cold. I wasn't cold.

Driving home from that party through the black woods and gray roads, three to a car, the least drunk in front, our headlights caught a leaping fawn. The day before, I had almost walked into a snake as it curled up in the cut grass in the path before me.

I kept interrupting nature with everything I did.

Still, I was sometimes amazed at the way it worked out, like earlier in the bright aisles of the grocery store with $117 in cash and a list of liquids to buy with it: two cases of beer, as much wine as I could, some not bad, if possible. I was once in love with a star chef who brought home bottles. I was amazed I remembered what he had taught me: this is drinkable, this is not, this is the right year, the hostess will like this one. Even with snacks for the long car ride into the mountains, we came out within a dollar to spare.

I knew some things still.

I wanted to learn more. I wanted to go back, to learn the ancient languages, how to can fruits, how to grow them. I wanted suddenly, in the liquor-store parking lot, looking up, to re-learn the names of the stars, their stories, the moon phases, memorize how to make good soup, memorize the old histories, memorize the worn lyrics to Dylan and Springsteen and Johnny Cash songs, always I wanted a way back.

I wanted to know him—know something—by heart other than my heart.

Like many things, I came to him late.

In fall of 2003, I was eating breakfast in my house in Michigan. The windows were open, the cats were in the windows. I turned on the television. For some reason, it was turned to a music channel, and for some even rarer reason, they were showing videos. I saw a music video: an old man sitting at a table, playing a piano, a guitar, a big house, a closed-down museum, a smashed record, lemons, a fish full of flies, a beautiful woman.

The song was "Hurt," and the man was Johnny Cash.

I started to cry. It was instant and physical. The song and its sepia images prickled the skin on my arms, sharpened the skin on my neck. My heart sliced open. There were rings on his heavy knuckles, wine sloshed over the table.

I turned off the television and switched on the radio. I heard the news.

I ran down the hill without a coat to the store where my boyfriend, a musician, worked.

Johnny Cash died, I said. Johnny Cash died.

Johnny Cash was born in Arkansas. His older brother died in childhood. He listened to the radio and sang in church. On a school trip to the Grand Ole Opry, he saw former child star June Carter, and told his friends he was going to marry her. He joined the Air Force at eighteen, and four years later, married a girl he had met at the roller rink before he shipped out. Overseas, he started writing songs. Upon his return, he worked as a door-to-door salesman.

What he said, when homeowners opened the door, was: "Hi. I'm JR Cash."

He formed a band made up of two auto mechanics, auditioned for Sam Phillips, and got a deal. His first tour was with Elvis Presley, Jerry Lee Lewis, and June Carter. He met her backstage at the Grand Ole Opry when he was tuning his guitar. He got down on his knees and asked her to marry him.

Both were married to other people at the time.

He was addicted to amphetamines, tranquilizers, and pain killers. He was arrested for possession. He got divorced once; June divorced twice. He was attacked by an ostrich. He tried to kill himself by crawling into a cave. He found religion. He recorded a live album in a prison. He took out an ad in *Billboard* after he won a Grammy which featured a full page picture of him with his middle finger raised.

These are facts.

He was the first rock 'n' roll star, before Elvis. Unlike Elvis, he lived. He did not die on a bathroom floor. He did not die of a drug overdose. He lived, which is much, much harder.

He was father or stepfather to seven children: six daughters and one son. He asked June Carter to marry him, onstage, in 1968, and she said yes. They were together more than thirty years until her death in 2003. He followed her a few months later.

And I?

I grew up wanting. I grew up in Georgia. I grew up, years later, a girl without heroes. I found them as a young adult. I found them in a poet who grew up in a factory town, and a pianist who had been raped, and a songwriter who lived. James Wright, Tori Amos, Johnny Cash, a motley crew.

My heroes lived, and the things they wrote, lived, and I want to live. I don't want to write a good poem. I don't want to write a good story. The world has enough good things. Pretty is not enough. Nice is not enough. It must be life or death. It must change. It must be a way to survive, to save. And live, and live.

You have five minutes. What are you going to say?

I am going to say this.

Nothing comes.

Sometimes I wish I smoked, like tonight. It's evening already, dark. I hate smoke. I'm a young woman, and I hate it, the smell, the staleness. I'm allergic to it. I don't want it, really. What I want is stillness. What I want is space. What I want is sitting, no questions, the time alone, the time. No one questions a woman smoking, slumped against a step. No one wonders what she is thinking, but she must be thinking, sitting there.

What will *people* think? I asked my boyfriend on one of many days when he dropped me off in the middle of nowhere to write, the mountains, the wilderness, because I wouldn't do it otherwise, wouldn't work in the house with its entrances and exits and TV and lights.

A woman alone *with* a notebook?

You have to stop *worrying* about what people think, he said.

No one would bother if I had ash in my hand instead of a pencil.

I forgot to mention: Muzak was invented in 1954. Then Johnny Cash came on the scene.

I forgot to mention: when Johnny Cash came on the scene, "How Much is that Doggy in the Window?" was the number one song on the radio.

Merle Haggard was in the front row of Cash's Folsom Prison concert. After the show, every man wanted to play the guitar. Every man wanted to play the guitar, but I wanted to play piano. I wanted to be an actress, then a singer, then a dancer. I wanted.

I forgot to mention, I am eating a Pink Lady apple. I am eating a Pink Lady apple instead of smoking, my placeholder, my space.

Leave me alone, I am a woman swallowing.

Leave me alone, I am a woman thinking thoughts. I am a woman who came after a man, and I am not nearly as brave as that man, but I have loved two lives and ruined my life already and begun again, and I am here, here with time, here to start again, here to say something. If I could, I would sit on the back steps and listen to the rain turn to ice. If I could, I would stand out in the cold. I would have a small flame to keep me warm. I have a small flame to keep me warm and it is called this, this thing I do, this speech, this hope, this song inside, inheritance. It doesn't burn.

•

ALISON STINE is the author of a poetry chapbook, *Lot of my Sister* (Kent State University Press, 2001), winner of the Wick Prize. Her poetry and prose have appeared in *The Paris Review*, *The Kenyon Review*, *Poetry*, *The Antioch Review*, *Tin House*, *The Beloit Poetry Journal*, *Gulf Coast*, *Black Warrior Review*, *Crab Orchard Review*, *Fugue*, *Hayden's Ferry Review*, and others. Her awards include scholarships from the Bread Loaf Writers' Conference, an Academy of American Poets Prize, and two Pushcart Prize nominations. Formerly the Emerging Writer at Gettysburg College, she is currently a Wallace Stegner Fellow at Stanford University, where she is completing her first novel.

Edward J. Rielly

SAUL (AND CASH) ON THE ROAD TO DAMASCUS: *THE MAN IN WHITE*

JOHNNY CASH WAS A STORYTELLER. He told many stories in song, stories of love, death, violence, country life, the alienated and forsaken, and, of course, religious faith. Cash told these stories in lyrics he composed and in songs written by others that he made very much his own. He also told his life story at considerable length, twice, first in *Man in Black*, and then later, and at greater length, in *Johnny Cash: The Autobiography*, which he wrote with Patrick Carr. These stories are well known to Cash fans.

Not so well known, though, is the novel *Man in White*, but it should be, both for its own sake and because of what it tells readers about its author. It is unusual to find a singer writing a novel, but the story of Saul, now known as Paul, the author of the New Testament Epistles bearing his name, is more than a novelty, even if its author claims in the introduction that he has no status as a novelist. Cash is, however, a storyteller, which seems enough, if one tells a story well and at some length, to qualify as a novelist. As Cash writes, "I found a story to tell in those few verses [the biographical details about Paul found in the Bible] and the story I tell around those verses is my own" (8).

When Cash says that the story is his own, he means, first, that he has made up much of the narrative. However, the story of Saul becoming Paul is also the story of Johnny Cash on his way to Damascus, or, more literally, on his lifelong struggle to find his spiritual way. The novel is one of three lengthy attempts by Cash over three decades to chronicle his spiritual journey. The first, *Man in Black*, from the 1970s, Cash acknowledges to be a "spiritual odyssey" (13). *Johnny Cash: The Autobiography*, written in the 1990s, takes the story further and presents it in greater autobiographical context, but the heart of the account remains Cash's spiritual struggle. *Man in White* comes between the two, in the 1980s.

Johnny Cash did not live his spiritual life in secret. He increasingly sang and talked about it. Cash publicly declared his life as a Christian and commitment to God on his television show, *The Johnny Cash Show*, on November 18, 1970 (*Autobiography* 274–75). He also wrote about it. Sharing was a way of testifying to the truth as he saw it.

In the prefatory "Personal Note" to *Man in Black*, he thanks friends and fans for living the story with him and expresses the belief that "if only one person turns to God through the story which I tell, it will all have been worthwhile" (13). Similarly, in the introduction to the novel, he writes, "by novelization of the activity and reality surrounding a tiny grain of truth, great truths can be illuminated and activated" (8). His purpose is surely much humbler that Milton's in *Paradise Lost*, where the poet offers to "justify the ways of God to men" (I, 26). For Cash, God's ways are obviously right and need no justification or defense. The onus is on humans to study, pray, and struggle toward the right; sharing one's personal story, though, may encourage others in their struggles.

The idea for *Man in White* came to Cash as he completed the last in a series of correspondence courses that he and his wife, June Carter Cash, took from Christian International in Phoenix. The course was on the life and epistles of St. Paul. Paul immediately interested Cash and set him on a mission to learn as much as possible about the early follower of Christ. In his autobiography, Cash notes that Paul fascinated him because of his "dramatic conversion" and "trials of faith." Also striking, he writes, were the parallels he saw between Paul and himself:

> He went out to conquer the world in the name of Jesus Christ; we in the music business, or at least those of us with my kind of drive, want our music heard all over the world. He was a man who always had a mission, who would never stop, who was always going here, going there, starting

> this, planning that; a life of ease and retirement wasn't on his agenda, just as it isn't on mine. I'm much more interested in keeping on down the roads I know and whatever new ones might reveal themselves to me, trying to tap that strength Paul found: the power of God that's inside me, that's there for me if only I seek it (312).

That Paul found his Savior—the Man in White—on the road, fit well with Cash's journey theme. As surely as any medieval pilgrim, Cash saw life as a spiritual pilgrimage. Cash recalls in *Man in Black* that after connecting with Sam Phillips at the Sun Record Company, he wrote a song entitled "My Prayer" (renamed "Lead Me, Father" when he recorded it three years later). He repeatedly sang the song in his mind or aloud every few days for years, calling on God to walk beside him, strengthen him, and pick him up when he stumbled (75).

Dave Urbanski, in *The Man Comes Around: The Spiritual Journey of Johnny Cash*, quotes Cash regarding the song "Meet Me in Heaven," which he recorded on the *Unchained* album. Cash explained that he wrote the song for June, though the title comes from words on the tombstones for his brother Jack and their father, and that the song is about people "'going down a trail together forever'" (150). Cash chose well for the concluding song to *Solitary Man*—the old country spiritual "Wayfaring Stranger." The individual is a stranger because his true home is across the Jordan and that is where he is traveling, to see loved ones again and, of course, to be with his savior.

Although congruent with Cash's own spiritual vision and personal spiritual journey, *Man in White* also merits respect as a carefully constructed novel. This observation should not be particularly surprising. Obviously, Cash could write. His many songs testify to his ability to narrate stories, use metaphors, develop themes, and engage the listener/reader. Trying something as extensive as a novel, though, was a unique effort for him, and he struggled with the novel on and off for almost a decade, beginning in 1977. It was finally published in 1986. As Steve Turner points out in his *The Man Called Cash*, "For someone used to telling stories in three verses and a chorus, a ninety-thousand-word novel had been an ambitious task" (180). Cash acknowledged the challenge: "It took me a long time, years and years during which my energies focused for a spell, then went somewhere else—music, drug abuse—but I kept at it. . . . " (*Autobiography* 311).

The attractiveness of the novel begins with its title, recalling by contrast the phrase the "Man in Black"—both Cash's performing attire and the title of his first autobiographical book. Although Saul/Paul is the protagonist, the title refers to the ultimate hero, Jesus. White refers to the radiance of the sinless and divine Christ, especially the image of the Resurrected Christ that Saul first sees when he is struck down on the road to Damascus and that returns to him many times. The sin and redemption theme is conveyed by the black/white contrast, but not in a simplistic all-or-nothing way. All humans are sinners, Cash believed, more or less a standard Christian concept. Everyone needs redemption. For Cash, the movement through life is a journey, progressing through fits and starts, toward that redemption.

The black-and-white contrast is only a partial antithesis. Cash explained much later one dimension of the symbolism in connection with the two dogs on the cover of the album *American Recordings*: one black with some white, the other primarily white with a smattering of black. Although he named the dogs Sin and Redemption, he noted that even in sin a person is not all bad, and conversely, no one is ever perfectly sinless (Urbanski 142).

Yet black is also a symbol of compassion for and solidarity with the sufferers and sinners of the world, an attitude best conveyed in the song "Man in Black" from 1971. Cash, according to the lyrics, dresses in black for those who are hopeless, hungry, imprisoned, sick, and lonely, as well as for those who have died in war and those who have missed out on the words of Jesus. Surely much of these misfortunes are caused by people's sins, sometimes the sufferers' own sins, but that is no impediment to compassion. Instead, it marks a source of community between Cash and humankind, including St. Paul, a shared experience of sin and the need for redemption.

Early in *Man in White*, Saul appears as a largely unsympathetic character, his primary attributes zeal and hatred: a zealous commitment to serving God and hatred for those who approach God in other ways, especially for those who follow the crucified Jesus. Cash uses contrasting characters and irony effectively in establishing what Saul is like and, consequently, the extent to which he changes after his conversion.

Cash introduces characters that contrast with Saul especially regarding a matter dear to the author's heart: religious tolerance. Saul is determined to destroy Jesus' followers, but others take a sharply different approach. When Peter and John are arrested, Gamaliel, a respected teacher and member of the Sanhedrin, speaks in opposition to trying to eradicate the Christians. In doing so, he expresses greater faith in God than does the ardent Saul: "I advise you, leave these men alone and let them go. If their activity is of human origin, it will fail. But if it is from God, you cannot stop them. You will be fighting against God" (26). The exhortation by Gamaliel carries the day, and, after a cautionary scourging, Peter and John are released. Saul stands watching: "He had never felt such hatred. 'What idiotic fanaticism!' he thought. 'It would be better if all Israel were rid of these religious lepers. . . .'" (27).

Undeterred, Saul embarks upon his mission to eliminate Jesus' disciples. He brings Stephen before the Sanhedrin and, with the aid of testimony from two brothers, Shemei and Cononiah, who serve Saul as informers, succeeds in gaining a guilty verdict. Stephen, whose story is told in Acts of the Apostles (6.8–8.2), is beaten and stoned to death, his official crime being blasphemy.

The novel makes Saul more responsible for the incident than does Acts, where he is described as being one of the men who approved the execution. However, in Acts the witnesses lay their coats at Saul's feet, which implies a special role for Saul. In the introduction, Cash recounts having many questions about Paul as he began studying him, including why those who killed Stephen laid their garments at his feet. Serious biblical research brought him many answers, as in this incident, when the elder and Temple guards remove their robes so "no one could later prove that this execution was carried out with Temple sanction" (45).

After the execution, Saul encounters Nicodemus, a former member of the Sanhedrin who had not been present for Stephen's conviction. The two men disagree regarding the execution, and Nicodemus assures Saul that he would not have voted for Stephen's death (47). Saul is also contrasted with Baanah ben David, an elderly rabbi who is also Saul's landlord, the rabbi's solicitous concern for Saul's mental and physical well-being at odds with the young man's passionate obsession with exterminating the Christians (62–63, 84–85).

Saul defends his efforts in terms of his commitment to the One God. He explains to Nicodemus that the first prayer he had memorized as a child was the Shema, a declaration of the Jewish belief in the unity of God. The prayer, which comes from Deuteronomy (6.4–5), Cash renders as "Hear O Israel: The Lord our God, the Lord he is One." The irony of Saul's reciting this prayer lies in his failure, from the novelistic point of view, to understand his initial misapplication of it. Initially, he sees in this basic principle of faith the rationale for destroying the Christian community. Much later, as one of the most important figures in the rise of Christianity, he will offer the same prayer, but with a radically different view of God and of his own spiritual role (49, 219).

A serious flaw in Saul within both the narrative of the novel and Cash's own personal credo is his intolerance. He believes in one God in a certain way and cannot tolerate those who believe in God in other ways. Cash makes his point clear in *Man in Black*:

> I'm sure denominations are important for bringing a body of believers together and giving them strength and motivation, but when this or that denomination begins to feel or, still worse, begins to teach that their particular interpretation of the Word opens the only door to heaven, then I feel it's dangerous. True, such preaching may convict [a term Cash often uses instead of *convert*] some people and win them over. But how many more nonbelievers are alienated and will shy away from any further look at the plan of God?
>
> Telling others is part of our faith all right, but the way we live it speaks louder than we can say it. The gospel of Christ must always be an open door with a welcome sign for all (33).

This issue of tolerance also appears in Cash's novelistic depiction of disagreements among the early Christians; the disagreement parallels the distinction quoted above between speaking one's faith and living it. After Saul's conversion and his later return to Jerusalem, he finds himself arguing with James about faith versus good works. James argues for good works, while Paul urges seeking converts on the basis of faith alone. "'So you say you have faith,' said James. 'And I say I have works.'" Paul then seeks conciliation by accepting James's position that they must live their faith through their actions, adding that the followers of the Lord "are justified by faith in him, that the righteousness of the Law is attained by total faith in him" (206). Saul's ability to find common ground demonstrates how far he has evolved from the earlier unbending zealot.

Another imaginative use of irony occurs in the rat episode shortly before Stephen's trial and execution. Saul, who lives in a cellar room beneath Baanah ben David's synagogue, discovers that a rat has been chewing on one of his biblical scrolls. He catches the rat and, filled with loathing for it, plans to kill the animal, only to be brought up short by the realization that the rat now contains within its stomach fragments of the sacred Scriptures.

Unable to kill something that possesses a bit of divine truth, Saul tosses the rat outside. Ironically, Saul has no trouble arranging for Stephen's death later that day, unable to comprehend that the martyr may also possess at least a fragment of divine truth. No less ironic is the prayer that Saul utters after receiving authorization from the high priest, Jonothan ben Annas, to leave Jerusalem to search out Jesus' followers. He praises a God that is "unchanging, all mighty, merciful, gracious, slow to anger, abounding in kindness and in truth, remembering loving kindness for a thousand generations, forgiving iniquity and transgressions and sins, and giving pardon to the penitent" (55–56). The reader will search in vain for much evidence of these qualities in Saul at this point in the story.

Among the novel's structural successes is a series of deaths that increasingly impacts Saul. First, of course, there is the death that occurred prior to the opening of the novel, that of Jesus. Then Stephen is stoned to death, "his face covered with blood but his countenance joyous" (45). The next important death is narrated through Saul's memory of an earlier event: the death of his friend Michael.

Still in Jerusalem prior to his setting forth for Damascus, Saul recalls returning from an earlier trip to find that in his absence a group of young men had gathered to protest the raising of a Roman standard over one of the city gates. Roman soldiers attempted to disperse the group, the confrontation turned violent, and a large number of protesters were either killed outright or crucified. One of the latter was Michael. Saul finds his friend still alive on the cross and asks why he engaged in such a foolish action. "'For you,' Michael whispered. 'And for Israel.'" In Saul's dreams, Stephen, Jesus, and Michael mingle, a disturbing combination for the self-proclaimed persecutor (69).

Dreams and visions run throughout the novel, as they do throughout Cash's life. In a recurring dream, Saul is standing in a river of blood, sometimes with Gentiles calling to him for help, a foreshadowing of the mission he will later undertake to bring Christianity to the Gentiles, as well as to the Jews. In one version of the dream, he is lying in the blood with his arms around the foot of a cross. Pulling himself up, he is blinded by the light emanating from the cross but is able to make out the sign for Jesus the Nazarene. Interpreting the dream is not difficult for Saul—Jesus' blood offered as a sacrifice for humankind with Saul's role to save others through the blood of the Savior—but accepting the message is not yet possible for him (72–73, 77–78).

Saul finds himself living a real-life version of the dream during the scene in which he leads an assault on the Christians worshipping in the Synagogue of the Isles of the Sea. Aristotle of Crete is scourged, and when Saul kicks Aristotle's wife in the stomach, Barnabas intervenes, leading Saul to take a sword from one of the Temple guards and hold its tip to Barnabas's throat. In a fit of rage, Saul hits Barnabas on the head with the flat of the blade, knocking him unconscious; he then stabs an elderly man in his hip when he refuses to stop praying. In the aftermath of the violence, Saul finds himself standing in a pool of blood. The terror he felt during his recurring dream returns, and to counter it he shouts the aforementioned Shema (95–97).

The spiritual line between visions and dreams was very fine in Cash's life, and both had great impact on him. Two especially significant examples involved his brother Jack and his father, Ray Cash. Both related to death and the next life. Jack was fatally injured in a table-saw accident in 1944 at the age of fourteen and died about a week later. Shortly before his death, Jack, calm and seemingly quite rational, spoke to his family surrounding his deathbed of a beautiful river that was going to take him away and of angels singing (*Autobiography* 35–36). In his accounts of the event, Cash never seems to doubt the truth of his brother's vision.

In the case of his father, the vision was Cash's own. Ray died on December 23, 1985. On Christmas night, after returning from the funeral home, Cash decided for the sake of the children in the family to set off the fireworks he had purchased earlier and that were a traditional part of Christmas for the Cash family. When he later went to bed, he dreamed that a silver car pulled up and deposited his father. As Johnny reached out to shake his father's hand, a great row of light flashed up between them, widening and separating the two men.

The following morning, Cash went to pick his mother up for the funeral and shared with her his father's message that he was happy and comfortable where he was. Again Cash seems to accept the visionary nature of the experience and its essential reality. He describes the experience in the introduction to *Man in White* (14–15) because, although he admits that he never had an experience comparable to Paul's vision near Damascus, the dream about his father was the closest he ever came. As he writes, "I was never privileged to have an experience like Paul did just outside Damascus, but on Christmas night 1985 I had a visionlike dream and saw a light that was unearthly and much more beautiful than the whole box of fireworks" (15).

Saul's life-altering encounter with Christ is described in terms of such an overpowering light: "a light far greater than the sun" that blisters his face, singes his hair, and blinds him. For just a second, Saul had seen the Man in White, and the figure remains on the back of his eyelids as a negative image (118–19). The story of the great light, Saul's blinding, and his later recovery of sight comes from Acts of the Apostles (9.3–18, 22.6–13, 26.12–18).

Neither in Acts nor in Paul's Epistles does one find any indication that Saul was anything but fully committed to persecuting the Christian church. In *Man in White*, though, Cash looks toward fictional credibility and psychological complexity in depicting a Saul who is growing ever readier for a conversion experience. Saul has undergone the troubling dreams about Stephen, Michael, Jesus, and the bloody stream already mentioned, certainly signs of a mind in torment. Then, as he approaches Damascus, he does so after days of uncertainty: "Fears and doubts had plagued him for the last six days." Further, "the purging of the Nazarenes in the city of God had brought him no real satisfaction," and every night he has been dreaming of Stephen, the executed Christian's face "in a blissful smile" (118). The questions continue: "Should he abandon his mission? How many would die in Damascus in the fulfillment of his task? The thought of the dying men, women, and children overwhelmed him, and he was almost sick to his stomach. . . . " (118).

At this moment, though, he pulls himself back from such doubts, worrying that "The Evil One is working against God's work" in his mind (118). Then comes the light, and Saul, as a character in a novel, is primed for the great change. The miracle may be decreased by the psychological preparation of Saul, but in terms of plot and character development the troubled portrait adds greater credibility to the story.

Not only the road on which Saul treads but his entire life has led to this moment. Having witnessed the Lord and been so transformed, Saul has reached a point that is both crisis and climax. This is the great turning point in his life and in the character Cash has drawn. Yet it necessarily is also the high point of the narrative. After witnessing God so immediately, what can the character possibly do to compete with this moment? After the miracle on the way to Damascus, all must, to some extent, be anticlimactic. Yet the rest of the novel is not without artistry and interest, even if on the whole it lacks the emotional power of the narrative up to Saul's conversion.

In a later incident also demonstrating Cash's ability to identify with his protagonist, Paul escapes from Damascus by being lowered in a basket from a city wall, an incident, like many in the novel, based on much sketchier biblical treatment (Acts 9.23–25). The novel adds a mishap as Paul lands in a thorn bush.

The powerful song "The Man Comes Around" from the album of the same title refers to a whirlwind in a thorn tree as part of the phenomena accompanying the return of Christ at the end of the world. In the liner notes to the album, Cash said that the phrase came to him in a dream in which Queen Elizabeth (certainly an unlikely subject for a dream) tells Cash that he is like "a thorn tree in a whirlwind."

Cash later recalls a similar reference in the Book of Job. The song, though, follows the novel by several years; any cause-to-effect relationship regarding this passage in the novel as effect instead likely involves another dream of Cash's, one he experienced repeatedly when he was attempting to recover from drug use in 1967. As he recalls in *Man in Black*, a glass ball would begin expanding in his stomach and eventually lift him off his bed. Then the ball would explode, sending pieces of glass through his body. Sometimes he also would dream of pulling briars, splinters of wood, and thorns out of his flesh (145).

Psychologically, the thorns in Paul's flesh, like those within Cash's dream, convey the lingering guilt of past transgressions. Paul is no longer the Saul who persecutes Christians, but he still remembers his earlier sins. His past also makes it difficult for some Christians to get beyond his earlier actions, including those who flee when Peter introduces Saul upon his return to Jerusalem (202).

Prior to returning to Jerusalem, Saul makes a pilgrimage to Mt. Sinai, ascending "The Stairway to Heaven" and, after undergoing a beating at the hands of two young men descending the mountain, finally reaches the top and an arch called "The Gateway to Heaven." Passing through the "Gateway," he reaches the place where tradition said Moses had been visited by God.

With night approaching, he gathers branches and leaves for a bed and, just as he is about to fall asleep, sees the Man in White. He hears the voice of Jesus and receives both his new mission to confirm the Lord's "new covenant" and a vision of the future destruction of Jerusalem (173–82). After witnessing the destruction until "not one stone was left upon another," he recalls that much earlier incident with the rat chewing one of his scrolls. Now the scriptural passage that the rat devoured comes back to him: "'This house which I have sanctified in my name will I cast out . . .'" (183). The return to this earlier incident with the rat effectively bookends the long portion of the protagonist's life stretching from his career as ardent persecutor through his conversion and his reception on Mt. Sinai of his new calling: to make his body "the temple of the Most High" and carry the new covenant to the Gentiles (178). The old house of faith has given way to the new one, as the Old Jerusalem, in the long tradition of Christian eschatological doctrine, yields to the New Jerusalem.

Saul is now ready to set out on his mission to spread the news of Jesus. First, he returns to Jerusalem, where he encounters Barnabas, whom he earlier had knocked unconscious after holding the point of a sword to his neck. Barnabas is again beaten, this time suffering at the hands of the Roman soldiers and the chief priests and elders. After Saul receives his new name, Paul, in another vision of the Man in White, he encounters the bleeding Barnabas. Now, however, Paul, armed with his faith, his new name, and his great mission, is the healer. He and Peter pray with their hands upon Barnabas. The image of the Man in White appears again behind Paul's eyelids, and when he opens his eyes the scar that Paul's sword had left on Barnabas's neck is gone along with his other wounds (217).

Johnny Cash has written the story of Paul up to his embarking on his many journeys to help establish and stabilize a number of Christian communities. Paul's subsequent activities are beyond the scope of the author's intentions, and so the novel, except for a brief epilogue and some song lyrics by Cash, ends here. However, the section concludes with the unusual note: "THIS STORY HAS NO END" (219).

Novels, of course, are supposed to have ends, and this one is no exception. Cash is writing, though, a narrative within the much longer story often known as salvation history. That history, for Cash, continues, and will continue until the end of the world when Jesus comes again, as he is described doing in "The Man Comes Around."

The individual story of Paul, however, does have an end, although Cash seemingly has no desire to write a fictional account of his missionary work that produced the epistles, an account that would make the novel much longer and certainly less focused. So the novel jumps over those endeavors and concludes with a brief, impressionistic account of Paul's impending death, including again the image of the Man in White (223–26).

The lyrics that follow the epilogue recount going to Damascus and standing at the spot where Saul had seen his great light (227). The lyrics point out, though, that the moment of revelation and conversion need not be on the road to Damascus. It could be anywhere, even in a closet. Johnny Cash walked that road to Damascus in his novel about Paul. He also walked his own personal Damascus road throughout his life, walking from sin to redemption, hoping that he would get there and stay there. The novel certainly helped with that. It also turned out to be a good novel.

•

EDWARD J. RIELLY chairs the English department at Saint Joseph's College of Maine. In addition to ten volumes of his own poetry, he has published several nonfiction books. His recent publications include *The 1960s* (Greenwood), *Baseball: An Encyclopedia of Popular Culture* (ABC-Clio; recently released in paper by the University of Nebraska Press), *Baseball and American Culture: Across the Diamond* (a collection of essays from Haworth), and *F. Scott Fitzgerald: A Biography* (Greenwood). He is editing *Baseball in the Classroom: Teaching America's National Pastime*, a collection of essays on baseball as pedagogy, for McFarland; and is writing *Sitting Bull: A Biography* (Greenwood) and *Football: An Encyclopedia of Popular Culture* (University of Nebraska Press). He also writes a newspaper column on baseball and has published many individual articles, book reviews, short stories, and poems.

Works Cited

Cash, Johnny. *American IV: The Man Comes Around*. American Recordings, 2002.

——. *American Recordings*. American Recordings, 1994.

——. *Johnny Cash: The Songs*. Ed. Don Cusic. New York: Thunder's Mouth Press, 2004.

——. *Man in Black*. Grand Rapids, MI: Zondervan Publishing House, 1975.

——. *Man in White: A Novel*. New York: HarperSanFrancisco, 1987.

——, with Patrick Carr. *Johnny Cash: The Autobiography*. New York: HarperPaperbacks, 1998.

Milton, John. *Complete Poems and Major Prose*. Ed. Merritt Y. Hughes. New York: Odyssey Press, 1957.

The Oxford Study Bible: Revised English Bible with the Apocrypha. Ed. M. Jack Suggs, Katharine Doob Sakenfield, and James R. Mueller. New York: Oxford University Press, 1992.

Turner, Steve. *The Man Called Cash: The Life, Love, and Faith of an American Legend.* Nashville: W Publishing Group, 2004.

Urbanski, Dave. *The Man Comes Around: The Spiritual Journey of Johnny Cash.* Lake Mary, FL: Relevant Media Group, 2003.

Robert G. Weiner

THE MAN IN BLACK ON DVD: A SELECTED FILMOGRAPHIC ESSAY

"I like a messy bed."
—JOHNNY CASH in *Door-to-Door Maniac*

"Mystery I had read somewhere is not the absence of meaning, but the presence of more meaning that we can comprehend."
—DENNIS COVINGTON in *Salvation of Sand Mountain*

THE MATERIAL COVERED HERE EXAMINES JOHNNY CASH from his first appearances in the 1950s to the last material he recorded in 2002. Cash's career as epitomized by these DVDs reveals a deep sense of mystery and meaning that ran throughout all of Cash's work, whether his music or acting. Professor Dennis Covington's comment that "mystery... is the presence of more meaning than (one) could possibly comprehend" correlates to Cash's body of work. The Man in Black's mysterious aura permeated his music and his whole career.

Cash considered himself a simple man and yet his presence commanded the respect of people as influential as President George W. Bush and the Reverend Billy Graham, to prominent rock bands like U2 and the Grateful Dead, along with songwriters such as Bob Dylan, Merle Haggard, and Kris Kristofferson and performance art Punk icons like G. G. Allen and the Murder Junkies. Cash had a broad range of appeal that included hardened convicts, murderers, and criminals, Native Americans, patriots, and Armed Forces personnel to punk rockers, Goths, college fraternities, and women, young and old.

Cash's music has so much honesty and meaning that he transcends all those class and professional barriers, which are so often a part of people's everyday lives. From the very beginning of his career, it has been difficult (if not impossible) to pigeonhole Johnny Cash as one type of artist (despite his often being considered a country artist). His music was popular, not only on the country charts, but the rock charts as well. From his first single, "Cry Cry Cry," to his last, "Hurt," his music always had an edge that made him different from the typical musical artist.

The same edge that separated his music from the rest could be applied to Cash's film career. His movie and television roles show him to a be a artist of great depth, from playing murderers in *Door-to-Door Maniac* and *Columbo*, to an illiterate but loving father in *The Pride of Jesse Helm*, to honest officers of the law in *Murder in Coweta County* and *Stagecoach*. In every role he played, every song he recorded, and every concert he gave he remained the "Man in Black: Johnny Cash." He was a complicated, but a very simple man, and it is utterly impossible to compartmentalize him and say, "This is what Johnny Cash was." The DVDs discussed here are a testament to that power.

This essay covers many of the appearances of Johnny Cash on DVD, ranging from well-known ones to the more obscure. I do not cover Cash on VHS, which at this point is a much larger body of work. However, that does point out the need for more Cash-related items to be transferred to DVD. It is divided into the following sections: documentaries, concert films (and videos), and acting appearances. Not every appearance of Cash on DVD is included, but I have tried to cover some of the major and more interesting ones that have significant Cash content. There is also a short list of other Cash-related DVDs toward the end of the essay, ones not analyzed in detail, because if a writer attempted to catalog every Cash appearance it would fill volumes.

Documentaries

Johnny Cash—The Man, His World, His Music, 1969

Originally produced for British Television in 1969, this ninety-minute film documents the world of Johnny Cash during the late sixties. Produced by Arthur and Evelyn Barron and directed by Robert Elfstrom (*Nashville Sound*, *Gospel Road Story of Jesus* [also featuring Cash], and cinematographer for *American Experience*) this film is a combination of concert, studio, and interview footage. It includes an inside look at the day-to-day life of Cash and his wife, June, on the road. In it, Cash comments that, "Love is the main theme of all music," and talks about the true sadness of country music that describes a "simple way of life."

We are treated to Carl Perkins singing "Blue Suede Shoes" and footage of Cash and Perkins playing "Devil to Pay" together. One of the most amazing sequences is footage of Cash signing autographs and listening to several songwriters sing and play their songs for him. He shows great patience in talking to the public and would-be songwriters. After hearing two songs from one folksinger, he goes the extra mile and gets the budding writer an audition for Columbia records.

Throughout the film, Cash drives the tour bus as he tells stories from his childhood. He even takes his family back to his childhood home where he worked as a "water boy," and the film provides a glimpse into early Southern life when the sharecropper's quarters are viewed.

There is a wonderful studio sequence with Cash and Bob Dylan during the *Nashville Skyline* sessions. Johnny and June attend the Second Annual Country Music Awards, where he is awarded album of the year for *Johnny Cash at Folsom Prison*. The most moving scene in the film is when Cash plays for some Native Americans and goes to Wounded Knee.

The end of the film shows Cash and the Carter family playing for a group of convicts. He states that he likes to play for convicts because "a prison is a prison and that's all it is." Cash sees convicts as real people instead of outcasts, which no doubt was responsible for his appeal. The concert footage features a smoking version of "Big River." This film is an amazing examination of Cash, covering all aspects of his life as an artist. The film also shows more than just Johnny Cash the artist and really portrays Johnny Cash the man. It presents his warmth and gives a historic glimpse into the South and life on the road.

Good Rockin' Tonight—Legacy of Sun Records, 2001

This documentary is part of the American Masters series. It traces the history of Sun Records from its humble beginnings (January 3, 1950), when it recorded rhythm and blues, to becoming the first to record rock greats like Elvis Presley, Jerry Lee Lewis, Carl Perkins, Billy Lee Riley, Roy Orbison, and, of course, Johnny Cash. The early recordings featured artists like B. B. King, Howlin's Wolf, Junior Parker, and many others. Sun's motto was, "We Record Anything."

This film features interviews with key musicians (Scotty Moore), producers (e.g., Jack Clement), and songwriters, including founder Sam Phillips. Considering Phillips has been in the business for more than fifty years, he looks surprisingly hip and is lucid throughout. Phillips's vision was to turn white kids on to black music or "race records," and black kids on to white artists. He wanted to get artists who were just learning their craft, and Sun captured the rawness, energy, and hunger of these artists. It broke all the existing rules for recording and made magic. Sun Records stands as the longest living independent label in history.

This film also serves as a modern-day tribute to Sun Records. Atlantic Records founder Ahmet Ertegun put together a CD tribute as a companion to the film. We see various artists reworking some Sun classics. This includes Paul McCartney in the studio with Scotty Moore doing the Elvis classic "That's All Right" and Ben Folds doing "Honey Don't."

The best performances on the DVD include Sonny Burgess doing "Ain't Got a Thing" and Billy Lee Riley doing "Red Hot." Matchbox 20 also plays with Jerry Lee Lewis on "Great Balls of Fire." Some of the other artists featured include Led Zeppelin's Jimmy Page and Robert Plant, Brian Ferry, Mark Knopfler, Johnny Hallyday, Malcolm Yelvington, and Kid Rock, among others.

In this documentary, Cash is neither interviewed nor discussed very much. However, what is said about Cash is worth hearing. As Phillips states, [Johnny Cash] "has a special way of being Johnny Cash." He is one of the "great writers of all time, and the stories in his songs are real and true. Cash has the ability to hit on both joy and sadness, and listeners knew he was the real thing." According to those interviewed, Cash is the "perfect songwriter" and can't be put into a box.

The band Live pays tribute to Cash, playing its version of "I Walk the Line." The band members then discuss how Cash is an inspiration because "Cash is real" and his words come from a life lived. There is also a version of "Cry Cry Cry" done by Third Ear Band, which is listless and cold with no energy, and should have been left out. Despite there being little Cash content on this DVD, it should be watched by Cash aficionados and anyone interested in the history of rock 'n' roll.

Amazing Grace with Bill Moyers, 1990

This 1990 documentary traces the story of what could possibly be the most well-known song in the English-speaking world, "Amazing Grace." No other song recorded and sung has the power to move people as much. Englishman John Newton wrote the song as part of the Olney Hymns series (circa 1760–1770). Newton, a former slave trader and rogue, had such a profound conversion experience that he wrote several songs about it. The song has gone through numerous melodies and re-envisioning throughout its long tenure.

The real gem in this documentary is Johnny Cash singing "Amazing Grace" live. Cash talks about singing the song while working in the cotton fields when he was a boy in Dyess, Arkansas, and how they sang the song when his brother died. According to Cash, there are all kinds of prisons created by drugs, alcohol, or some other kind of habit. One could be in a "dungeon (and be) free as bird" while singing this song. "This is a song with no guilt that frees the spirit," he said. It is a song that makes a difference in people's lives. The lyrics are "straight ahead and honest at a guttural heart level."

Seeing Cash perform and hearing how it influenced him makes this documentary worth watching. Certainly no other song has become a part of our everyday culture for such a long period.

Johnny Cash Ridin' the Rails: The Great American Train Story, 1974

This 1974 documentary on the history of the railroad features Johnny Cash narrating and performing throughout. Nicholas Webster, who also directed the infamous *Santa Claus Conquers the Martians* (one of the worst movies of all time), directed this fifty-minute film. Cash describes how, from his childhood on, he has been fascinated with railroads and his imagination was stirred by hearing that "lonesome whistle cutting through the night." As a boy, the railroads inspired him to think that "anything would be possible" in life.

Interspersed with footage and historical information on the early railroad is Cash performing. He sings a traditional song that describes how the railroads became "the curse of the country" to those employed in the Waggoner and Canal, and suggest that the "devil take the man who came up with the plan" of the railroads.

The April 1862 hijacking of "The Confederate General" by Union spies is the most well-known event retold in the documentary (and the subject of the brilliant Buster Keaton movie, *The General*). This segment features Cash singing The Band's "The Night They Drove Old Dixie Down."

One of the ways men received some relief from the hard drudgery of building the railroads was through the power of song. A caller would sing out a verse and the rest of the men would follow his lead. Cash sings the song about the legendary African-American folk hero, John Henry—"The Legend of John Henry's Hammer"—and similar songs that became inspirations to the working man.

Cash then describes how the early cowboys, after their long cattle drives, would get much-needed relief in drink, song, and women in the railroad towns. In addition to the commerce of transporting freight, the railroads afforded ordinary folks the ability to buy land from the railroad companies, thus furthering Westward Expansion. By the early twentieth century, stories and songs about the railroads were firmly in place in the American consciousness. Cash sings the story of the most famous locomotive engineer, "Ballad of Casey Jones" (also performed and recorded in an excellent version by the Jerry Garcia Acoustic Band. The Grateful Dead also performed the traditional ballad as well as an original song based on it called "Casey Jones").

Cash sings songs that lament the decline of the railroads as new innovations, like the automobile, became the nation's primary means of transportation. He laments the fact that no one comes to the train station and "nobody knows his name." There are great shots of Cash and the trains at night.

It is to Rhino's credit that they have released this excellent documentary on DVD. Each historical segment also features Cash singing a song with his voice in good form. The extras on the disc feature various outtakes and footage of Cash, so it is a little more than the bare bones found on many documentaries of this kind. Other songs include "Train Robbers," "City of New Orleans," "The L&N Don't Stop Here Anymore," "Collage of Yesterday," "Doesn't Anybody Know My Name" (see above), and "Shave and a Hot Bath," among other traditional pieces.

Johnny Cash: The Anthology, 2001

Johnny Cash: The Anthology contains two separate documentaries examining the life and career of the legendary musician. One is a fifty-minute documentary featuring videos for songs throughout Cash's career through 1994. It features interviews with producers, friends, songwriters, and Cash's contemporaries, like Merle Haggard, Waylon Jennings, and George Jones, as well more recent artists like Marty Stuart and Rodney Crowell. There are a total of fifteen performances on this film.

Cash had more than 100 hit singles throughout his career, and the *Anthology* portion features a few of those numbers. Most of the songs are in black and white and there is no indication of the source footage. The "Folsom Prison Blues" video starts out with Jennings as the backup guitarist and solo lead.

During an interview session, Jennings points out that Cash would have been a star in any era. He describes Cash as the most intelligent man he knows, with the ability to understand the simplicity of life, as well as the big issues. Some of the other tracks include "Big River," "Cry Cry Cry," "If I Were A Carpenter," "Daddy Sang Bass," "Bird on a Wire," and the autobiographical "Man in Black."

The most interesting story is about the formation of the song "Ring of Fire." A former producer describes how Cash had a dream about "Ring of Fire," hearing Mexican trumpets in the background. Nobody at the time of the song's release had attempted such an approach to a pop song.

The real gem in this collection is the ninety-minute *Johnny Cash: Half Mile A Day*. It features many of the video clips and interviews from *Anthology*, but also includes interviews with folks like Billy Bob Thorton, Judy Collins, and Kris Kristofferson.

Cash discusses being stationed in Germany during a stint in the Armed Forces in the early fifties. On a whim, he took the last five dollars he had and walked through a terrible snowstorm just to buy a guitar. In an interview, producer and Sun Record's founder Sam Phillips is interviewed. He describes how Cash landed at Sun and the artist's first single, "Cry Cry Cry," going to number one.

Rodney Crowell describes how he first heard "I Walk the Line," written for Cash's first wife. Crowell says he had never heard anything like that before; it was raw, powerful, and yet, personal. Marty Stuart describes Cash as a larger-than-life character in the same league as Paul Bunyan and Davy Crockett.

Cash's entire career is covered, from his storybook romance with June Carter to his infamous performances at Carnegie Hall when he had laryngitis. The disk includes his cause for Indian rights and history, the start of his playing to prisoners, and his problems with drugs.

Merle Haggard discusses how Cash convinced him to talk about his prison time before an American audience when he performed. He told Haggard, "People will be on your side if you are honest."

By the 1990s, Cash considered retiring from recording and touring. He did not have a record label, but Rick Ruben, who produced the Beastie Boys and Red Hot Chile Peppers, asked Cash to make a record with him. Cash's *American Recordings* renewed his career both critically and with the record-buying public. Cash suddenly was cool again with a new audience. Ruben stripped Cash down to the basics of the man and his guitar with great songs and no slickness.

Despite the fact that there is no complete video of any song without some kind of narration or interview, these two documentaries are worth watching. With the success of the movie *Walk the Line*, the public's fascination with Cash is far from over. Those who liked the movie should watch this documentary to supplement the movie's story.

The Unauthorized Biography of Johnny Cash, 2005

This film starts out with a photoplay of Cash smashing up a hotel room in Des Moines, Iowa, in 1961. The narrator describes Cash as a "devout Christian who sinned." The narrator describes Cash as a split personality—Johnny is the good boy and Cash is evil.

The DVD begins with a description of Cash's early life in Dyess, Arkansas. It includes early footage of him from the *Singing Brakeman* film. The documentary ably covers Cash's early life, including his first marriage, time in the Air Force, and relationship with June Carter. However, the focus is on Cash's drug use and his wild antics.

Long before bands like Led Zeppelin and The Who made headlines by trashing hotel rooms, Cash and his group were trashing hotel rooms and getting away with it. Cash's arrests, self-destruction at a Grand Ole Opry performance, airplane antics (which caused an early landing), and drug use are the main focus of this film.

The makers of this film completely ignore Cash's career from the 1970s to 1990s, except to say that by the latter decade, Cash was a "has been" who was saved by producer Rick Ruben. This documentary is fairly good on Cash's early career and there are some interesting clips and photos, but as a portrait of Cash's life it fails miserably. There is too much focus on the negative and the scandalous parts of Cash's life and not on his career as a whole, thus a good reason why it is "unauthorized." The company that produced this has done other similar films that are sensationalistic.

This does not mean, however, that Cash fans should simply avoid this DVD altogether. There are more than thirty minutes of interviews featuring Cash's brother, Tommy, and his drummer, W. S. Holland. Tommy's interview provides a unique insight into Cash's childhood and early career. Drummer W. S. Holland's interview is a goldmine of information about life on the road during the early years of rock.

Biography: Johnny Cash, 1998

This is a re-release of the 1998 *Biography* program on Johnny Cash. It begins by describing Cash's genealogy. Within the first five minutes of this program, the viewer learns more pertinent information about Cash's life than in many of the other documentaries about the legendary musician.

Throughout the program, Cash's sister Louise is interviewed, as is daughter Roseanne and brother Tommy. The "single most significant event" in Cash's life was the death of his brother, according to his daughter Roseanne. The film contains footage of various rare forty-five-picture sleeves and a poster that is a real treat. Cash's drug use is mentioned throughout, but it is never emphasized in a sensational way.

The DVD has no extras, but is the most balanced of the biographical documentaries. Watching it, a viewer really can see why Cash earned the nickname, "Quintessential American Troubadour."

I Walk the Line: Country Legends, 2005

This CD/DVD package (filmed after Cash's death) features a DVD of the program *County Legends* that pays homage to Cash. After this brief introduction with footage— but none of Cash's music—the film goes into a tribute by various musicians, friends, and producers.

The people interviewed include Randall Jamaill, Billy Joe Shaver, Mitch Jacobs, John Evans, Jason Allen, Jamie Richards, and Mark Zeus, who tell personal stories about knowing Cash or stories about how he influenced their careers. They all discuss how Cash did things on his own terms and never followed trends. He was the first true "outlaw" musician. As Billy Joe Shaver states, "Like Frank Sinatra, Cash picked the best songs to record."

In this film, several musicians play their own songs, displaying how Cash influenced their style. *Country Legends* is really less of a documentary than a tribute to the man and his music. The thirty-minute CD includes some of the best of Cash, including "I Walk the Line," "Folsom Prison Blues," "Big River," and "Ways of a Woman in Love." While this package is a good deal—priced under ten dollars—there is little to recommend it to anyone but hardcore Cash fanatics. The *Country Legends* program is interesting in parts, but it really contains no new information or Cash music and it is obvious why it is unauthorized.

Concert Films and Videos

Johnny Cash Live at Montreux, 1994

This DVD documents Cash's 1994 performance at the Montreux Jazz Festival in Sweden. Hot on the heels of his first *American Recordings* release, Cash performs with renewed vigor and enthusiasm. His band featured his son, John Carter Cash, Bob Wooton on guitar, Dave Roe on bass, and long-time (thirty-five-plus years) drummer W. S. Holland. Holland plays like he is on fire and it is very apparent why Cash stuck with him all those years. While the transfer is fairly good, there is a blue tint throughout that is sometimes distracting.

There are an astounding twenty songs in the sixty-five-minute DVD. Cash opens up with a fine version of "Folsom Prison Blues," and then goes into a sprightly version of "Get Rhythm." "Ring of Fire" is upbeat, despite no horns, and then there's a terrific "I Walk the Line," which Cash prefaces with a story about when he first heard Holland's drumming on Carl Perkins' "Blue Suede Shoes."

In the middle of the show, Cash showcases a couple of acoustic numbers from the *American Recordings*, which are conveyed with a personal intimacy. He explains the rationale behind the "stripped down" album, which contains songs that communicate both the dark and the light sides of Cash's personality. Some of the songs performed include "Bird on a Wire," "Delia," "Beast in Me," and a song that relates Cash's long-time love of the railroads, "Let the Train Blow the Whistle." He wraps up the acoustic set with a lovely "Redemption." Then the band goes into a terrific version of "Big River," but the highlight of the concert is Cash's performance with his wife, June Carter, on "Jackson," followed by the old Carter family's gospel theme "Will the Circle Be Unbroken." The concert wraps up with "Orange Blossom Special," "San Quentin," and the "Next Time I'm in Town." There are no extras on the DVD, but there is a booklet featuring liner notes by writer Michael Heatley.

Road to Nashville, 1967

Road to Nashville packs thirty-eight songs in its 102 minutes and is touted as the "biggest country music jamboree ever filmed." Unfortunately, the producers (one of whom was Marty Robbins) decided to film *Road to Nashville* as a variety show when just taping the music would have been more appropriate. Directed by Will Zens, who directed *Hell on Wheels*, *To the Shores of Hell*, and *Hot Summer in Barefoot Country*, this film provides a glimpse of country music in 1967.

In the film, a Hollywood bigwig (Richard Arlen) sends his bumbling assistant Colonel Feitlebaum (Doodles Weaver) to go to Nashville and scout for talent for (what else) a country music film in Nashville. Weaver is so cornball that it is almost painful to watch, and the jokes are not even funny (e.g., Batman doesn't get kissed much because of his "batbreath"). At the time, I suppose this was high humor for the masses, but it did not age well.

The real meat of this DVD is the performances. They provide an interesting look at some legendary and not-so-legendary country music performers. There are amazing versions of Waylon Jennings' "Anita," Marty Robbins "Begging to You," and "Devil Woman," with "El Paso" closing the show. Some of the other artists include Hank Snow, Bill Anderson, the "Queen of Country" Kitty Wells, The Osborne Brothers, Porter Wagonner, Dottie West, and the now forgotten Margie Singleton and Bobby Sykes. The Stonemans do an instrumental that makes them look more like a 1960s swinging combo rock group than a traditional family of country musicians. There is also a bizarre attempt at humorous music in the vein of Homer and Jethro by Quinine Gumstump & Buck, which leaves the viewer scratching his head.

The Carter family does Cash's "I Walk the Line" in fine form, and with the Man in Black himself they perform a rousing "Were You There" with deep feeling and honesty. Solo, Cash performs "The One on the Right." While this film is a disappointment for fans wanting a high dose of Cash, it does provide insight into popular country music in 1967. As a historical document, *Road to Nashville* is priceless and, thank goodness, the chapter stops are for the songs, so that much of Weaver's excruciating humor can be left out.

Johnny Cash: A Concert Behind Prison Walls, 1977

This 1977 television special (directed by Johnny Carson's brother Dick) documents a variety show featuring Cash at the Tennessee State Prison. Cash's backup band, which includes Carl Perkins, is tight throughout. Cash begins with "Folsom Prison Blues" and Kris Kristofferson's "Sunday Morning Coming Down." The producers tell Cash not to include the word "stoned" in the lyrics because he was performing to inmates, but in typical Cash fashion, he does what he wants to and sings the verse. Cash then sings a heartfelt version of "Jacob Green" as though he were talking to the convicts directly.

"America's favorite drunk" Foster Brooks does a brief comedic sketch, which certainly seems out of place, telling drunken jokes to a group of prisoner inmates. There is some sort of weird irony there. His humor feels very dated, despite coming off as a "well-oiled" machine. A very young and adorable Linda Ronstadt (in a very skimpy dress) does versions of "Desperado" and "You're No Good," then later during the second half of the show, sings "Silver Thread and Golden Needles."

Cash wraps up this sixty-minute program with rousing versions of "Hey Porter" and "Orange Blossom Special," playing the harmonica as though it were an extension of his body. The show wraps up with what is the definitive live version of "A Boy Named Sue." Cash is on fire when he does this number for the inmates.

While there is simply not enough of Cash on this release, it is still a fine record of the event. Watching brings to light how badly those who own the rights to Cash's other televisions specials and *The Johnny Cash Show* need to sort out their financial concerns and release that material on DVD. This DVD is also packaged with an audio CD that has some extra tracks.

Pete Seeger's Rainbow Quest: Johnny Cash and Roscoe Holcombe

This DVD documents *Rainbow Quest* folk singer Pete Seeger's music program from the mid-1960s. While the transfer is a little muddy and jerky, considering the rareness of this material, it holds up well. The first part of this two-hour program features Seeger and Cash singing, telling stories, and improvising together. Seeger does the opening melody and introduces the program. He has such a conversational style that one feels as though he is actually in your living room. He talks about how the Carter family influenced his career and life.

Cash comes out and performs "I Am a Pilgrim." June then discusses the early Carter family and together they perform "Worried Man's Blues" (trading verses) at Seeger's request. Cash talks about his life as a child and the first songs he ever learned. Then he performs a nice version of "There's a Mother Always Waiting."

Cash discusses the origins of "Five Feet High and Rising" and performs "Pickin' Time." Each song is prefaced with stories. Cash and Seeger discuss their love for Native American songwriter Peter Lafarge. Cash talks about having Cherokee blood and they both do their favorite Lafarge compositions. Seeger sings the tribute to the canine coyote "Ki Yo Ti," and Cash does "As Long as the Grass Shall Grow."

Cash and Seeger hold a fascinating discussion about how the Cherokee language originated before chatting about the "Ballad of the Talking Leaves" and its history. This provides interesting tidbits about a too often overlooked songwriter and activist. Cash requests that Seeger sing "Cripple Creek," and then June finishes the show with "I'm Thinking Tonight of My Blue Eyes." There are no extras on this disc, but it is well worth seeking out as a true glimpse into the mind and world of Cash.

Johnny Cash: Hurt, 2003

This is a promotional video for the song "Hurt," Cash's last major hit before his death. "Hurt" is taken from his critically acclaimed 2002 album *American IV: The Man Comes Around.* Written by Nine Inch Nails mastermind Trent Reznor, and performed on the *Downward Spirial* album (1994), *Hurt* is directed by music video and feature film (*One Hour Photo*) director Mark Romanek.

The video features Cash singing, while playing his guitar, at the dinner table with his wife, June, hovering in the background. The food on the table looks rotten, which makes the overall effect of the film all that more potent. Throughout this four-minute piece the viewer is treated to various snippets of Cash throughout his career. Cash memorabilia, which is scattered around, includes a broken gold record and the House of Cash museum sign. Images of Christ nailed to the cross make the ache of the song all the more apparent. During the climax, Cash pours wine all over the dinner table and the film's end shows him putting the cover over the piano. Cash's frail state and the heart-wrenching lyrics make the pain of the song all the more apparent.

The video won the 2003 Country Music Award for Video of the Year and the 2004 Grammy Award for Best Short Form Music Video. This is the definitive version of the song, and even Trent Reznor has claimed that he no longer owns it after hearing and seeing Cash's version.

While watching the song over and over again is enjoyable and enlightening, the director could have included a commentary or interview describing his experience with Cash and what he was trying to achieve with the video. The producer, Rick Rubin, should also have been interviewed to explain why he asked Cash to record this song. The video is also featured on the CD and on the DVD *The Work of Director Mark Romanek* (Palm Pictures 2005). Considering that June Carter Cash died two months after the filming and Cash died four months later, this video is a haunting epitaph to his career.

The Highwaymen—On the Road Again, 1993

Country music's only real supergroup, the Highwaymen featured Johnny Cash, Willie Nelson, Waylon Jennings, and Kris Kristofferson for a couple of critically acclaimed albums and tours. This DVD features the group in Aberdeen, Scotland, during its 1992 tour. The video packs seventeen songs into this sixty-minute program, which also features interviews with the audience, June Cash, and the band members. One can see the confidence of the four as they take the stage.

Cash does nice tight versions of "Folsom Prison Blues," "Get Rhythm," and a song that the Grateful Dead covered no less than 397 times from 1971–1995, "Big River." Cash is in fine form during these numbers. There is also footage of the band backstage.

During the interview segments, the band members describe how much they enjoy playing together and how since they don't really "have to tour," playing together is a real joy. They describe how wonderful it is to "bring freedom" to country music away from record company suits, producers, and executives. Cash talks about how his family roots are in Scotland and that in 1667 the first Cash came to America.

Both Jennings and Cash wax philosophically as to how long they will keep playing. The back-up band is tight but very subdued, and no member is showcased. This is appropriate because the real stars of the show are the "big four." This DVD stands as a nice testament to one of the most important historic events in the history of country music.

There is also a videotape of a 1990 Highwaymen's concert in New York, *Highwaymen Live!* (2000), but it has not been released on DVD. Since two of the members have already died, a DVD release of that concert is needed.

Johnny Cash at Town Hall Party, 1958–1959

This amazing concert performance of Johnny Cash and the Tennessee Two was taken from two appearances (November 15, 1958 and August 8, 1959) on the television show *Town Hall Party*. Cash historian Peter Lewry briefly describes the history of the show in the liner notes. *Town Hall Party* aired from 1952–1961 and was country music's largest "barn dance." It was broadcast every Saturday night from Compton, California, a suburb of Los Angeles. The show is a kinescope or "kinny," which, according to the liner notes, "is motion picture of a live television program... taken by photographing the picture directly off of a television screen."

Cash begins the set with a nice "Get Rhythm" with Luther Perkins' guitar solos being spotlighted. The band then goes into "You're the Nearest Thing to Heaven" and the current Sun single, the gospel-tinged, "I Was There When It Happened." Cash's persona is modest throughout. His first Columbia album (*The Fabulous Johnny Cash*) was just about to come out and they play a number of western album tracks, including "Don't Take Your Guns To Town" and "Frankie's Man Johnny." The second set opens with the hit "I Walk the Line," to roaring applause. Cash plays the somber "The Ways of a Woman In Love" and "Give My Love to Rose." This performance ends on a gospel note with "It Was Jesus" and "Suppertime."

The August 8, 1959 performance begins with the countrified "Guess Things Happen That Way" and the autobiographical single "Five Feet High and Rising," which the audience seems to recognize. Cash introduces his back-up band, which includes a drummer and piano player in addition to the Tennessee Two. He does his latest single, the jailhouse number "I Got Stripes," which is performed also as the encore by audience demand. There are a number of repeats from the 1958 show: "The Ways of a Woman in Love," "I Walk the Line," "Frankie Man's Johnny," "I Was There When It Happened," and "Don't Take Your Guns to Town." Cash and his band are on fire when they rip through a fantastic "Big River" and "Folsom Prison Blues." They perform another autobiographical number, "Pickin' Time," about Cash's boyhood days in the cotton fields. The highlight of the program is Cash impersonating Elvis Presley, even to the point of changing his hair. Cash claims that he is impersonating an Elvis impersonator. He does an impromptu "Heartbreak Hotel" with the crowd egging him on and laughing while he pretends to be out of breath. During "I Walk the Line," the camera pans over to some girls in the audience who are swaying in what looks to be like an attempted dance of some kind.

As with all of the Bear Family releases, the packaging is fantastic, with a beautiful color booklet and informative liner notes. It is a shame that Cash's first 1957 *Town Hall* appearance is not included (if it even exists), but what is available is a real gem and worth the extra money that most Bear Family releases cost. The program is in black and white and the footage is a little spotty at times, but considering how little footage of Cash and the Tennessee Two exists, the *Town Hall Party* performances are a welcome and vital addition to Cash products on DVD. This is Cash "without a net" at his rawest and most energetic best.

Johnny Cash Live From Austin, 1987

On January 3, 1987, Cash took the stage on one of the world's most beloved music programs: *Austin City Limits*. Only about thirty minutes of the concert was actually shown on PBS, but this DVD presents the entire fifty-minute program. The band starts up with a wonderful "Ring of Fire" complete with horns. It goes into an upbeat "Folsom Prison Blues," with a smooth guitar solo by Bob Wooton. Next, Cash introduces Kris Kristofferson's "Sunday Morning Coming Down," and then sings "I Walk the Line," with drummer W. S. Holland, who is obviously enjoying himself. Cash does a number of rarities during this concert, including the prison suicide song "The Wall," merging into "Long Black Veil," and the obligatory "Big River." He performs Tom T. Hall's "I'll Go Somewhere and Sing My Songs Again" and Texan Guy Clark's "Let Him Roll." The band performs a fine "Ghost Riders in the Sky," but the highlight of this DVD is June Carter and Cash performing Dave Loggins's "Where Did We Go Right." Although not written by Cash, the song tells the real tale of June and Johnny's relationship and romance. It is heartwarming to see them hold hands while performing. The show ends with an "I Walk the Line" reprise.

While Cash's voice is in fine form throughout this concert, his band is just too subdued and slick. The rawness and energy that is a Johnny Cash concert is lacking in this release (despite some critics' arguments that this was one of Cash's finest performances). It is certainly heartfelt and honest, but the band is too well-produced and sounds sterile. However, the fact that this DVD contains songs not on other DVDs makes it a worthy purchase for Cash aficionados. The DVD comes with a small booklet that has liner notes by *Austin City Limits* producer Terry Lickona.

Feature Film and Television Appearances

Murder in Coweta County, 1983

This 1983 made-for-television movie features both Johnny Cash and Andy Griffith in major roles. It was directed by Gary Nelson, who directed *Murder Me, Murder You*, *Kojak*, *The Pride of Jesse Helm* (see review below), and many other television movies and series. This film was based on a true story documented in the book *Murder in Coweta County* by Margaret Anne Barnes.

The basic story is set in Merriwether County, Georgia, in 1948, where John Wallace, played by Griffith, brutally murders another man to "teach" him a lesson. The hero of the story is the sheriff of Coweta County, Lamar Potts, played by Cash, who smells something fishy about the death, which actually occurred in Coweta. Wallace believes that he owns Merriwether County and is above the law because of his wealth and community standing. He pretends to be a God-fearing man who cares about the community, but he is a mean and heartless man.

Griffith is simply incredible in this role—the personification of evil and a far cry from the sheriff of the *Andy Griffith Show* and the lawyer of *Matlock*. The ability to capture the true essence of a person like Wallace shows Griffith's versatility as an actor.

Cash is amazing as Potts. The way he deduces that Wallace committed cold-blooded murder makes for an interesting mystery and story. He plays the role straight, with gusto, portraying Potts as an honest man seeking to do what is right regardless of the unpopular consequences. Watch for June Carter Cash as the psychic. This DVD has no extras, which is really a shame for such a good film. The director could have at least produced a commentary track or interview. This film was also released on video as *Last Blood*.

The Last Days of Frank and Jesse James, 1986

This 1986 television movie features three of the Highwaymen—Johnny Cash, Kris Kristofferson, and Willie Nelson (in a cameo)—and does a decent job of documenting the last days of outlaws Frank and Jesse James. Kristofferson plays Jesse James with grace, class, and recklessness. Cash plays his brother Frank with zest and is as sensible and ornery as one would expect. Frank James was a man of contradictions, which Cash portrays admirably. When Cash says, "I murdered a man," the viewer believes him. The bulk of the movie is about the last couple of raids the brothers did. Frank seeks to just "get out" of the business of robbing. Frank only wants to farm and take care of his family. In fact, when he finally faces trial for murder, he is so popular that he is acquitted.

June Carter Cash plays the James brothers' mother and her role, though small, is vital to the story. For a television film, it is a pretty good telling of the real-life story. Jesse's killer, Bob Ford, made a cottage industry out of telling "How He Killed Jesse James." Frank waited ten long years to get his revenge, only to have Bob killed by someone else. Cash sings the opening and closing song for the picture. This DVD has no extras, but a director's commentary or interview would have been nice.

Little House on the Prairie: The Collection, 1976

This 1976 episode of *Little House on the Prairie: The Collection* features both Johnny Cash and June Carter Cash in major roles. Directed by star Michael Landon, it features Cash as Caleb Hodgekiss, a conman posing as a minister in an attempt to take advantage of the people of Walnut Grove. June plays Hodegkiss' wife, Mattie, who is distraught over her husband's plans. Cash has one of the best lines when he explains his rationale to his wife: "Take what you can when you can get it or it gets taken away from you and that's the way the world is." Cash's character is gathering money on the pretext of helping the folks in the town, Grave's Corner, whose lives had been decimated by a fire. He learns that perhaps he was wrong in attempting to "pull one over" on the good folks of Walnut Grove and finds humility and understanding. The most moving scene is when he comforts a little girl who lost her puppy.

Columbo: Swan Song, 1974

Johnny Cash is featured in the 1974 *Columbo* television movie *Swan Song*, also starring Peter Faulk. In this movie, Cash plays Tommy Brown, a popular gospel/country singer. Brown's wife (based on Tammy Faye Baker and played by the legendary Ida Lupino) is blackmailing him to squeeze money from his songs and concert appearances. Apparently Brown had an affair with a sixteen-year-old girl and is threatened by his wife with exposure if he does not comply with her wishes.

Brown poisons a thermos of coffee with sleeping pills and, while flying an airplane, parachutes out while his wife and the sixteen-year-old girl plummet to their deaths. At the request of Brown's brother-in-law (who believes his sister was murdered), the LAPD sends Lieutenant Columbo to investigate. After the plane crash, Cash's character is free to pursue his carnal pleasures of wine, young women, and song.

Cash plays Brown with much believability, and it is obvious he enjoys the role. Since both Brown and Columbo are "smooth operators," it is fun to watch them try to "out smooth" one another and pit their wits against each other, while playing a game of words. There is one particularly funny moment when Columbo eats some squirrel chili. Throughout the movie, Cash's music, including "I Saw the Light" and "Sunday Morning Coming Down," is featured.

Any fan of Cash should not miss this movie. It is featured on the *Columbo: The Complete Third Season* DVD set. As Columbo states after Cash's character gives himself up, "Any man who can sing like that can't be all bad." Indeed!

The Pride of Jesse Hallam, 1981

The 1981 television movie stars Cash (as Jesse Hallam) and Brenda Vaccaro. Directed by Gary Nelson, the movie tells the story of Hallam, a widower who must move his daughter and son from their home in Kentucky to the big city of Cincinnati, Ohio, in order for his daughter to have special spinal surgery. Hallam, however, is illiterate and, when he tries to find work to support his family, doors keep slamming shut. Eventually, he realizes that in order to survive in the big city, he must learn to read.

The film, supposedly based on real-life events, is a touching "feel good" story. Cash's character goes through all the human emotions one might expect, from denial and pride to humility and acceptance. Cash should have won an Emmy for this performance, because it is one of the most honest and emotive roles in his filmography. The viewer empathizes with his frustration of attempting to survive in a world where reading is imperative.

There are several very touching sequences in the film, one of which involves Hallam reading to his daughter in the hospital and another when he starts reading Hemingway's *The Old Man and the Sea* with his tutor. By the end of the movie, Hallam goes to ninth grade with his son and is proud to be there. As he states in the film, "We're goin' to high school and we're goin' to graduate and nobody or nothin's goin' to stop us. We're goin' to learn to read."

Cash's music for the film includes three originals, "Moving Up," "I'm Just an Old Chunk of Coal," and "Paradise." The only extras on this DVD are two trailers, and Madacy did not use the best print—this one is scratchy and poorly edited. The content more than makes up for that, however.

There are supposedly several versions of the film on DVD, including one that includes a CD interview with Cash, published by Westlake Entertainment and also released by Unicorn Entertainment as *Johnny Cash 2 on 1* with *Five Minutes to Live*. With more than twenty-four million functional illiterates in the United States, this film brings to the surface the problems these people face. *The Pride of Jesse Hallam* is an honest tribute to the human will and not to be missed.

Five Minutes to Live: A.K.A. Door-to-Door Maniac, 1961

Cash made his feature film debut in 1961's *Five Minutes to Live*, also the last movie by Bill Karn, who directed *Ma Barker's Killer Brood*, *Gun's Don't Argue*, and *Dangerous Assignment*. Cash plays Johnny Cabot, a hood on the run from the law because he was "fingered" for killing a couple of police officers during a "heist" that went bad.

This black-and-white film was one of the last true *film noir* movies—in the same vein as Stanley Kubrick's 1956 *The Killing* and 1961's *Night Tide*, which featured a very young Dennis Hopper. In typical *film noir* style, Dorella narrates Cabot's story while in custody. On the run from the police, Cabot is holed up in a hotel waiting for some action. He finds out that a certain crime boss, who also knows the person that sold Cabot out to the police, needs a "good heater man."

Cabot's girlfriend has something to do with snitching on him, so he promptly kills her. Dorella comes up with a scheme to rob a Federal Trust bank by kidnapping Nancy Wilson (played by screenwriter Kay Forrester), who is the wife of bank vice president Ken Wilson (played by Donald Woods). The plan is not a very good one. While Cabot holds Wilson captive in her home, under threat of death unless a certain phone call is received, Dorella goes into the bank and demands the money.

In typical Cash fashion, he plays Cabot as smooth, but with an edginess that is not found in some of his other roles. While Dorella and Cabot are casing the bank officer's house in a nice suburban neighborhood, Cabot states that he "never saw so much nothing." Dorella responds, "People here live the lives magazine ads tell about." Without reading too much into these statements, they do seem to indicate that suburbia may not be all that it is cracked up to be.

The scene shifts to inside the home of the bank vice president and his wife while they are having breakfast. Little Ronnie Howard's character complains about having to "eat mush" (the oatmeal does not look very appetizing). This family is not the picture-perfect family of suburbia. Ken and Nancy are arguing about nothing in particular, and the bank officer actually plans on asking his wife for a divorce. He is having an affair and plans to run off with his girlfriend, but Nancy won't let him get a word in edgewise, and he does not ask her for the divorce.

While Dorella goes to the bank to get the ransom money, Cabot goes up to the house and pretends to be a door-to-door salesman, selling musical instruments. He is very cool and collected as a salesman. Nancy does not want to take the time to talk to him, but Cabot asks for some water and goes into the house with gun in hand, much to the horror of his captive.

The criminal sings her the song "Five Minutes to Live," which Cash also wrote. When asked if he was an entertainer, Cabot replies, "No, I'm a killer." Cabot tells her to dress up, since he "likes a broad to look sharp." When she goes to the bedroom to make the bed, Cabot delivers one of the best lines in history of film:, "I like a messy bed." When he attempts to violently rape her, the oven buzzer going off saves her. Cabot continues to act psychotic and begins smashing things in the house, but strangely enough has a soft spot for kids.

This is an interesting film, not just for Cash aficionados, but for anyone who likes a gritty crime drama and is a fan of the genre. The print on this DVD is actually pretty good considering the fact that *Five Minutes to Live*, which had its title changed to *Door-Door-Maniac* in 1965, would probably be a forgotten film if not for Cash's involvement.

The Critic's Choice DVD has as an extra feature, the twenty-minute, 1962 TV Western television pilot *The Night Rider*, starring Cash, Merle Travis, Eddy Dean, Johnny Western, and Dick Jones. This photoplay was filmed before a live television audience as part of the Galloway House showcase. Cash's portrayal of Johnny Laredo is the highlight of an otherwise dismal show.

The premise is an interpretation of the song "Don't Take Your Guns to Town," but the script is flimsy. Half of the program consists of songs done by Travis and others, but little Cash. The story is so poorly written that it is not surprising that the series never made it into primetime. However, Cash is always Cash and plays the character with charm, despite weak dialogue and story. The print on this DVD is very good and is in color.

Bear Family records has released both *Five Minutes to Live* and *Night Rider* as separate deluxe editions on DVD. Like with all Bear Family products, they used the best masters and the packaging is outstanding. Their versions are the first time the films have been remastered from the original 35mm film and both come with extensive booklets, filled with photographs, tidbits of information, and notes by friend Johnny Western. There is even a trailer for the *Door-to-Door Maniac* version of the film.

Considering how expensive Bear Family releases are, it is odd that they released these films as separate DVDs. The Critics Choice version is not bad, so unless one is a hardcore Cash collector, it will do the job as well as the Bear Family releases.

This Is Your Life: Ultimate Collection Volume 1, 1953–1987

This is one of the oddest Cash-related programs on DVD. The three-disc set features various episodes of *This Is Your Life*. Cash's show, which originally aired on February 28, 1971, is on the first disc. The show is preceded by a 1986 introduction by Ralph Edwards. The show was filmed before a live audience at the Grand Ole Opry and its first guest is the Reverend Billy Graham, who gives a heartfelt tribute to Cash via video.

From the beginning, Cash seems overwhelmed and gets choked up several times during the show. Cash's grade-school teacher is brought out and talks about how Cash sang and acted in the school plays. His first band, the Landsberg Barbarians, formed when he was stationed in Germany, is also featured, along with a rare recording playing in the background. Tennessee Two bassist Marshall Grant then comes out. Both men give heartfelt praises of the late guitarist Luther Perkins. Cash's former manager, Stu Carnall, then tells the story of how they once took 100 baby chickens on tour with them. Edwards describes Cash's drug use and personal problems, as well as his advocacy for prisoners and Native Americans. The man who once gave Cash a room for a night in a Lafayette Georgia jailhouse, Sheriff Ralph Jones, also appears, and prisoner Glen Sherely, who composed "Greystone Chapel," tells via video how much he appreciates the fact that Cash reached out to him. At this point, Cash is practically in tears.

June Carter then arrives, as do Cash's mother, father, brothers, and sisters. His daughters also wish him well via video from California, and Maybelle Carter and his baby son, John Carter, come out to end the show. Despite the guests saying Cash is the "tallest man" they ever saw, Cash is shown to be a man of great feeling and humility. This DVD set also features Boris Karloff, Betty White, Laurel and Hardy, Jayne Mansfield, and Vincent Price, among others. A booklet detailing each episode comes with the set. It is a bizarre, but interesting, Cash appearance on DVD.

Stagecoach, 1986

This television remake of the John Ford/John Wayne classic stars the four Highwaymen: Cash as Sheriff Curly, Waylon Jennings as Hatfield, Willie Nelson as Doc Holliday, and Kris Kristofferson as Ringo Kid. Guest stars include Waylon's wife Jesse Coulter, June Carter Cash, and a brief appearance by Cash's son John Carter. Willie Nelson produced the film and orchestrated the music along with David Allen Coe.

Cash plays the role of Sheriff Curly straightforward, much like he played his role as sheriff in *Murder in Coweta County*. He is a man that believes in justice, and when he learns that the Ringo Kid is innocent of the charges against him, he lets him go. Everything you expect from a western is in this film: wide-open spaces, the outlaw, Indian raids, gamblers, tough-talking women, and, most of all, the great shootout at the end where justice is finally served.

While no film could ever live up to the 1939 John Ford original, this is a fun film to watch. Seeing the Highwaymen together on one screen is a real treat. When all four highwaymen walk the street together, it is awe-inspiring. Despite the fact that every single Western cliché is embedded in this film, it is a better film than the 1966 Gordon Douglas remake.

Other appearances of Cash on DVD

This section provides a quick look at other Cash appearances on DVD.

Johnny Cash Singing at his Best, Passport Video, 2004

This DVD is a complete rip-off of the Bear Family *Town Hall* DVD, with three extra songs. It also uses footage from *The Anthology* DVD. The quality and print is not as good, and how Passport got the rights to put out this shoddy product is a mystery. Get the real, complete DVDs discussed above; it is obvious as to why this is unauthorized.

The Appalachians, Evening Star Productions, 2005

This three-DVD set tells the story of the people and the land of

Appalachia. It features interviews and rare excerpts from a July 2003 interview with Cash. It is highly recommended.

Festival! The Newport Folk Festival, performances gathered from 1963–1965

On this DVD, Johnny Cash performs "I Walk the Line," and the performance also features Bob Dylan, Pete Seeger, Son House, Peter, Paul and Mary, and many others.

Johnny Cash: The Man in Black A Documentary, Timeless Media Group, 2005

This is a seventy-five-minute documentary about Cash's life. The bonus features includes short documentaries on "Origins of Country" and "The Fifties"—not a bad documentary at all.

Johnny Cash: Legend Box Set Limited Edition, Columbia/Legacy, 2005

This expensive, limited, four-CD book features a bonus DVD that includes some rare footage/sounds, including Cash's old "Home Equipment Company Advertisements" and other gems. It also has *Johnny Cash: The First 25 Years*, the complete 1980 CBS TV special, and a lithograph portrait of Cash by Marc Burkhardt.

The Gospel Road, Twentieth Century Fox, 1973

Robert Elstrom directed this eighty-four-minute movie written by Cash, who narrates and performs, along with June Carter, Mary Magdalene, and Kris Kristofferson. It is a biographical tale about the life of Jesus Christ that forces the viewer to experience the life of Christ in vivid detail. It is much better than most "Jesus" movies and highly recommended.

Walk the Line, Twentieth Century Fox, 2005

The Oscar-nominated biopic stars Joaquin Phoenix as Cash and Oscar-winner Reese Witherspoon as June. The special edition features commentary, deleted scenes with commentary, and three extended music sequences featuring Joaquin Phoenix and Reese Witherspoon. The special edition also contains the documentary "Celebrating the Man in Black: The Making of *Walk the Line*," and features interviews with Rosanne Cash, Kris Kristofferson, Sheryl Crow, John Mellencamp, Willie Nelson, and Kid Rock. The DVD includes the featurettes "Folsom, Cash and the Comeback" and "Ring of Fire: The Passion of Johnny and June."

I Walk the Line, Sony Pictures, 1970

The 1970 John Frankenheimer movie stars Gregory Peck and was inspired by Cash's music. The basic story is that a sheriff falls in love with a teenage girl and has an affair. He also gets involved in various "gray" activities, which cannot remain secret in a small Tennessee town.

North and South, BBC Warner, 1985

This groundbreaking Civil War television series features Cash throughout.

Flip Wilson Show Parts 3 & 4, 1970

Johnny Cash and Flip perform "Oklahoma Hills" together.

Hee Haw Collection Volume 2, 1973

Cash performs "Big River" and "City of New Orleans."

Willie Nelson My Life, White Star, 2000

Features an interview with Cash.

Tribute to Hank Williams and His Music, Eagle Eye Media, 2002

Cash performs "Men With Broken Hearts" and "Kaw-Liga."

Dr. Quinn, Medicine Woman, CBS, 1993–1998

Cash plays Kid Cole and June Carter plays Sister Ruth.

George Jones Same Ole Me, 1969

Features an interview with Cash.

Country Legends Live, Time Life, 2005

Cash performs "Sixteen Tons."

Country Legends Live Volume 2, Time Life, 2005

Cash performs "Folsom Prison Blues."

Roger Miller: Life on the Road, White Star, 2003

Features an interview with Cash.

Skiffle, Video Beat, 2004

Features an interview with Cash.

Special thanks go to Emily Smith; her work in interlibrary loans made this essay possible. Also, thanks to Texas Tech University staff.

•

ROBERT G. WEINER first became interested in Johnny Cash when he saw the Grateful Dead perform "Big River," and he sought out the original version. He bought a tape of Cash's Greatest Hits, which he quickly wore out. In 1986, on his way to a Public Image Limited Concert in Dallas, he read Cash's autobiography, *Man in Black*, and on the trip back, he read Cash's novel about St. Paul, *Man in White*. He is co-author of *The Grateful Dead and the Deadheads* and editor of *Perspectives on the Grateful Dead*. Weiner's articles about Lubbock and gospel music appear in *West Texas Historical Journal* and the *East Texas Historical Journal*. He published the article "Atomic Music: Country Conservatism: Folk Discontent" in *On the Culture of the American South*, edited by Dennis Hall, and the "Cowboy Songs in Nature" in the *Cowboy Way*, edited by Paul Carlson. He most recently has book chapters in *The Gospel of Superheroes* and *Landscape of Hollywood Westerns*. Currently, Weiner can be seen in the music documentary "Lubbock Lights;" see www.lubbock-lights.com for more information about this film. Weiner also wrote the Johnny Cash article featured in the *Guide to United States Popular Culture*, edited by Ray and Pat Browne. He has graduate degrees in history and information science and is currently a reference librarian at the Mahon Library in Lubbock, Texas.

Works Cited

Amazing Grace with Bill Moyers. Films for the Humanities, Inc., 2003.

Biography: Johnny Cash. A&E Home Video, 2005 (1998).

Five Minutes to Live a.k.a. Door-to-Door Maniac. Dir. Bill Karn. Perf. Johnny Cash and Donald Woods. Critics Choice, 2006 (1961).

Good Rockin' Tonight—Legacy of Sun Records. Dir. Bruce Sinofsky. Image Entertainment, 2001.

The Highwaymen—On the Road Again. White Star, 2003 (1993).

I Walk the Line: Country Legends. BCI Eclipse Company, 2005.

Johnny Cash: The Anthology. Dir. Al Greenfield. Image Entertainment, 2002 (2000).

Johnny Cash at Town Hall Party 1958–59. Dir. Wesley Tuttle. Bear Family, 2002.

Johnny Cash: A Concert Behind Prison Walls. Dir. Dick Carson, Eagle Vision USA, 2003 (1977).

Johnny Cash Live at Montreux 1994. Eagle Vision USA, 2005 (1994).

Johnny Cash Live from Austin TX. New West Records, 2005 (1987).

Johnny Cash—The Man, His World, His Music. Dir. Robert Elfstrom. Sanctuary Records, 2005 (1969).

Johnny Cash—Ridin' the Rails: The Great American Train Story. Dir. Nicholas Webster. Rhino, 2005 (1986).

The Last Days of Frank and Jesse James. Dir. William A. Graham. Perf. Johnny Cash and Kris Kristofferson. Lions Gate, 2003 (1986).

Little House on the Prairie: The Collection. Dir. Michael Landon. Perf. Melissa Gilbert and Michael Landon. Good Times Video, 2001 (1976).

Murder in Coweta County. Dir. Gary Nelson. Perf. Johnny Cash and Andy Griffith. Sterling Entertainment, 2001 (1983).

Pete Seeger's Rainbow Quest, Shanachie, 2005.

The Pride of Jesse Hallam. Dir. Gary Nelson. Perf. Johnny Cash and Brenda Vaccaro. Westlake Entertainment, 2003 (1981).

Road to Nashville. Dir. Will Zens. Rhino, 2000 (1967).

Reznor, Trent. *Hurt*. Dir. Mark Romanek. Perf. Johnny Cash. American Recordings/Lost Highway, 2003.

Stagecoach. Dir. Ted Post. Perf. Willie Nelson, Kris Kristofferson, Johnny Cash, Waylon Jennings. MGM, 2006 (1986).

"Swan Song," *Columbo*. Dir. Nicholas Colasanto. Perf. Peter Faulk, Johnny Cash, and Ida Lupino. Universal Studios Home Entertainment, 2005 (1974).

This is Your Life: Ultimate Collection Volume 1. Dir. Richard Gottlieb, Axel Gruenberg. Perf. Ralph Edwards, Bob Warren. R2 Entertainment, 2005 (1953–1987).

The Unauthorized Biography of Johnny Cash. Highland Video, 2005.

Todd M. Callais

JOHNNY CASH AND THE CRIMINAL MIND: THE MAN IN BLACK'S EXPANSION OF THE PUBLIC CRIME NARRATIVE

Introduction

The day that Johnny Cash died, an MTV news reporter started her historic announcement of the event by stating, "Johnny Cash, the man who sang the famous lyric 'but I shot a man in Reno, just to watch him die,' died today." Since almost the start of his musical career Cash has been inextricably linked with a criminal persona. Explaining the criminal mind to the public seems to be at least a hobby to Cash, although perhaps it is more important to think of it as a mission.

Early in his autobiography Cash describes a "violent home invasion" that he, his wife, June Carter, and assorted family and friends faced in their Jamaica home, Cinnamon Hill, on Christmas Day, 1982 (48). Cash's account of this event begins as a violent, abrupt intrusion during dinner, and evolves into a humanizing description of the three men who had come into their home. He discusses how young they were, how awkward they seemed to be in their crime, and their decision to let Cash and his family finish their dinner by giving them a plate full of turkey. Eventually all three robbers were caught and killed by Jamaican police; Cash reflects upon this, stating:

> How do I feel about it? What's my emotional response to the fact (or at least the distinct possibility) that the desperate junkie boys that threatened and traumatized my family and might easily have killed us all (perhaps never intending any such thing) were executed for their act-or murdered, or shot down like dogs, have it how you will? I'm out of answers. My only certainties are that I grieve for desperate young men and the societies that produce and suffer so many of them, and I felt that I knew those boys. We had a kinship, they and I: I knew how they thought, I knew how they needed. They were like me (55–56).

This quote illuminates Cash's unique perspective on criminal behavior. While Cash has been quick in his life to condemn criminal behavior and violence, it is clear that he has a deep understanding of where these criminal desires originate, not just in evil hearts that are formed at conception, but in social structure and home environment.

In other words, Cash consistently presents two themes regarding crime in his music and politics. The first is a call for *redemption* for those individuals caught up in criminal behavior, and the second is a *contestation* of the external causes of that criminal behavior.

Cash cared about people—this is evident from his history and music. What set him apart is that he cared about people that few of the powerful seemed to care about: the criminal, the poor, and the subjugated. By openly discussing the impact of crime and the complexity of individuals who engaged in criminal behavior, Johnny Cash expanded the generally binary public narrative, which defined criminals as absolutely bad people. In addition, this humanizing of criminals serves to directly and indirectly contest the fairly repressive criminal justice model that was in place for the first decade and a half of Cash's musical career.

Initiatives toward symbolic social change are most effective when they are able to reach large groups of people; Cash's charismatic appeal and musical talent make this possible. In fact, Johnny Cash has sold more than fifty million albums worldwide (*Launch Radio Networks* 2003). The ability to push forth frames of contestation and redemption in the area of crime and justice during an era of strict and repressive prisons and criminal justice should not be understated. Though its true impact can not be measured, Johnny Cash's public persona, his innovative prison albums, and his expansive catalog of songs that focus on crime and criminals as a major theme expanded the public crime narrative and demonstrate a re-conceptualization of criminal identity and the identity of the criminal justice system.

The Persona of Johnny Cash

At times Cash is spoken of in mythic proportions. A review of his album covers demonstrates an abundance of different images that Cash tried to convey to the large population of music fans that awaited each new record. Whether sitting on top of a train, embracing his Native American heritage, presenting himself as a potentially dangerous gunslinger, or silently sitting in black, his favorite color, it becomes clear that Cash wanted to present something different, something provocative, to his audience.

In his autobiography, Cash explains three questions that are always asked of him by reporters; two of them relate directly to his public persona and its importance to expanding the public crime narrative. Cash states:

> Question One: Why was I in prison? I never was. That got started because I wrote and sang "Folsom Prison Blues," my 1955 hit, from the perspective of a convicted, unrepentant killer, and twelve years later I made a concert album, *Johnny Cash at Folsom Prison*. In fact, I've never served any time at all in any correctional institution anywhere (76).

Cash goes on to state that many people refuse to believe that he never spent any time in prison. This is likely because of the sincerity and intensity with which he sings about criminals and criminal behavior. His success as a musician combined with the public's belief that he is a criminal creates an interesting public phenomena. Cash's criminal persona seems so authentic, yet he is so beloved by the nation, meaning that he has the unique ability to contribute to his audiences' perspective on criminality.

Adding to Cash's politically progressive attitude that expands the public crime narrative is his peculiar decision to wear one color of clothing, leading to the moniker the "Man in Black." In his autobiography Cash discusses:

> Question Three is simple: Why do I always wear black?...First there's the song "Man in Black," which I wrote in 1971. I had my network TV show at the time, and so many reporters were asking me Question Two that I saw an opportunity to answer with a message. I wore the black, I sang, "for the poor and beaten down, livin' in the hopeless, hungry side of town." I wore it "for the prisoner who has long paid for his crime, but is there because he's a victim of the times." I wore it for "the sick and

> lonely old" and "the reckless whose bad trip left from them cold...." I still do, and wearing it still means something to me. It's still my symbol of rebellion-against a stagnant status quo, against our hypocritical houses of God, against people whose minds are closed to others' ideas (85–87).

This symbolic presentation of black clothing places Cash in a continual state of protest. The fact that he wears black while performing makes him a symbol of the fallen, the downtrodden, and the criminal. The personas put forth by Johnny Cash contribute just as much to the reorientation of criminal identity as anything that he wrote or performed.

The Importance of the Prison Albums

Johnny Cash sold 6.5 million albums worldwide in 1969, even more than the Beatles sold that year (*Launch Radio Networks* 2003). The sales were driven by the overwhelming success of Cash's live albums recorded in Folsom Prison (1968) and San Quentin Prison (1969). Cash recorded *At Folsom Prison* in 1968, and the surprising success of this album led to the recording of *At San Quentin* the next year. Although *At Folsom Prison* has received more critical acclaim, both albums are legendary. What makes these albums so unique is that listeners hear not only Cash, but also the response from the audience of prisoners to his music and message. The audience's reactions, combined with themes that are present in Johnny Cash music, provide an ideal learning opportunity for listeners.

In his performance at San Quentin in 1969, Cash sings a song that is incredibly popular with the prisoners: a song titled "San Quentin." In the song, Cash sings to San Quentin from the perspective of an inmate. Cash tells the prison that he wishes for it to fall to the ground and "burn in hell." Cash closes one of the stanzas with the hope that all of the world will find out that San Quentin prison was able to do no good for its inmates (2000). Cash's ability to actively contest the prison-industrial complex in such a divisive environment by itself is an interesting public statement. The crowd erupts during the first and fourth lines of this stanza. While the reaction to Cash telling San Quentin to burn in hell is understandable, the reaction to the last line is significant. Wishing for the world to find out that San Quentin has done no good is an active contestation of the deterrence model of criminal justice. The vibrant crowd reaction illustrates skepticism toward the idea that prison rehabilitates offenders and protects society. With his prison albums, a unique dynamic is reached that has never been paralleled.

The songs on these albums contain themes of marginality, religion, deviance, and criminal justice. According to writer Michael Streissguth, the Folsom prison album is:

> a social statement on behalf of disenfranchised peoples . . . for by appearing in front of America's modern day lepers and recording and releasing what came of it, he unapologetically told his listeners that these locked-away men deserved the compassion, if not the liberation, that the 1960s offered. He used his art as a battering ram to smash through conventional notions of prisoners and prisons (Streissguth 13).

As an example, at Folsom Prison Cash sings "The Wall," a song about a prisoner who attempts a risky escape plan that he knows will end in him being killed. In "The Wall" Cash somberly discusses an inmate who becomes obsessed with a wall that he might be able to climb, which would allow him to escape from prison (1968). The inmate is consistently warned throughout the song how risky of a feat this would be. In the end the inmate attempts to climb the wall. Cash states that newspapers called the attempt a jailbreak plan, but in Cash's opinion it was a suicide. While understandably, this song doesn't elicit a rowdy response from the crowd, it was important for Cash to include this track, because it demonstrates a side of prison that isn't included in the mainstream prison narrative.

Cash often styled himself as a non-conformist or an outlaw—the "Man in Black" interested in social justice. He also had serious problems with drugs while on tour, and nearly committed suicide in despair over his addiction. As a result, while he didn't spend as much time in jail as some people think, he was adopted by convicts as "one of their own," or at least as somebody who had a difficult life and told the truth about prisons and social injustice.

Although he would not have put it this way, Cash established himself as an artist who would sing songs about marginalized men. And although these particular prison tours took place nearly four decades ago, Cash's music still remains relevant:

> Transcending the decade of its birth, the [Folsom prison] album still resonates in the early 21st century, when criminal justice remains anything but rational and man has never appeared more insensitive to his fellow man (Streissguth 14).

Diversifying the Explanation of Criminal Experience

When considering the long discography and over four decades of performance history of Johnny Cash, there are a number of important themes that emerge from Cash's lyrics. In a three-disc box set arranged by Cash, the titles *Love*, *God*, and *Murder* were given to the discs to denote what Cash acknowledged were the primary foci of his writing (2000). What makes Cash's coverage of crime and the criminal persona so important isn't that he takes an overly political tone or that he is especially sympathetic to criminals; it is that he presents a diverse picture of the criminal experience that spans a wide spectrum of theoretical understanding of criminals.

What's amazing about Cash's crime-themed music is how illustrative it is of theoretical traditions in the fields of criminology and criminal justice. To the extent that these theoretical traditions are trying to inform policy and public opinion, Johnny Cash's music can be viewed as a public service announcement serving the interests of theoretical criminologists. Cash's music is very diverse and clearly demonstrates the classical, positivist, and constructionist perspectives on crime.

The Classical Tradition

The classical model of human behavior is the oldest tradition still considered relevant by social scientists and those who are interested in criminal behavior. The rational choice theory assumes that criminals rationally consider the benefits of committing a crime, the certainty that they might get caught, and the consequences of punishment. Therefore those individuals who commit crime rationally calculate the costs and benefits of committing a crime (Exum).

In the liner notes to the disc titled *Murder*, Cash says of his collection of songs, "Here is my personal selection of my recordings of songs of robbers, liars and murderers. These songs are just for listening and singing. Don't go out and do it" (2000b). Consider the lyrics from Cash's "Folsom Prison Blues" (1968). Cash begins the song with a discussion of his upbringing. His mother tells him definitively that she does not want Johnny to get involved with guns and violence. She implores him to be a good person. Her statements have little impact, because Johnny commits a cold-blooded murder illustrated by Cash's famous statement about taking the life of a man in Reno. In his autobiography Cash relays that when writing this song he tried to think of the worst reason to kill someone that he possibly could: "to watch him die." As the song progresses, Cash's character ends up in prison, where he begins to learn the error of his ways. He thinks about the lives of persons not in prison and he makes a promise to himself that if he were ever able to get out of prison he would lead a life that was different. This song reifies the interest of the justice system; that effective punishment will convince bad people to stop committing crime. The character in this song ignores advice from his parents and perhaps natural instincts so that he can attain the benefit of murder; the ability to watch someone die.

Later in the song he considers the consequences of his actions and realizes that his choice to kill was a poor choice. He basically indicates that the disadvantages to murder outweigh the advantages, so if he were to leave Folsom Prison he would abstain from bad behavior. The prison-industrial complex could not ask for a better advertisement.

There is an abundance of rational choice in Cash's musical collection. An element of rational choice theory is the corresponding criminal justice strategy of deterrence which focuses on the punishment of bad people to set an example for others considering crime; this is referred to as general deterrence. Take for consideration the narrative of the song "Cocaine Blues" and its use on the albums *Murder* (2000) and *At Folsom Prison* (1968). It is the story of a person who succumbs to addiction and commits a horrible act; Cash starts his performance by discussing a morning when he woke up, took some cocaine, and killed his woman. The song later reveals that Cash's character committed the murder because his partner was cheating on him. This establishes the character in the song as a bad person with a lack of guilt.

After the capture of this individual the following scenario plays out. A juror brings out the verdict for the character; a guilty verdict. The judge sentences the murderer in the song to ninety-nine years in Folsom prison. The criminal asks for mercy but it is too late; he receives a harsh punishment and learns a lesson about right and wrong. This song is entertaining, but also teaches a lesson about the dangers of addiction to alcohol and cocaine and the use of violence. In many ways it could be claimed that Cash's work here reifies the system, and in many ways it does. These messages have to be considered, however, in the larger context of Johnny Cash's musical collection.

The Positivist Tradition

While Johnny Cash presented clear and vivid representations of the classical perspective that appealed to a broad population of people, he also expanded the crime narrative by vividly demonstrating theoretical perspectives of the positivist tradition. Criminal positivism attempts to explain why people would commit crime. Why do some of us violate rules? Why do others obey rules? Why do some members of society commit violent crimes, drink to the point of alcoholism, and engage in other criminal endeavors? In the liner notes to the disc titled *Murder*, Cash says of his collection of songs, "We, the people, put ourselves in the shoes of the singer. We want to feel his pain, his loneliness. We want to be part of that rebellion" (2000b).

One example of positivism is the *strain* explanation of criminal behavior. Strain theory argues that crime results from the disparity between the ideals of society and opportunity that is available. An individual who cannot achieve the traditional goals of society, such as wealth, family, and respect, will resort to illegitimate means to achieve those goals: crime (Merton). In his concert at Folsom prison, Cash performed the song "Busted" to an enthusiastic crowd. As you read the lyrics toward the end of this song it becomes clear that being "busted" or broke is used by the man singing this song as a justification for the use of illegitimate means of achieving middle-class goals. The last two stanzas of the song perfectly demonstrate the strain theory (1968).

The song begins by establishing that the gentleman in the song has consistently attempted to use legitimate means to attain money, such as working, even begging. Cash discusses attempts to get a loan, scrape up money by selling things, and growing crops to sell. The song then establishes the problems in the family, such as poverty, extreme illness, and a general lack of pride. Cash finally states that while he is not a criminal, his situation allows him to understand how a man can steal when "he's busted" (1968).

The importance of this statement can barely be overstated. Cash in this song is demonstrating that the traditional idea that hard work will always yield results is flawed, and therefore the economic system can legitimate, and arguably create, criminals. In a different type of system this gentleman would not have to commit crime; in our economy he does.

A second positivist explanation for criminal behavior is control theory. Control theorists believe that all people would naturally commit criminal behavior if left to their own devices. Therefore, what is most interesting is why people don't commit crime. Control theorists believe that there are social restraints on each person and crime occurs when restraining forces are weakened (Gottfredson and Hirschi). Consider a few famous lines from a Cash and the Tennessee Two song, "I Walk the Line." In "I Walk the Line" Cash talks about how the love of a woman that he is with causes him to walk the line between good and evil. These words from Cash's famous song "I Walk the Line" (1956) are interpreted correctly by many to mean that Cash abstains from infidelity because of the positive controlling effect of the relationship in which he is involved (Cash's autobiography and other sources have noted the irony of this song being performed by Johnny Cash).

It is important to note that this song generally notes the controlling effect of family. This same analysis can be understood in terms of "walking the line" between crime and the straight life. Another example is the song "The Ballad of the Harpweaver" (1960), which chronicles a family so poor that they cannot afford to eat or supply clothes for each other. While this could be seen as a scenario where crime is a natural result, faith and a sense of family prevent the people in the song from considering it.

These controlling agents are not only used to prevent people from entering crime, in fact they often help people to escape from their criminal involvement. Take the song "Greystone Chapel" (1968), which Cash performed at Folsom Prison. An inmate at Folsom named Glenn Shirley wrote the song. Cash explained this to the audience and identified it as a source of legitimacy for the song. The song considers the value of religious faith as a controlling agent that prevents crime (1968). The perspective of the song is that while some persons may be physically in prison they are not spiritually bound by any structure. In Folsom, there is a chapel that allows inmates to define and reinforce moral boundaries.

The inmate discusses prison as a "den of sin," ironically a world free of moral controlling agents, with the exception of the greystone chapel. This chapel instills a belief system strong enough to prevent some or many of the inmates in Folsom from having an undesirable values system in relation to controlling crime. Cash pushes songs indicating the importance of social and moral controlling agents to any person who abstains from crime; in fact this is the only thing that delineates persons in similar socioeconomic and social situations.

A third explanation of criminal behavior is differential association theory, which basically states that people commit crime when they have learned definitions (rationalizations and attitudes) favorable to crime in excess of definitions unfavorable to committing crime; in other words, people learn by example to be criminals (Sutherland and Cressey). One of Johnny Cash's best-known songs is "A Boy Named Sue," which gained notoriety after it was performed at San Quentin Prison (1969). The story of Sue begins with his father leaving him at the age of three. Sue reveals that his father left almost nothing for the family, but he did give Sue his name before he left.

The narrative Sue continues as he finds himself consistently getting into fights and getting embarrassed in front of women because of his name. Much later in life he has a chance encounter; they get into a fight, and when Sue has the chance to kill his father, his father attempts to explain himself. The father explains that he knew he would be leaving Sue and his mother so he wanted his son to be as tough as humanly possible. The route that he picked to achieve this goal was to give his son a name that would cause him to get made fun of and get into many fights: Sue. The father in this story put his son in a position where learning positive definitions of violence would be necessary for survival. He did this because he would not be there for Sue to teach him how to fight. Sue is a violent person, but circumstances made him that way; this is not an idea common to the public crime narrative.

The Constructionist Tradition

When Johnny Cash discusses inequality, a corrupt prison system, and prison guards and police officers who aren't doing their jobs, he is pushing forth a contestation of the current system. In addition, he is discussing and reorienting the construction of criminal identity. The constructionist perspective is broad, and attempts to explain the creation of deviant categories. Why do certain rules exist? How do rules get enforced? What are the consequences?

In the liner notes to *Murder*, Cash says of his collection of songs, "We sang about Machine Gun Kelly, Pretty Boy Floyd, John Dillinger, and a host of others in the 20th century. Our heroes in song were, for the most part, anti-establishment. The loot and their bounty was the U.S. Mail, the U.S. Government or the rich man wielding power over the poor man" (2000b). This indicates Cash's infatuation with crime as a contestation of power and inequality. This infatuation is clearly represented through Cash's musical catalog.

The labeling perspective attempts to explain individual responses to criminal and deviant labels. Labeling theorists argue that criminal and deviant behavior originates in any number of biological, psychological, or social contexts in a person's life (e.g., juvenile playgroups in urban neighborhoods; physical and emotional abuse at home; rational choices made by bad individuals). These actions occur in early life and elicit a negative reaction from the general population. This reaction, or label, is placed on an individual and limits the options for that individual. Eventually, the person will begin to take on elements of these labels (Lemert).

Although this is a fairly common example throughout Cash's entire life, the clearest example is in the introduction to the song "Slow Rider" on *Ride This Train* (1960), a concept album that allowed Cash to demonstrate the perspective of numerous persons and experiences throughout American history. In "Slow Rider," Cash takes on the persona of famed gunfighter John Wesley Harding.

In the song, Cash explains the social construction of a notorious murderer. He doesn't explain why the gunman was in a position where he had to kill someone to save his life, but he does discuss the impact that it had on young John Wesley. The label placed on Harding is inescapable, even as he tries to move toward a straight and narrow life. Harding discusses how he is going to disappear in the hopes that some day he can live a life where no one thinks of him as the killer that he once was. Cash's humanizing of a supposed cold-blooded killer is a statement on the construction of criminal identity.

A second constructionist idea illustrated by Cash is conflict theory. Conflict criminology argues that the interests of the powerful ultimately determine what we classify as values. The organized state does not represent common interests, but instead represents the interests of those with sufficient power to control its operation. As a result the more powerful people are legally freer to pursue self-interests, while less powerful people who pursue self-interest are more likely to be officially defined and processed as criminal. Cash discusses the criminal justice system as a wrangler of the poor in his performance of "Starkville City Jail" (1969). The potentially autobiographical song discusses police officers as units that patrol the streets looking for nameless faces to place in jail in an attempt to maintain the boundaries of society. This song is about the social construction of crime. The character in this story is thrown in jail for something that he perceives to be ridiculous (and that a large proportion of the population might feel is ridiculous), a curfew. He is rounded up for his status and thrown in jail to create the appearance of safety at night. While Cash doesn't overtly explain the tenets of conflict theory, he gives clear examples of the perspective.

In "San Quentin," a song immensely popular with the prisoners in San Quentin prison, Cash again contests the intentions and value of the criminal justice system by taking on the persona of a prisoner talking to prison (1969). He speaks of how much he hates San Quentin because of the emotional cuts and scars that it has placed upon him.

The powerful statement being made here is that the prison system fails. The song also addresses the government's silent endorsement of a system that fails, and arguably, has the opposite effect of what is intended. This idea is put forth when Cash asks San Quentin whether it thinks any good actually comes from its existence. The person singing the song argues no, and in fact any difference is in the direction that the prison system would not hope for.

The Legacy of Johnny Cash

The strength of Cash's discography is not that it lends support or proves something significant about one theoretical tradition. The strength of Cash is that he demonstrates the diversity of criminal experiences and allows audiences to gain insight into the criminal mind. By demonstrating and advertising the classical, positivist, and constructionist perspective, Cash contests the hegemonic narrative of the evil criminal who always needs to be punished. Cash forces crime to be considered in the context of economic, family, and social structure in addition to criminals being bad people.

In the realm of popular culture, it is fair to say that Johnny Cash has reached legendary status. He has meant so much to so many people, but perhaps the population that has been most impacted by his music and life are those stigmatized and disempowered groups that he tried so hard to present to the public. Cash's ability to transcend himself through his public persona, the classic prison albums that he created, and the diverse musical catalog that greatly expands the public crime narrative means that Cash's message will continue long past his life. Pushing forth redemption and contestation represents a dramatic departure from the hegemonic script on the "evil criminal."

•

TODD M. CALLAIS is a Ph.D. candidate in the department of sociology at Ohio State University. His research interests are criminology, inequality, and the sociology of culture. His recent research has focused on the social impact of popular culture as well as stigma management techniques for people leaving prison. Most recently his work has been published in the book *How Real is Reality TV: Essays on Representation and Truth*. Todd lives in Columbus, Ohio, with his wife, Melissa, and his dogs, Mr. Bojangles and Cash: The Dog in Black.

Works Cited

Cash, Johnny. *At San Quentin (The Complete 1969 Concert)*. Columbia Records, 2000.

——.*Murder.* American Recordings, 2000. Compact disc.

——. *At Folsom Prison*. Columbia Records, 1968.

——. *Ride This Train*. Columbia Records, 1960.

Cash, Johnny and the Tennessee Two. *The Complete Original Sun Singles*. Sun Entertainment, 1999.

Cash, Johnny with Patrick Carr. *Johnny Cash: The Autobiography.* New York: Harper, 1998.

Exum, M. Lynn. "The Application and Robustness of the Rational Choice Perspective in the Study of Intoxicated and Angry Intentions to Aggress." *Criminology* 40 (2002): 933–966.

Gottfredson, Michael and Travis Hirschi. *A General Theory of Crime*. Stanford: Stanford UP, 1990.

"Johnny Cash Albums Sales Soar." *Launch Radio Networks* (18 November 2003) http://launch.yahoo.com/read/news.asp?contentID=214647.

Lemert, Edwin M. *Social Pathology*. New York: McGraw-Hill, 1951.

Mansfield, Brian. *Ring of Fire: A Tribute to Johnny Cash*. Nashville: Routledge Hill Press, 2003.

Merton, Robert K. "Social Structure and Anomie." *American Sociological Review* 41 (1938): 660–675.

Reiman, Jeffrey. *The Rich Get Richer and the Poor Get Prison: Ideology, Class, and Criminal Justice*. Boston: Allyn & Bacon, 1995.

Streissguth, Michael. *Johnny Cash at Folsom Prison: The Making of a Masterpiece*. Cambridge, MA: Da Capo Press, 2004.

Sutherland, Edwin H. and Donald R. Cressey. *Criminology, 10th Edition*. New York: Harper & Row, 1978.